Hubert
Memories of events
we sha...
G000113564

With
HEALING
HANDS

With HEALING HANDS

The untold story of the Australian civilian
surgical teams in Vietnam

GARY McKAY and **ELIZABETH STEWART**

ALLEN&UNWIN

First published in 2009

Copyright © Gary McKay and Elizabeth Stewart 2009

All rights reserved. No part of this book may be reproduced or transmitted in any form or by any means, electronic or mechanical, including photocopying, recording or by any information storage and retrieval system, without prior permission in writing from the publisher. The Australian *Copyright Act 1968* (the Act) allows a maximum of one chapter or 10 per cent of this book, whichever is the greater, to be photocopied by any educational institution for its educational purposes provided that the educational institution (or body that administers it) has given a remuneration notice to Copyright Agency Limited (CAL) under the Act.

Allen & Unwin
83 Alexander Street
Crows Nest NSW 2065
Australia
Phone: (61 2) 8425 0100
Fax: (61 2) 9906 2218
Email: info@allenandunwin.com
Web: www.allenandunwin.com

Cataloguing-in-Publication details are available
from the National Library of Australia
www.librariesaustralia.nla.gov.au

ISBN 978 1 74175 074 4

Map by Ian Faulkner
Text design by Squirt Creative
Set in 12/16 pt Adobe Jenson Pro by Midland Typesetters, Australia
Printed and bound in Australia by Griffin Press

10 9 8 7 6 5 4 3 2 1

To the doctors, nurses and other medical personnel
who so willingly gave of themselves to assist others

Contents

Foreword

With Healing Hands is the magnificent, previously untold story of many of Australia's finest medical specialists, men and women, who volunteered to serve our country by treating civilian sick and wounded war casualties in Vietnam from 1964 to 1972. They were asked to help, and they responded in the true spirit of Florence Nightingale and the Hippocratic Oath.

This book adds a great deal to our understanding of the longest war in which Australian servicemen have participated. Both authors have considerable experience and knowledge: Gary served many years in the Australian Army, and served in the Vietnam War as an infantry platoon commander where he was severely wounded and awarded a Military Cross for gallantry. Elizabeth Stewart is an historian in the Military History Section at the Australian War Memorial and has worked on the *Official History of Australia's Involvement in Southeast Asian Conflicts*.

Australia was involved in the Vietnam War from 1962 to 1973. All who lived through that period will remember it as one of deep national division. But it was more than that, and it was different to any other war we have served in, for our involvement was aimed not at defeating an aggressor but at preventing the spread of communism throughout Asia, and we were assisting another nation in that role.

The book describes in detail the work of the civilian surgical teams who served so well in several civilian hospitals in South Vietnam. The

Australian Department of External Affairs, not the Defence Department, developed and ran the program, which was a crucial part of winning the hearts and minds of a divided country. When the government called for appropriate experienced surgical specialists, nurses and other staff to volunteer for civilian surgical teams to assist in Vietnam, the response from the Australian medical and nursing professions was outstanding. Major hospitals throughout Australia willingly formed teams consisting of surgeons, physicians and radiographers, as well as specialist nurses in operating theatre tasks and general nursing.

The first surgical team to leave Australia, in 1964, was from the Royal Melbourne Hospital and worked at the provincial hospital in Long Xuyen in the province of An Giang in the southwest of South Vietnam. Australian teams continued to work in Long Xuyen until December 1970. From 1966 additional Australian surgical teams were placed in hospitals in other locations including Bien Hoa, Vung Tau and Ba Ria. The teams came from hospitals in Victoria, New South Wales, Queensland, Western Australia and South Australia, and there was also an Australian SEATO composite team. Precise details of team membership and each hospital team are well documented in the appendices.

The task of the surgical teams was daunting, working in conditions that ranged from barely adequate to appalling. They had to work with very limited equipment and services; where equipment existed it was often primitive or simply broken down. The accounts of the problems faced by both surgical staff and ward-nursing members is often heartrending, but through it all evidence of great skill, vast experience and an overwhelming will to do the job well shines through proudly.

In these difficult conditions, the question of tours' duration is an important one; it is remarkable that the Department of External Affairs did not undertake investigation and proper management of the problems the teams endured. As described, the hospitals were clearly in a wretched condition, and herculean efforts and dedication were required to achieve the level of medical service that the patients deserved and the teams wished to provide. The stress placed on the teams was immense, with poor living accommodation, extremely long working hours and few opportunities for rest periods. The teams seemed to receive little or no intelligence briefing on the war, and indeed, during the Tet Offensive in 1968 they often came under mortar or small-arms attack.

The workload achieved by the surgical teams during their tours was remarkable, and team leaders' reports indicate huge numbers of surgical procedures undertaken—some in excess of 300 patients per month. Added to this was the challenging and diverse work taken on by the nursing staff in wards. They describe the lack of bed linen, two patients to a bed due to inadequate ward space, and even worse crowding in the paediatric wards.

Little credit can be given to the Department of External Affairs for the administrative arrangements of the commitment. Teams were developed without sound knowledge of the work they would be undertaking. They were not advised of the living conditions, the quality of the hospitals, or the availability of supplies; nor were they briefed on the type of equipment and clothing they would require. Furthermore, briefings were not provided despite thorough reports being submitted by very senior medical specialists who were specifically sent to provide advice to the Department of External Affairs on the program. At the completion of their tours, returning team leaders also submitted reports that seemingly were not used for briefing material.

Particular reference is made to the considerable assistance provided to the teams by the military forces of both Australia and the United States. The servicemen of both countries went to great lengths to assist in provision of medical supplies, vehicle repair and maintenance, travel assistance and security support.

The book includes comments and opinions from a wide range of people involved in the program, discussing the attitudes of the Vietnamese patients and staff, and the character of the patients—indeed, their extraordinary stoicism under horrific conditions, and their gratitude for the care given by the teams, are nothing short of inspirational.

The practical details also make this book a useful source of information on the undertaking of the organisation of medical care in a foreign country. Naturally, the issue of language is crucial; interpreters or (ideally) prior language training should be provided. While the lesson in Vietnam was that the local people were overwhelmingly thankful for the care that was provided, language was always a problem and clearly should be considered as a primary issue for similar aid programs.

With Healing Hands is a beautiful story of Australian men and women, amidst the horror of war, providing superb care and succour to often forgotten people—the local civilian families. Villagers caught in a war zone and coping with tragedy, bereavement, pain and more. Australia can be proud of and grateful for the work of these wonderfully dedicated medical teams, who volunteered to help.

W.B. Digger James
Major General (Retd)
16 May 2009

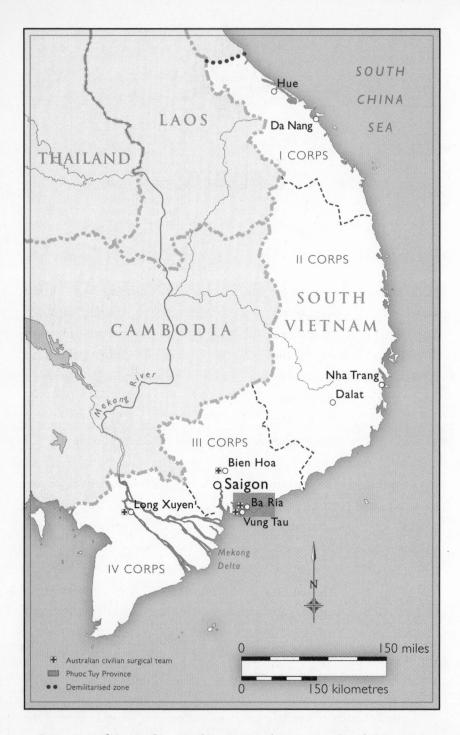

Location of Australian civilian surgical teams in South Vietnam

Preface

In 2005, while researching women's roles in the Vietnam War for the Australian War Memorial's new Vietnam gallery, author Elizabeth Stewart came across the remarkable war story of nursing sister Dorothy 'Dot' Angell. Serving for four months with an Alfred Hospital civilian surgical team in the war-ravaged city of Bien Hoa in 1967, Dot wrote a series of candid and emotional letters home to her family. Reading these letters, Elizabeth became aware that Dot was part of a large and distinguished group of medical professionals whose war story was yet to be told.

Dealing with minor burns, broken limbs and mild illnesses, delivering babies, and treating patients with plague, tetanus, malaria, advanced cancer, horrific war wounds and severe facial deformities, the teams worked through floods, enervating heat, and enemy attack to bring medical relief to an exhausted and traumatised Vietnamese population. The nearly 500 Australian men and women who signed up to work on surgical teams during the eight years they operated in South Vietnam did so for a variety of reasons: adventure, excitement, professional challenge, empathy for a people at war. All found themselves at times confronted, scared, angry, exhausted and challenged, but few, if any, regretted their decision to go to Vietnam.

Important as the teams' work was, there was another reason for writing this history. Although they were sent by Australia under the auspices of the Southeast Asia Treaty Organisation (SEATO) and administered by the Department of External Affairs (now the Department of Foreign Affairs and Trade), all of the teams had close links with the United States, South Vietnamese and Australian military. Indeed, most could not have operated without the support of military personnel and the supplies they provided. As well, although team members were working as civilians, they, like their military counterparts, were exposed daily to the sights, sounds and physical toll of life in a war zone, and many suffered from stress, nightmares, flashbacks and unexplained illness on their return home. Their experiences were similar in many ways to those of the medical personnel who worked in Australian Army field hospitals, but this has never been officially recognised.

In 2000, and again in 2002, former team members petitioned the federal government to have their medical conditions recognised and brought under the *Veterans' Entitlements Act*. This would give them proper compensation and access to correct medical care for illnesses and depression that resulted from their Vietnam service. On both occasions their representations failed, for reasons outlined in the epilogue. This book was written in part to bring the teams' service to light and to provide historical background for any future claims for official recognition.

It could not have been written without the generous support and encouragement of many former surgical team members. As well as being the inspiration for the book, Dot Angell provided names, contact details—indeed, placed her vast database on former team members at our disposal. With this we were able to construct a wide-ranging interview program, and we thank her for her generosity. Dot also provided documents, and her PhD thesis on the experiences of civilian nurses in Vietnam was a useful starting point. Other team members, such as Veronica 'Von' Clinch, Beth Scott, Jenny O'Neill, Peter Last, Gavan O'Connor, Jan Bell and Joan Rose provided documents, letters and diaries that helped bring their oral stories to life. All of those we interviewed provided us with invaluable information, copious tea and coffee, and some fantastic meals. We thank them all for opening their homes and their hearts to us while reliving what were at times painful memories.

We would also like to thank our publisher, Ian Bowring, for enabling us to bring this story into the public domain, and for his patience: the book was written in a difficult period during which both authors had bouts of illness. Our appreciation is also extended to our editor, Clara Finlay.

Both our families were tolerant of our absences during the long interview process. Elizabeth thanks Jerry, Katherine and Emily for their patience, and Gary thanks his partner, Margot. It has been a privilege and a pleasure to learn and write about the experiences of civilian doctors and nurses in South Vietnam, and we hope we have done justice to the information we have been so freely given.

Elizabeth Stewart and Gary McKay

Introduction

For centuries before the United States and its allies became involved in Vietnam, the country had been almost continuously at war, either fighting off invaders or embroiled in disputes between north and south.

French colonial rule over Indochina (Vietnam, Cambodia and Laos)[1] began in the 1860s. It was notably cruel and deeply unpopular, particularly in the north. Opposition to the French was led by the Indochinese Communist Party, launched in 1930 by Ho Chi Minh. After a series of failed uprisings, in 1941 a coalition of nationalists and communists formed the League for the Independence of Vietnam, later known as the Viet Minh.

During the Second World War, the Japanese invasion temporarily drove out the French, and the Viet Minh, with support from both the US and China, focused on fighting the new enemy. Weeks after the Japanese surrender in August 1945, Ho Chi Minh declared in Hanoi, the northern capital, the independence of the Democratic Republic of Vietnam (DRV).

At the allies' Potsdam Conference in July 1945, it had been agreed that the territory of Vietnam would be divided at the 16th parallel: the French would take the Japanese surrender in the south; the Chinese in the north. Since Free French forces were not yet ready to move in, the British temporarily replaced them. However, by late 1945 the French—

who had never recognised Ho Chi Minh's DRV—were in control again throughout most of the country. The Viet Minh began liaising more closely with the Chinese communists in the north while maintaining control over a network of revolutionaries in the south.

The Viet Minh eventually drove the French out of Vietnam after a bitterly fought campaign that culminated in the overrunning of French forces at Dien Bien Phu, in the country's far northwest, in 1954. This marked the end of what is often termed the First Indochina War.

By this time, the 1949 victory of the communists in China and communist-inspired insurgencies in Indonesia, Thailand, Malaya, the Philippines and Burma, in addition to Indochina, had persuaded the US that much of Asia could fall under communist control.[2] In April 1950, General Omar Bradley, chairman of the Joint Chiefs of Staff, advised the US Secretary of Defense that 'South East Asia is a vital segment in the line of containment of communism stretching from Japan southward and around to the Indian Peninsula.'[3] After the 1950 invasion of South Korea by the Chinese- and Soviet-backed North, President Harry S. Truman ordered an 'acceleration in the furnishing of military assistance to the forces of France and the Associated States in Indochina.'[4]

After the French defeat in 1954, the Geneva Accords recognised Indochinese independence from France. Vietnam was divided along the 17th parallel, known as the Demilitarised Zone, or DMZ. Internationally supervised elections, which the communists expected to win, were to be held in 1956. As the French exited the south, the French-installed emperor, Bao Dai, sought to retain control over his State of Vietnam. He appointed as prime minister Ngo Dinh Diem, who soon deposed him via referendum and in October 1955 declared the Republic of Vietnam. Diem refused to be bound by the Geneva Accords, and the elections were never held.

Meanwhile, as large numbers of anticommunists, notably Catholics, migrated from north to south, the communists in the south formed the National Liberation Front, better known as the Viet Cong, with the goal of unifying Vietnam under communist rule. The Viet Cong began a campaign of insurgency against the Republic of South Vietnam, supported from 1959 by the Vietnam Communist Party, which moved soldiers and weapons into the south via the clandestine land route that was soon dubbed the Ho Chi Minh Trail. This marked the start of the Second Indochina War, known inside Vietnam as the American War.

The American War

The US began providing advisers to the South Vietnamese in 1954 under President Dwight D. Eisenhower. Asked at a news conference to 'comment on the strategic importance of Indochina to the free world', Eisenhower replied with a summation of what he called the 'falling domino principle. You have a row of dominoes set up, you knock over the first one, and what will happen to the last one is the certainty that it will go over very quickly . . . The possible consequences of the loss [of free Southeast Asian nations] are just incalculable to the free world.'[5]

In 1961 the so-called Domino Theory gained fresh currency when a three-way political struggle arose in Laos, which shared borders with Vietnam, China, Burma, Thailand and Cambodia. The US supported royalist forces against the communist Pathet Lao, which had fought with the Viet Minh against the French and which hosted several thousand North Vietnamese troops in areas under its control. The Soviet Union and China both competed for the allegiance of the Lao communists. Handing over to President John F. Kennedy in 1961, Eisenhower told his successor that if Laos were to fall to communism, it would be 'just a question of time' before its neighbours fell too.[6]

In mid 1962, a coalition government was formed and Laos was declared neutral. However, North Vietnam continued to use Laotian territory as a transit route to South Vietnam. The Kennedy Administration accordingly boosted defence aid and civil-project support to the south.

Also fuelling US involvement in South Vietnam was the growing unpopularity of the Diem government and the perceived ineptitude of the Army of the Republic of Vietnam (ARVN). President Kennedy was urged to send in combat forces to bolster the ARVN, but instead sent US Special Forces (Green Berets) to help the South Vietnamese develop a counterinsurgency program. In November 1963, Diem was murdered in a military coup that had tacit US support. Soon afterwards, Kennedy was assassinated.

His successor, President Lyndon Johnson, increased the number of US advisers to more than 16,000 in 1964. Determined not to let South Vietnam fall to the communists, he launched covert attacks on North Vietnamese infrastructure and military installations, as well as the Ho Chi Minh Trail. In August 1964, US ships reported (falsely, as now appears) that they had been fired on by North Vietnamese vessels. The so-called Gulf of Tonkin incident led the US Congress to hand over its war-making powers to the president. In March 1965, after North Vietnamese troops launched surprise attacks on a US helicopter base and a military quarters, Johnson ordered a sustained bombing campaign against North Vietnam and sent in ground troops to protect the air bases in the south. When the first group of 3500 Marines landed at Da Nang, they were welcomed with garlands of flowers. By June 1964 the US had 75,000 combat troops in South Vietnam; by the end of 1965 it had committed 200,000.

Australia's involvement

Australia's formal links with South Vietnam began in November 1952, when Canberra sent to Saigon an accredited Minister for Vietnam, Cambodia and Laos. In February 1955, Australia became a member of SEATO after ratifying the collective defence treaty of the same name. SEATO aimed to limit communist gains in the region by improving the economic condition of Southeast Asian states. While Vietnam was not a member, it was included as a territory under SEATO protection.

In 1959, the Australian legation in South Vietnam became an embassy with the appointment of an Australian ambassador to South Vietnam (and Minister to Laos). Two years later, Canberra's concerns about the communist threat to the region reached new heights as Indonesian President Sukarno claimed Netherlands New Guinea (today's West Irian) for Indonesia. Warning that he would use force if necessary to bring the territory under Indonesian control, he secured the support of the Soviet Union and the People's Republic of China. Against Australia's wishes, West Irian was transferred to Indonesia. Now increasingly relying on the Indonesian Communist Party for support, Sukarno also opposed the British-backed Federation of Malaysia and launched a policy of confrontation (*Konfrontasi*) to stop the union. Australia grew increasingly worried that it could soon have a communist-controlled state at its northern 'back door'. In 1963, the government of Sir Robert Menzies identified Indonesia as the main strategic threat to Australia and its territories.[7]

The previous year, after repeated requests from President Diem, Canberra had sent the first Australian Army Training Team Vietnam (AATTV) contingent of thirty advisers to South Vietnam.[8] In 1964, as US troop numbers approached 70,000, the AATTV's strength was increased to eighty. Though its members were not directly involved in combat operations at first, it was increasingly difficult for them to avoid combat. On 6 July, Warrant Officer Kevin Conway became the first Australian soldier to be killed in action in Vietnam, during an attack on his special forces camp at Nam Dong. The following month, the Royal Australian Air Force sent six Caribou transport planes to the coastal town of Vung Tau. In November 1964, chiefly over fears about Indonesia and *Konfrontasi*, the Australian government introduced selective conscription by ballot under the *National Service Act*. National Servicemen were obliged to serve full-time for two years.

The first Australian combat troops arrived in Vietnam in April 1965, when the Menzies Government sent the 1st Battalion, Royal Australian Regiment (1RAR) to Bien Hoa to serve with the US 173rd Airborne Brigade. As the US war effort escalated, and as Australia tagged along 'all the way with LBJ', the Australian military commitment also grew. In 1965 full-time National Servicemen were made liable for 'special overseas service' in Malaysia or Vietnam. The first 'Nashos' landed in South Vietnam in mid 1966 as part of an allied force that, aside from the US, included servicemen from New Zealand, Thailand, the Philippines and South Korea. The Vietnam War would generate Australia's longest ever commitment to any armed conflict and—partly as a result of conscription—its most divisive.

The teams

Australia sent its first civilian surgical team to the Republic of Vietnam (South Vietnam) in 1964. Prior to that, the country had been receiving civilian aid from Australia as a member of the Colombo Plan, but as a member of SEATO, South Vietnam was entitled to further aid under Australia's SEATO aid program. The country desperately needed medical assistance. South Vietnam had a population of about 16 million, and of the country's approximately 850 doctors, only 158 were available to care for the civilian population. The rest had been conscripted into the army.

Given the dire lack of medical care for its people, the government of South Vietnam appealed to the United States Agency for International Development (USAID) for medical teams. USAID was the body that arranged and distributed all American and allied civilian aid to South Vietnam, eventually including the Australian surgical teams. After some discussion, it was decided to ask various nations to send civilian surgical teams to work at provincial hospitals throughout South Vietnam. To accommodate the teams, USAID began building new surgical suites and improving existing buildings in many of the country's French-built hospitals. By the end of 1963, twenty-six of thirty-eight provincial hospitals had been equipped for modern surgery.[1] Despite the improvements, Australian surgical team members were to find conditions very different from those they were used to at home.

The first three American surgical teams arrived in South Vietnam in January 1963 and were based in the towns of Da Nang, Nha Trang and Can Tho. A New Zealand team arrived a short time later, operating out of Qui Nhon. Teams were also sent from South Korea, the Philippines, the United Kingdom, China, Switzerland, Iran, Spain, France and Cuba, and a German hospital ship, the *Helgoland*, was moored in the Saigon River. In addition, around 770 doctors, male nurses and technicians from the United States armed forces were organised into Military Provincial Hospital Assistance Program teams, which served as advisers in district dispensaries and lived and worked with groups attached to the South Vietnamese Army.[2]

In 1962, after USAID relayed the South Vietnamese request for medical support to the Australian government, the Department of External Affairs (DEA) sent a leading Melbourne neurologist, Dr John Game, to South Vietnam to assess what was needed. In his report, Dr Game said 'the request for surgical teams appears to be based on a sound concept and offers a means ... to give immediate aid, the benefits of which will extend through the whole country'. Furthermore, it would be 'a form of aid which would be at once visible to the local populace and the world', but not one that would involve Australia in a continuous commitment.[3] He recommended that a surgical team (only one in the first instance) be sent to the town of Nha Trang, on the central coast. Although the location of the first team was later changed to Long Xuyen, in the Mekong delta, Dr Game's second recommendation, that the team be raised from one of the major teaching hospitals, was adopted.

Despite Dr Game's comprehensive report and the Australian government's support for the scheme, it was another two years before the first Australian civilian surgical team was sent to Vietnam. The aims of the teams were threefold: to provide a quality general surgical and medical service for the South Vietnamese population; to teach the Vietnamese medical staff (mainly by example); and, as Dr Game had foreseen, to serve as evidence of Australia's support and concern for the people of South Vietnam. Although these aims appeared straightforward, they were to prove ambiguous and difficult to implement, and many team members later questioned why the teams were sent at all.

Team composition

The first Australian surgical team, from the Royal Melbourne Hospital, arrived in Long Xuyen, the capital of An Giang province in the Mekong delta, in October 1964. It served as something of a template for later teams, coming as it did from a major teaching hospital and comprising experienced doctors, nurses and other personnel hand picked for the job. As time went on, and the number of medical staff wanting to join the teams declined, the DEA sought teams from Repatriation hospitals across the country. When this pool too proved inadequate, composite teams were formed from hospitals around Australia. These, however, sometimes lacked the close bonds and unity of purpose of the earlier, single-hospital-based teams.

As it became harder to recruit people, less experienced and younger men and women were chosen. Some older team members felt that these people adapted less successfully to conditions in Vietnam, and that their inexperience led to team disunity. John Game's original view had been that the first team to go must be made up of experienced, mature staff: at minimum, a surgeon 'with experience and judgement' (preferably an outpatient surgeon of a teaching hospital), a more junior doctor or experienced general practitioner, an anaesthetist, a theatre sister, a ward sister, a laboratory technician and a radiographer. His preference was for team members who had already worked together, presumably because this would help with team cohesion. The theatre sister, he noted, 'should be a resourceful woman, physically robust and with experience'. Terms of service, Game thought, should be three months for the senior surgeon and twelve months for the junior. Team members should be replaced one at a time, to help maintain continuity and local knowledge.[4]

Practical experience in Vietnam and difficulties with recruiting ensured that many of Dr Game's recommendations were eventually laid aside. As the volume of work grew, it became clear that many more staff would be needed. By 1967 it was recommended that teams should have at least ten members, with, in addition, a paediatrician, an administrative officer and extra nursing sisters.[5] Later on, teams of sixteen or more were not uncommon. Length of service also varied from Dr Game's recommendations. One constant problem was the amount of time senior surgeons could take away from their work. Many had heavy responsibilities at their home hospitals, as they were often leading specialists in their field, or had private practices that could not be left for long periods. Three to four months was the longest that most could afford to be away. Still, a significant number felt they had more to contribute after their first tour and returned to South Vietnam a second or even third time. Junior surgeons also faced difficulty in getting away. An absence of several months could make a significant difference to the progress of their career. On the other hand, some applied because they thought experience gained in Vietnam would benefit their careers.

Nursing and other medical staff often joined the teams for six months. Most felt this was enough time to feel they had achieved something, but by the end of it they had had enough of the difficult conditions and pressures of the work in Vietnam. A small number of teams were sent for one year but that was uncommon, since it soon became clear that twelve-month tours led to high rates of burnout, illness and exhaustion.

Two of the most important team roles were those of the leader and the administrator. In a 1965 report on team progress in Long Xuyen, it was emphasised that 'good leadership, of vital importance in the functioning of armed forces, is perhaps more important in small civilian teams isolated in a foreign community, where the cultivation and maintenance of good relations between the team and the host civilian population poses further demands on team members'.[6] The team leader, usually the senior surgeon, was responsible for looking after other team members, settling disputes and ensuring that their mental and physical needs were met. A good leader united his team; a poor one could damage morale and lower work standards.

The administrator's job, as outlined in 1967, was to relieve the leader of most of the daily non-medical chores,[7] but the lack of a clear duty statement was frustrating for some who took up this role. Bill Townsend, who was team administrator in Vung Tau in 1968–69, remembers attending a DEA briefing where he was given a letter outlining his duties and told that 'the success of the mission depends upon you'. In fact, the letter gave him only the most basic guidance and he had to learn most of the job on the run,[8] finding ways to maintain supplies, organise pay, arrange maintenance and repairs both at the hospitals and the team members' housing, look after team vehicles, and ensure the smooth running of the team.

Administration and conditions

Australian surgical teams were administered by the DEA. The Department organised team members' travel arrangements, vaccinations, pay and briefings. In Saigon, the capital of South Vietnam, teams were officially under the auspices of the Australian embassy but in fact had little contact with it. Teams were usually met in Saigon by embassy staff, and occasionally briefed by them, but after that formal contact was mainly limited to meetings between the team administrator and the embassy's Counsellor for Aid, though team members sometimes attended official embassy functions.

In 1967 the DEA decided to rely on the Vietnamese for all the teams' supplies and equipment.[9] This did not work out well. Team members often carried basic medicines and equipment to Vietnam in their luggage, but ongoing supplies were always a problem. When the first teams arrived at the four provincial hospitals to which Australian teams were sent, they found that medical supplies and equipment were almost nonexistent. The team in Vung Tau had to spend two weeks cleaning the hospital and installing basic equipment before they could even begin to deliver medical services. Teams in Bien Hoa, Long Xuyen and Ba Ria had similar problems. Generally, they relied on USAID and American and Australian military hospitals to provide them with the necessary supplies. This was not a perfect arrangement and took valuable time away from their primary work, but it was unavoidable. Later teams, which had administrators, were spared much of the scrounging for supplies that their predecessors were forced to do, but even so, shortages of such basic items as blood supplies continued.

Before leaving for Vietnam, all team members were given medical examinations by the Department of Health and were vaccinated against smallpox, plague, cholera and typhoid. Throughout the tour they took antimalarial pills. The Vietnamese Ministry of Health housed the teams, usually in a single building, but in Vung Tau in two buildings. Teams were provided with Vietnamese staff to do their laundry, cleaning and cooking; their food came from the local markets. It was part of the team administrator's job to run the team house, pay local staff and, most importantly, make sure 'that the beer supplies were kept going too'.[10]

Team members were paid according to their status. The leaders received the highest salary, plus an allowance for their extra responsibilities. All team members were given a daily allowance of $6.25 to cover extra expenses. Because their food and accommodation were paid for, this was usually found to be enough.

Many team members found conditions in South Vietnam difficult and exhausting, especially if their tour of duty was long. Leave was deemed essential, and most leaders made provision for each member to have a weekend away every few weeks. Those on six-month contracts got one week's leave; those in Vietnam for a year were given three weeks off. During longer breaks, many took the opportunity to explore neighbouring countries, and Cambodia and Thailand were popular destinations. On shorter breaks, members sometimes travelled in small groups to other towns in South Vietnam, especially Da Nang, Nha Trang, and Dalat, in the mountains. For weekend trips many went to the seaside resort town of Vung Tau, visiting their local counterparts and enjoying the beach. Vung Tau teams in turn visited Bien Hoa and Long Xuyen, which was set in a relatively quiet and peaceful location on the Bassac River.

Preparation

Surgical teams were formed in various ways. Early teams were often hand picked by senior surgeons in the teaching hospitals. Dr Mervyn Smith, who took the first Royal Adelaide Hospital team to Bien Hoa in 1967, was a persuasive recruiter. He approached a number of the hospital's experienced doctors, nurses and other medical specialists and eventually assembled a team of twelve, most of whom signed up for a six-month tour. Dr Smith was exceptionally well liked, and his care in choosing his team was rewarded with a tightly knit, harmonious group of men and women who worked and lived together without major problems.

Even where teams were not hand picked, they generally bonded into happy working units. Often vacancies were advertised on hospital noticeboards, and applicants were interviewed either by the team leader or senior hospital staff. Janet Brewster's (née Glasson) selection was typical. She was working as a nurse at the Royal Prince Alfred Hospital in Sydney and had read some of the letters sent back from a Prince Alfred team in Long Xuyen. They inspired her to apply when positions on a New South Wales state team were advertised:

> I was only twenty-four at the time and they wanted them twenty-five plus. I very brazenly went to this interview thinking 'Oh, well.' There were people lined up everywhere

for interviews. There was a panel of six, I think. And then I got notification to say I was chosen ... It was [because] I had all the qualifications [and] because I had been to a boarding school and they knew I wouldn't get homesick.[11]

New recruits often had very little time to prepare themselves for the adventure ahead. In some cases nurses had only a few weeks to obtain passports, get vaccinated, buy and pack the necessary supplies and clothing, and farewell their families. Surgeons usually had a slightly longer lead time, as it was a complicated business leaving a practice or senior hospital position, even for three months.

Few team members were briefed by the DEA before they left. Those who were—they were flown to Canberra for the purpose—received advice on issues like what clothing to take and how to be good representatives of Australia. Very few people received useful advice on how to cope with living in a war zone, what safety precautions to take, or what Vietnamese customs they needed to be aware of to avoid giving offence to their hosts. A few team members were offered, and took up, the opportunity to learn basic Vietnamese, but most were told not to bother: rudimentary French would do. This did not prove to be the case.

Every former team member interviewed for this book was critical of the lack of preparation he or she had been given for work in Vietnam. The early teams, being the pioneers, were forced to learn on the spot. However, they were never asked to formally brief later teams, who would have benefited greatly from their experience. Information was sometimes passed informally from those who had returned from Vietnam to those preparing to go, but this process was ad hoc and relatively uncommon.

Dr Peter Last, a paediatrician and anaesthetist in Bien Hoa in 1967, wrote a detailed report towards the end of his tour with the aim of improving conditions for later teams. About departmental briefings he wrote:

No attempt whatever was made to prepare us for the considerable difficulties and frustrations of the Asian temperament and Vietnamese customs. Only after many weeks did we discover that these people must not be beckoned to with one finger, spoken to in a loud voice, touched upon the back, or pointed to . . . If this sort of information is not known to the Department, it certainly should be, and it should be promulgated before members leave.[12]

Peter Last's was not the only report written during or after a tour by a team member determined to make things easier for his successors, yet it seems that such information was rarely, if ever, passed on.

Sometimes, when team members did receive briefings or written notes, they were inaccurate. John Morriss remembers being reminded by his team leader about 'the construction of deep trench latrines and the use of duckboards in tented camps in the tropics'. Expecting primitive accommodation, he was pleasantly surprised to find that the team house in Long Xuyen 'was in a French colonial villa with eleven bedrooms and seven bathrooms'.[13] The advice given to Kay Dabovich, a nurse in Long Xuyen in 1969, included not wearing shorts or other revealing clothing in public and preferably not wearing trousers; apart from that, she recalls, 'we were not given much information at all'.[14] Dot Angell, who served with the Alfred Hospital team in Bien Hoa in 1967, was very blunt about their poor preparation:

The preparation that we had was nothing. It was like a tour guide to sunny Vietnam. We had no idea what the living and working conditions would be like . . . And [there was] no discussion about what it would be like to be a woman in a war zone.[15]

Whether the lack of information and outright misinformation were the fault of the DEA or of the individual hospitals involved, or both, is not clear. Certainly, however, the team members felt that it was left to them to learn how to do their job and cope with wartime conditions as best they could once they arrived in Vietnam. It is to their credit that most coped extremely well with being thrown in the deep end. Some of those who struggled, however, still feel the effects of their Vietnam service today.

'Doing something worthwhile'

Motives for joining a team going to Vietnam varied greatly. Some nurses had previously worked in Third World countries and wanted to repeat the experience. Others were looking for adventure, or felt a strong desire to help civilians in a country at war. Dot Angell was one of many young women who wanted a change:

> I'm a daughter of the sixties and I'd just arrived back home after three and a half years in swinging London. I went back to my training hospital, the Alfred, and I found it very oppressive. So when they called for volunteers to join the Alfred Hospital team to go to Vietnam, of course I volunteered.[16]

Jenny Hunter (née Dyason), who nursed in Long Xuyen in 1967 and Bien Hoa in 1969, had mixed motives. She too had been nursing in England and felt that Vietnam would be an adventure, but she also felt she had a duty to go because 'I was fit and well and a nurse'.[17]

Many men were also looking for an exciting opportunity. John Morriss joined the Royal Perth Hospital team in Long Xuyen in 1969. He had recently retired after serving for thirteen years in the British Army and 'had just begun to get itchy feet when the opportunity to go to Vietnam, as the team's administrative officer, arose. I jumped at the chance.'[18] Others believed that the opportunity would give them extra surgical skills or simply wanted to do some good in a war-torn country. Peter Last was typical of some doctors who wanted to emulate their teachers, men who had worked as surgeons during the Second World War or in Korea:

> I was just too young to get involved in the Second World War, and to have gone to Korea would have broken my medical course. But I always had a sense of inadequacy that I wasn't able to have those experiences . . . [so] the main drawcard was the feeling that I would actually be doing something worthwhile in a foreign setting . . . which would give me some wartime experience and exposure so I could look those ex-servicemen in the eye . . .[19]

Although there were a variety of reasons for people wanting to serve in a surgical team, a common theme was altruism. Whether they agreed with the reasons for the war or not, many were struck by the fact that millions of South Vietnamese were suffering and they felt a strong desire to help alleviate that suffering. Gavan O'Connor, a laboratory technician in Vung Tau and Bien Hoa in 1969, expressed this motivation in one of his first letters to his wife, Dolores:

> Darling, you can't possibly know how sorry I am to have upset you—but as you know, some things just have to be done. It's no good going through life leaving the hard work to other people. As has often been said, 'All that it needs for evil to conquer, is that good men do nothing.'[20]

His fellow team member Bill Townsend said that his decision to go had a political dimension. He has always been more of an opponent than a supporter of the war, but he strongly believed that there was a social solution to the conflict, and he wanted to be part of it.[21]

Gavan O'Connor's wife, Dolores, was one of many spouses who were less than thrilled to see their partner leave home for several months.

Many senior doctors had young families; several had children born while they were on their tour of duty. Graham Douglas Tracy (Doug) was the senior surgeon and team leader of the first team sent to work in Vung Tau in November 1966. As head of surgery at Prince Henry Hospital in Sydney, he was asked to form a team and did so at once. As he says, though, the timing wasn't perfect—'My wife was pregnant for the sixth time and . . . I don't think she was enthused, but . . . all my life I've been lucky to have someone who goes along with my plans and so she didn't put any blocks in my way.'[22] Doug Tracy's daughter was born while he was still in Vietnam, and he, like many of his colleagues, was deeply grateful to his wife for letting him go.

Other team members experienced varied reactions from their families. The news that she would be heading to Vietnam made Dot Angell's father 'very, very proud' because he had been unable to serve in the Second World War, but it made her mother very anxious. Jan Bell, a nurse in Vung Tau in 1968, said that as a Second World War veteran her father hated the idea of her going to Vietnam.

> He didn't even want me to be a nurse in the first place because you see men's genitalia . . . so he just hated the thought of me going to Vietnam. Thought it was a dreadful place. And my mother didn't like it at all either. [23]

A sense of adventure, a strong will, and a desire to help the Vietnamese were common to many of the nurses who served in Vietnam, whether their families approved or not.

Teams usually flew as a group to Vietnam. Sometimes the leader went a couple of weeks early, to look at conditions and work out the best way to deploy members. Doug Tracy was flown over early to assess conditions in Long Xuyen and Bien Hoa before being taken to Le Loi Hospital in Vung Tau, where his would be the first Australian team to operate. He was horrified at the state of the hospital and realised that his team would be spending a good while cleaning up before any surgery could take place.[24]

Teams who flew out together used the trip as an opportunity to get to know each other. The strict hierarchy that separated senior and junior surgeons and nursing staff in Australian hospitals began to soften on these flights. First-class Qantas service, complete with champagne, helped the process, as did a necessary stopover in Singapore. For those used to the tropics, Singapore was a pleasant interlude before the hard work began, but for many team members, especially the younger nurses, it was an eye-opener. The tropical weather and crowds of Asian faces touched off a culture shock that only grew once they landed in Saigon. For Joan Rose (née Pryor), a radiographer in Long Xuyen, the food on the trip over made an impression:

> I remember sitting first class . . . with Pat Maplestone, who was the anaesthetist, and Pat saying to me, 'Well this is caviar, Joan,' and I'm thinking 'Oh, right.' And I remember I wrote home and said something like it took us three hours to have our meal.[25]

Janet Brewster, who also worked in Long Xuyen, found the travel and arrival in Vietnam an intense experience:

> My biggest shock was seeing so many people my height. I was always the squirt. All these people in Singapore when we first landed there . . . There were millions of them, and they were all short people. And the hustle and bustle of the airport and landing in Saigon. The intensity of so much military and so many aircraft. It was quite an experience.[26]

It was important for team leaders to use this travel time to pull their teams together, because although few of those heading to Vietnam knew what to expect, they were certain that hard work would require team unity.

Whether they travelled in groups or individually, most team members have vivid memories of their arrival in Saigon. At that time the city's main airport, Tan Son Nhut, was one of the busiest in the world, buzzing with military aircraft and personnel. Team members were left in no doubt that they had arrived in a war zone, and for many, this was when the reality of their situation hit home. A common reaction to seeing the evidence of war was, 'What on earth have I got myself into?', followed by the realisation that it was too late to back out.

Dot Angell had a particularly rough introduction to the war. When her Pan Am flight from Singapore landed in Saigon, it was left sitting on the tarmac for two hours owing to a dispute between the South Vietnamese and American governments. As she remembers, they had no air-conditioning and nothing to drink, and the atmosphere was stifling:

> The plane was surrounded by South Vietnamese, all with M16 rifles. That . . . was quite a wake up. That we weren't in sunny Vietnam, that we were in a war zone and that was our first experience of how dangerous it was going to be . . . I think being so young it was all terribly exciting. But after a while, when we were on the ground, that excitement changed.[27]

Bill Townsend, heading for Vung Tau in late 1968, was typical of those who had second thoughts:

> You got off the plane and immediately the smells were differ-ent and you saw all this military hardware, rows and rows of it. And there were fighter aircraft . . . You looked around [at]

everyone in uniform and the scurry and the urgency of it. And I thought, gee whiz, have I done the right thing? . . . Too late for that now.[28]

Australian embassy staff met team members at the airport. Because they travelled on diplomatic passports, they cleared Customs fairly quickly. Teams were taken either to the embassy to be briefed or directly to their accommodation. Dot Angell's team received a briefing, but she was unimpressed when embassy officials left them standing, tired and thirsty, while telling them what they could and could not do in Vietnam.[29] After this initial contact, most team members saw little of embassy staff, whom they sometimes sensed were not interested in their work or their problems. In his September 1967 report on conditions in Bien Hoa, Peter Last noted that individual contact between team members and the embassy 'has been so minimal as hardly to exist'. He wrote that although the ambassador and his wife had visited the team for lunch, and that other foreign ambassadors had been brought to visit, other problems on which he had asked for help had been ignored or barely addressed. He urged the embassy to 'take a close and continuing interest in our work' because Bien Hoa was close to Saigon and could therefore be used as a showcase of Australia's aid contribution to South Vietnam.[30] But his and others' suggestions seem to have gone unheeded, and the lack of close contact between the Australian embassy and the surgical teams persisted.

In Saigon, team members stayed in what was called the Aid house, a residence run for much of the time by an Australian engineer, Ralph Pennington. It was a comfortable building with polished wood floors, described by surgeon Tom Hugh as 'like something out of a Somerset Maugham novel', with an interesting mix of government officials, judges, and other 'strange people' staying there.[31] It was a convenient place for team members to stay when they needed to travel to Saigon for any reason. Saigon too made an impression, not always favourable. Gavan O'Connor found the city 'a dismal sight' full of 'square concrete sort of buildings and . . . nothing very colourful.'[32] Others thought it a fascinating city and a good place to escape to, away from the endless work and the pressure of life in a provincial hospital. Most team members saw little of Saigon at first, as they were quickly taken to their final destinations. They usually did not mind, being keen to start work. Landing in Saigon was only the start of the adventure. Much more lay in store.

2

First in: Long Xuyen

The first Australian civilian surgical team sent to South Vietnam left for Saigon on 3 October 1964. The team was from the Royal Melbourne Hospital; its final destination was Long Xuyen, whose provincial hospital would host Australian surgical teams until their withdrawal in late 1970.

An Giang province, in the southwest of South Vietnam, shares a border with Cambodia. Its flat countryside is scored by hundreds of rivers, streams and canals, and in the 1960s its inhabitants were mainly fishermen and rice farmers. In 1964 the province had about 450,000 people and only seven doctors. Four of those worked in the provincial hospital; the rest were in private practice. There were no medically trained personnel working in the countryside. When most people in the province fell ill, medical or surgical treatment did not even occur to them; they generally sought help from practitioners of traditional medicine.

Long Xuyen was an attractive town located on the Bassac River, a tributary of the Mekong. During the war it was relatively immune from attack; in 1967 Dr Alister Brass, travelling in Vietnam as a special reporter for the *Medical Journal of Australia*, reported that the town was '97 per cent secure' from enemy attack.[1] The reason for this was the predominance within An Giang of the Hoa Hao sect, an offshoot of

Buddhism founded in 1939 by a native of the Mekong delta region. The sect emphasised simplicity of life and worship within the home; farming was espoused as the lifestyle most conducive to religious practice. In 1947 the sect's prophet, Huynh Phu So, was kidnapped and murdered by the Viet Minh. This assassination led to a universal hatred of the Viet Cong among Hoa Hao followers, who helped to protect the inhabitants of An Giang from the communists. As a result, Viet Cong forces largely stayed away from Long Xuyen, staging most of their attacks further out in the province, often close to or on the Cambodian border. It was also rumoured that Viet Cong fighters were disinclined to attack the town because they used it as a rest and recreation centre.

The Australians found Long Xuyen warm and friendly. It had '. . . a centre of curving, sun-faded, two-storey yellow buildings . . . and a bustling seven-days-a-week market notable for its seafood'.[2] Its 60,000 people were well fed from the plentiful supplies of rice, fruit, vegetables, poultry and fish that were grown and harvested in the region. On the other hand, poor sanitation, widespread stagnant water and crowded living conditions meant that many people had chronic illnesses or infections, which kept the hospital busy. The hospital itself had beds for about 450 patients but its patient load was often double that figure. As well as the four local doctors working there, Vietnamese staff included a nurse anaesthetist and a number of nurses. No major surgery was carried out at the hospital.

The Department of External Affairs initially asked the Royal Melbourne Hospital to supply a self-sufficient surgical unit made up of two surgeons, an anaesthetist, a physician, two theatre sisters, a ward sister and a radiographer. Two nurses on the team, Ann Boucher and Susan Terry, were prepared to stay for a full year. The rest of the team were relieved after three or four months, although Royal Melbourne continued to supply staff to Long Xuyen for the first twelve months.

Team members had only a month's notice before leaving. As Susan Terry recalled, everyone in the team worked up until the last minute, 'so there was little time for more formal meetings. I suppose everyone felt we could make up for it later, which we did!'[3]

Susan Terry's main recollection of the first-class Qantas flight via Singapore was of the food. She had been worried about their luggage limits—she was carrying the complete works of Shakespeare.[4] Anaesthetist Jim Villiers seemed less concerned: he arrived at Melbourne airport with eleven pieces of luggage. Although this provoked some teasing, Jim had had the foresight to pack, in pieces, a self-sufficient, portable anaesthetic apparatus. In his limited preparation time, Jim had asked DEA officials what anaesthetic equipment he would have to work with in Vietnam. They told him not to worry: 'the Americans will supply everything'. Having had previous experience with the armed forces in Korea, Jim resolved to be self-sufficient. His planning paid off: the anaesthetic equipment he found at the Long Xuyen hospital was unusable, so his own unit was all he had for some time.[5]

Susan Terry remembered flying towards Saigon over delta country that was 'lush green with rice paddies and jungle scrub'. Somewhere down there, she mused, was their new home, but she was disappointed that they were not far enough inland to see Long Xuyen.[6] The first indication that they were flying into a war zone was the pilot's warning that he would be making a steep descent into Saigon to avoid being shot at.

Any misgivings the team may have had about arriving in Vietnam in the middle of a war were soon allayed when they received a welcome so effusive it 'made its members feel in some small way like Liverpudlian Beatles'.[7] The Australian Ambassador, David Anderson, was there to meet them, together with a party of about thirty others including the Vietnamese Minister for Foreign Affairs and the Director General of Health. A large banner in the Customs lounge read 'Welcome the Australian Medical Team', and Vietnamese girls presented them with garlands of fresh flowers. There was also, according to Susan Terry, a full Saigon press pack, including Vietnamese, French and English journalists, taking still photos and film footage.[8] Photos of the arrival were published in all major South Vietnamese and Australian newspapers. Subsequent team arrivals were tame in comparison.

The team spent a week in Saigon acclimatising and receiving advice. Team members attended numerous receptions with Vietnamese officials, went on outings, and had briefings on Vietnam's geography and its complex history. They were 'given the life of the privileged classes—guests of ministers of the Republic, guests of the Club Nautique on the Saigon River . . . and guests of members of the Australian embassy, who entertained us most generously'.[9] More importantly, perhaps, they began to get an idea of the medical situation in South Vietnam, meeting Vietnamese medical and nursing colleagues, and visiting the Pasteur Institute of Pathology. They discovered that their food and equipment would be supplied by the United States Operations Mission (USOM), which was the United States aid program in Vietnam. The Australian surgical teams' relationship with USOM would become crucial for their survival.

On 12 October, the Royal Melbourne team boarded a military aircraft for its final destination. Radiographer Noelle Laidlaw (née Courtney) remembers an approach similar to the one at Saigon, where the pilot 'did a quick circle over Long Xuyen airport then whipped in quickly' to avoid gunfire. On the ground, it seemed the entire town had turned out to welcome them.[10] A report on the team's efforts after twelve months also noted that 'the warmth and kindness of the welcome which greeted the team . . . exceeded even that at Saigon'.[11] Loaded into government cars, the team was taken the seven kilometres into town, their route lined with smiling and waving schoolchildren. Susan Terry was deeply moved:

> As we approached the town bridge a policeman halted the traffic. Here people were two and three deep cheering and waving. There were banners and flags everywhere . . . I couldn't stop my tears. Those flags had been made for us.[12]

A formal reception followed, at which Colonel Tuoi, the Provincial Chief, expressed his gratitude. The Australians attempted to respond in Vietnamese, with limited success, to the amusement of the large crowd. After being presented with more garlands, they were treated to lunch at Colonel Tuoi's residence.

Afterwards, en route to the hospital, they had time to take in their surroundings. Although the town boasted some substantial French-built residences, most residents lived in small thatched huts huddled along the banks of the Bassac. Many were suspended over the river and connected to the shore by rickety bridges. Cooking facilities were minimal, and many people ate from street vendors who cooked on the spot. Sewerage facilities were nonexistent in these dwellings, and toilets were simply a box suspended over one of the many channels running through the area. This was one of the reasons, the team soon realised, for the high rates of diseases such as dysentery. Despite the poverty, the team found the surroundings pleasant and lush, the greenery and abundance of water giving the area a tropical feel.

Their first impressions of the hospital were also pleasing. Built by the French, it consisted of a number of separate pavilions connected by walkways and surrounded by verandahs. Its gardens were well kept and contained large trees for shade and shelter. Noelle Laidlaw remembered that 'it looked lovely, from the outside. But it was a bit of a shock when we went in . . . [with] families camped beside little narrow beds, two patients to each bed . . . that was a bit of an eye-opener.'[13] She was not the only one to be shocked by the conditions. The buildings were generally run down, and during the wet season, when the Bassac River overflowed and flooded the hospital grounds, duckboards had to be laid across the water so staff and patients could avoid the sewage and other debris floating around. In the wards, patients commonly slept two or more to a bed, and as patient care was left mostly to relatives, at night the floors around beds and on the verandahs were crowded with people cooking, sleeping and attending to the sick.

The hospital was run by the Chief Doctor, or Médecin Chef, and domestic arrangements were taken care of by eleven Catholic nuns. The sister in charge, Sister Clothilde, had a number of favourite pigs that ran in the hospital grounds, one of the first sights to greet the new team. Considering the animals a health hazard, the team asked if they could be removed, but Sister Clothilde was reluctant. In a face-saving gesture, she accepted the gift of several bags of cement to make borders for her flowerbeds and in return kept the pigs under a degree of control.

The role of the Royal Melbourne team was clear. They were in Long Xuyen not to take over the hospital but to provide a level of surgical support that had not previously been available. Their areas of concern were limited to the surgical units and pre- and post-surgical care, including radiography and anaesthesia. The team's nurses worked in the theatres and post-operative wards. A description of the facilities by a team member reflecting on a year's work gives a sense of what the first team faced:

> The wards themselves varied in their appointments. On the one hand there was the spotlessly tiled medical ward. On the other there was the corrugated iron subsidiary maternity ward. Throughout, toilet facilities and sewage disposal was scanty and primitive. The odour of some of the buildings, of course, paralleled these shortcomings. As the year went on, new buildings were erected, alterations were made to the wards, and a sewerage system was installed.[14]

Generally, team members adapted quickly to the conditions and began trying to teach better methods by example.

After their first look at the hospital, the new team was taken to its accommodation. A large residence had been set aside for them, but the building was still under repair so for the first six weeks they were given rooms at one of the town's supposedly good hotels, the Kim Tinh.

It [the hotel] is perhaps best euphemistically described as not primarily a residential establishment. Its windows contain no glass. Its beds contain no springs. Its pillows contain no resilience. Its kitchens prepared no food ... Its toilets were far from sweet smelling ... There were no cupboards ... [and] one's sleep is intermittent on account of unfamiliar circumstances, peculiar human, canine and mechanical noises, and the sight of occasional shadowy figures on nearby rooftops.[15]

Susan Terry recalled her first night at the Kim Tinh:

I sat up in bed that night to survey the situation. I was completely surrounded by mosquito net, but my huge double bed had no bedclothes save the mattress cover. The room, apart from the bed, contained only a wash basin, a small table and a very, very small rung for hanging clothes ... Outside we seemed to be getting the full eleven inches of October rainfall in one night, and two of us had veritable floods on our floors because one of the taps wouldn't turn off. The situation passed all expectations ...[16]

Although the hotel manager assured the team he had given the place a good clean before their arrival, they spent the first few days scrubbing walls, floors and bathrooms, and obtaining fresh linen from the hospital's stores.

The conditions were made more bearable by the presence and generosity of American soldiers. Long Xuyen housed a contingent of advisers from the Military Assistance Command Vietnam (MACV), who opened their arms, and their facilities, to the new arrivals. Their compound was located not far from the hotel, and team members were encouraged to visit often. They immediately took up the offer, eating their meals there, doing laundry, and resting in congenial surroundings.

The Americans welcomed the Australians, especially the nurses, with relief. They had heard that a number of Australian sisters were coming and had assumed they would be nuns. To find out they were nurses instead was something of a bonus, and the women found themselves surrounded with willing companions for the duration of their stay. Susan Terry was particularly appreciative of the Americans:

> They let us have showers when ours were not running, let us wash clothes in their beautiful hot water, and let us iron there for we had not an iron or an ironing board of our own. I believe unexpected military visitors did raise eyebrows at the sight of girls' dresses airing on the front verandah of the Army mess, but nothing deterred the boys.[17]

Having settled in to their new home, the team began work. The surgical suite they took over housed two theatres. Before any work could be done it had to be reorganised and restocked with linen and equipment. There was a sterilising department adjacent to the theatres, but the electrical steriliser housed there 'was inadequate to the task. It was supplemented with a kerosene-heated steriliser which looked something like the boiler of a railway train.'[18] Noelle Laidlaw found that the radiography machine she was to use was 'pretty ancient'. There were no X-ray films or developing fixer to be found, and constant electricity interruptions made what little work she was able to do almost impossible. She quickly put in an order to the Royal Melbourne Hospital for supplies, and Vietnamese workers repaired the darkroom after she complained of the lack of an exhaust fan or running water.[19]

Anaesthetist Jim Villiers also found some inadequacies:

> There was a big American anaesthetic machine which depended on having carbon dioxide . . . Well, there was no carbon dioxide. There was no nitrous oxide, which is the gas

we used. Oxygen was in short supply . . . So the uniform anaesthetic consisted of chloroform . . . in other words anaesthesia was at the stage it was in Europe before the 1914–1918 war . . .[20]

He recalled putting his portable anaesthetic machine to use on the first day of work. A five-year-old boy had been brought into the hospital with bad abdominal burns. Before arriving there he had had a wick put on his abdomen and set alight 'to draw all the vapours out'. Naturally this 'treatment' was adding to his pain. The Vietnamese doctor in charge of the case expected the Australians to operate and cure the boy immediately. The surgeons were nervous. If this first patient died on the table, their reputations would be in tatters, but if they didn't act, the boy would surely die. So they went to work, with Jim using his portable machine. Fortunately 'the patient survived and our reputation was unfazed'.[21]

Word soon spread about the 'bac si uc dai loi'—'Australian doctors'. New patients began to trickle in, and numbers grew rapidly as more people were cured. The types of cases varied. Surgical emergencies were either routine, such as acute appendicitis or peritonitis, bowel obstructions or stomach ulcer perforations, or they were traumatic injuries, usually war related. Typical of these were bullets located in the abdomen, head or chest, or grenade or mine injuries to limbs. In addition, the team began to see increasing numbers of people with chronic conditions. These included bowel perforations from ascaris worms, which most locals were infested with because of the polluted water they drank, and large goitres, caused by iodine deficiencies. Because goitres affected so much of the population, and their removal was not only relatively easy but obvious and effective, the team became well known throughout the delta.

New people would arrive daily to see us with stories of how bac si uc dai loi had operated on and saved their nephew after he had been sick for ten days ... or of how their next-door neighbour who had had an enormous goitre for as long as they could remember now looked normal except for a small scar round her throat. Their faith in us of whom they knew so little was almost frightening. It brought with it a tremendous sense of responsibility.[22]

Having launched into surgical work almost immediately, the new team quickly settled into a routine. The work rate was demanding: the hospital could cope with approximately 140 surgical cases a month, and this is what was achieved. The Australians and their Vietnamese counterparts slowly learned each other's ways. Jim Villiers undertook to train his Vietnamese nurse anaesthetist, Miss Chau, and was so successful that by the end of his three months' duty she was described as 'a capable specialist in this discipline' who was able to teach her compatriots.[23]

One of the biggest problems facing team members was the absence of a blood bank. Surgeons were losing people because of a lack of blood, so they made determined efforts to establish a bank. But the Vietnamese were extremely reluctant to donate blood, fearing that this would make them weak, and that their bodies would never replace the blood they lost. Even when a family member's survival was at stake, the hesitancy persisted. The Australians realised they had a difficult task on their hands. Only a few weeks after her arrival, Noelle Laidlaw (who helped Dr Tim Matthew oversee the blood-bank project) found herself donating blood to a man who had been brought in with extensive gunshot wounds to the abdomen. A mixture of her own, American and Vietnamese blood was used during surgery to save the man, who would otherwise have died. The facts that she showed no ill effects and that the patient recovered helped the blood-bank idea take hold. The team requested Red Cross badges from Australia, and these were handed out to donors, quickly becoming a sought-after item.

As time went on and enthusiasm for the blood bank subsided, the team had to offer new incentives, such as a meal, to persuade people to donate. Their efforts were largely successful, and by the end of the first year the blood bank was well established, run mainly by the Vietnamese themselves.[24]

After two months, the team was reported to be 'functioning as a busy and happy combination'.[25] The arrival of a new team member, Ian Russell, increased the amount of work that could be undertaken. Living arrangements also improved. After six weeks at the Kim Tinh, morale had declined and some of the women on the team had fallen ill. In late November, however, the Australians' house was finally ready: a large white building that had been used in the past by the French, Japanese, and some Vietnamese aristocracy. Immediately dubbed the White House, it was surrounded by lush, well-kept gardens, and guarded by local police who kept watch at the outside gates. Inside, it boasted eleven air-conditioned bedrooms, living and dining rooms, and a kitchen. Vietnamese house staff took care of the laundry, cooking and gardening.

> Not only was this house most comfortable, but it provided excellent facilities for privacy, rest and relaxation. The upper sundeck was frequently used during the midday siesta period mainly for sunbaking, reading, and French lessons. The space in the house afforded the opportunity to invite house guests, and to return some of the hospitality which had been showered on the team.[26]

Their high social and diplomatic profile continued. In the first two months, visits were received from Australian embassy officers, Australian servicemen, and news cameraman and filmmaker Neil Davis. In December, the leading surgeon Dr Edward Hughes visited the team on behalf of the Department of External Affairs to observe its work. He noted that 'morale was high . . . all members of the team were very fit

... they were sun-tanned and gave us a very happy welcome.[27] He was impressed that the team had become a cohesive unit, given that none of the team members knew each other before going to Vietnam and that conditions had been trying in the first few weeks. He credited the team's unity to its leader, Donald Macleish, who 'as leader of the team, has accomplished his task with the most conscientious endeavour'. In relation to its work, Hughes remarked that

> the team has established itself firmly. They all enjoy the work, and all the females seem keen to stay not only longer but perhaps the full twelve months. The work done has been very good, and the relationship with the Vietnamese has been excellent.[28]

He was well aware of the amount of attention the team had received, and felt it important 'not to let the team feel that it is forgotten'. He believed the best way to do this was to encourage visits by senior medical personnel, whom the Long Xuyen teams would host regularly in coming years.

By the end of their first year in Long Xuyen, Royal Melbourne teams had firmly established an Australian presence at the hospital, as their annual report indicated:

> From their formal expressions of gratitude on the one hand, to the most touching presentations of bananas or eggs by poor but grateful patients on the other, there is no doubt that the medical help given was deeply appreciated. It is a form of aid which must not stop.[29]

On a more practical level, the teams had increased the number and range of operations being performed at Long Xuyen, founded a blood bank and an outpatients clinic, created a new pharmacy, introduced a postgraduate nurse scholarship, and taught new techniques to the Vietnamese surgeon and to the anaesthetic and theatre nurses. The team was 'a respected, accepted and even indispensable part of the local scene.'[30]

Nurse Susan Terry had no regrets:

My year in Vietnam certainly was a wonderful one and I know I shall always look back with great happiness on those days. The friendship with which we were always met and the so very genuine appreciation of those we were able to help ... is something it would be impossible to forget, as too is the desperate, pathetic need for medical help among the many thousands still without it.[31]

Life at the hospital

After the last Royal Melbourne team left in late 1965, St Vincent's Hospital in Melbourne provided the second major contingent for Long Xuyen. Other hospitals to provide long-term support there included Prince Henry's Hospital in Melbourne and the Royal Perth Hospital. In 1967 it was noted that the provision of teams by individual hospitals had been outstandingly successful. The system took into account corporate spirit and the compatibility of team members, both essential to success. The system of rotating doctors every three to four months and nurses every four to six months, or longer, allowed for continuity and the maintenance of high standards and good relationships with the Vietnamese.[32] As the number of people available or willing to go to Vietnam dwindled, state-sponsored teams were arranged to fill the gaps, but at some cost in team spirit and unity.

By the time the St Vincent's team took over in Long Xuyen, the number of cases being dealt with had increased substantially, as had the range of ailments and injuries involved. The leading causes of death were

diseases that had been largely eradicated in the West, including tuberculosis, typhoid, malaria and dysentery. War trauma and traffic accidents
also caused many deaths. A distressing injury the team saw occasionally
occurred only in the river country. Young women would get their long
hair caught up in the outboard motors used on fishing boats, and they
were literally scalped. Burns from the small kerosene heaters used for
cooking were also common. The variety of cases kept surgeons on their
toes and gave them valuable experience. Simply operating on infants
made a huge difference:

> ... they [Vietnamese doctors] had never operated on young
> children. They were looked upon as being too young to be
> operated on. So this was another eye-opener [for the local
> people]. That you could operate on the very young and they
> could survive, and equally you could operate on the very old
> and they would survive.[33]

One of the greatest frustrations for surgeons was the fact that most
patients did not come to hospital until their illness was advanced. Having
had access only to traditional or Chinese medicine in the past, the local
people continued to pursue these avenues before deciding to try the 'uc
dai loi' at Long Xuyen. Chinese treatments ranged from cupping (placing
a glass—in which the air pressure had been reduced by heating—on the
skin to draw out a bruise) and the application of leeches, to the inser-
tion of tobacco and cow dung into open wounds or tumours for their
supposed healing properties. Large goitres were often pricked with sharp-
ened bamboo sticks in an attempt to reduce the swelling. Treatments such
as these worsened already serious conditions, so that by the time patients
reached the hospital it was often too late to save them. Another compli-
cating factor was the difficulty of travel around the province. Patients in
outlying areas would spend days in sampans or cyclos being brought to the
hospital, and in cases such as acute appendicitis could die on the way.

Resourcefulness was an essential part of the surgeon's work in Long Xuyen. Bernard Dunn, a surgeon with the Royal Melbourne team in 1965, remembers the case of a young boy brought in with a fruit pip lodged in his throat and unable to breathe. The nearest bronchoscope, which would normally be used to extract the pip, was sixty kilometres away on an unsafe road. Instead the team improvised:

> . . . we had a set-up whereby if I got into trouble I was going to put an intertracheal tube into the child and ram the pip down one side and let the kid breathe on the other side . . . And the surgeon did a tracheostomy and got the pip out of the way. There was a certain amount of resourcefulness necessary on everyone's part, and it was very rewarding doing some of these sorts of things.[34]

Surgeons often found it particularly satisfying to work on some of the region's children. A boy around eight years old whom they nick-named Pinocchio had been born without a nose. Australian surgeons constructed a new one for him from transplanted tissue. During his tour in 1968 radiographer Clive Bond encountered the boy, who repeatedly pointed to his nose with two fingers. Eventually the team realised that he wanted nostrils so he would look like other children:

> So one day we obliged, and [when the boy was] under anaes-thetic, one of our surgeons fashioned two nostrils. They weren't proper airways, but they looked the part. He was very, very pleased with this. Whenever we passed little Pinocchio on the streets he always waved and gave us a big smile.[35]

Surgeons' days were long and varied. Starting work at around 8 a.m., they would conduct rounds, seeing patients in the recovery room and the wards, often accompanied by a large crowd of interpreters, Australian and Vietnamese nurses, patients and relatives. They would then operate until midday, when everything stopped for the mandatory two-hour siesta. Further operations would take place in the afternoon, after which their work was usually finished, though at times they were called in to operate at night or on weekends. Surgeons and nurses alike were struck by the bravery of their patients:

> The patients . . . were the most stoic and enduring we had ever looked after. Most of them were seriously ill. Many were in great pain. Seldom did they complain at all, and never without more than adequate reason.[36]

In the early days, one of the main problems experienced by all team members was in communicating with patients. It was several weeks before the team acquired interpreters; until then medical problems were conveyed by sign language, and techniques could be conveyed to Vietnamese staff only by demonstration. Working in this way was extremely frustrating, so the employment of three interpreters came as a relief. Nam Phuong was a young woman who had seen the first Australian team arrive in Long Xuyen and was keen to work for them. She was delighted to be accepted as one of the first interpreters and found it a maturing experience:

> My everyday life was now woven into the activities of people who once did not know where Vietnam was . . . In the battle-fields, people were fighting to kill; at the hospital the surgeons, doctors and nurses were fighting to save . . . At the hospital I knew for the first time what suffering and death were like. I matured in my thinking and came out of myself a little.[37]

For the Australians, the arrival of the interpreters eased their work burden and brought new friendships:

It was astonishing how the hospital changed for us, and how much more we learnt, after the interpreters arrived ... [They] were far more than merely interpreters and fellow workers. They were people we trusted, respected and admired ...[38]

Working through interpreters, although an improvement, was not always ideal for surgeons. Alister Brass noted that it was hard to establish a normal doctor–patient relationship when all conversation had to be relayed through a third person. The Australians were often not sure how much of what they said regarding treatment and surgery was understood: 'We just operate, do the best we can, and they either get better or they don't.'[39]

Surgery was not the only practice that had changed dramatically with the arrival of the Australian teams. Where surgeons were performing about 120 operations a month, the outpatients clinic saw almost 1000 people. Many had only minor problems, but there was still a large number of patients for physicians to see on any one day. A quarter to a third of people who came to the clinic had tuberculosis. The large amount of medication dispensed to treat this problem did not always achieve its aim: the team learned that patients were often paid by the Viet Cong and others for their medication, which was resold on the black market. Other frequent complaints were a variety of transmissable diseases, ulcers, congenital abnormalities, anaemia, and malignancies, stomach cancer being the most common. Although doctors in the clinic also faced the problem of patients coming in with advanced conditions, they had a high degree of success.

The work of the Australian nurses was closely linked with that of the surgeons. They worked in the theatres, the recovery ward and in any other areas that needed their help and where they felt they could teach by example. Flexibility was essential, as they were called upon to carry out a wide range of duties. When disruptions to the electricity supply made Noelle Laidlaw's job of taking X-rays difficult, she would help out wherever she was needed: 'There were a lot of people that wanted X-rays, but we just couldn't do them . . . the bulk of my work was helping the others, virtually. I became multi-skilled.'[40]

The nurses often worked very long hours, sometimes late into the night and at weekends. Jenny O'Neill (née Antons) did a six-month tour in Long Xuyen in 1966–67 and recorded a typical case in her diary:

> At 9pm we were called to hospital—8 injured people, hit by grenade. 2 dead—an old man and baby, a boy of 4 years died on the table, he had shrapnel penetrating into bowels and stomach—I baptised him. They all were very shocked . . . It happened only 8 miles from here. Back from hospital 3am.[41]

Apart from caring for patients, nurses did as much teaching as they could. Well aware that they were not in Vietnam to impose Western standards on the Vietnamese, they walked a fine line in helping the local staff improve their methods without being overly assertive. Although there were some qualified Vietnamese nurses in the hospital, most of the nursing staff were untrained boys and girls, aged between fifteen and seventeen, who would do unpaid work for two years in the hope of eventually being hired as a nurse assistant. They were often illiterate, and the Australian nurses struggled to help them learn, as Susan Terry recalls:

> I was trying to explain why a little girl who had been shot through the head was hemiplegic [paralysed on one side as a result of brain injury]. After I had been talking only a few minutes, I was surrounded by a group of ominously blank faces . . . and one of the students asked, 'Please, what is the brain?'[42]

Apart from the locals' lack of basic knowledge, the language barrier and widespread superstition were also obstacles to teaching them basic nursing practices. Communication was helped somewhat by the use of interpreters, but fear and suspicion of Western ways were encouraged by practitioners of Chinese medicine, who saw the Australians as competitors for their business.

As time went on, the teaching of nurses shifted to a more formal basis. In late 1965 the St Vincent's team began a lecture course in anatomy, physiology, hygiene and surgical nursing. Patricia Reilly was included in the team specifically to deliver these lectures; she gave them in French, and they were translated by the chief Vietnamese nurse. The lectures were continued by later teams, but problems with translation and lack of attendance eventually brought them to an end. In late 1967 Jan Mills (née Rayner) was employed on a New South Wales combined team as a nurse educator to help establish a school of nursing. She set up the facilities on the first floor of the hospital, with teaching equipment provided by USAID. Entrance exams for the school were held locally and were extremely competitive—Jan heard that 250 applications from around the delta region were narrowed down to forty. During the exam, husbands and boyfriends passed notes through the window to the women inside, so keen were they to see them pass. The women selected for the school lived together in a dormitory and worked for no pay. Jan's role was to advise the principal of the school, and although she found the job frustrating at times—the worst part was dealing with the Vietnamese bureaucracy—she was proud of the women who graduated and of her role improving local health care.[43] Paediatrician Brian Kearney was another team member able to make an important difference by teaching at the school:

> The majority of patients [in the paediatric ward] are children
> of peasants. [These parents] show a remarkable devotion to
> their children, combined with an appalling ignorance of how
> to care for their physical health. Many of the student nurses
> [in the nurses' school] on graduation will be assigned to rural

areas as health workers and if well-grounded at a suitable level in child care will be ideally placed to begin the slow but fundamental problem of educating the parents.[44]

Australian Army anaesthetist Marshall Barr, who was based in Vung Tau, visited the school in early 1968 and was impressed:

> The classrooms were modern, uncluttered and equipped with comfortable desks, wall charts, anatomical models and other teaching aids. The students were enthusiastic young ladies in spotless white uniforms who greeted Jan with respect and affection. It could have been any first-class nursing school in Australia, except for the guards.[45]

The desire to leave something of permanence after their tour was shared by most team members, and a source of disappointment for those who felt their efforts were of no lasting value. Teaching was one area which, when successfully carried out, ensured that the help offered would endure.

The Australian nurses taught not only the Vietnamese nurses and students but also a large number of patients' relatives. As the relatives spent so much time caring for their family members, they felt they had a right to be instructed on the correct techniques. Susan Terry found that once a new skill had been taught and understood, relatives and nurses alike would carry it out 'with the utmost enthusiasm and vigour', continuing a particular treatment for twenty-four hours if necessary.[46] At other times, however, the Australians became frustrated and angry at the Vietnamese nurses' apparent lack of care for their patients, and their refusal to act at critical times. Jenny O'Neill wrote of a baby brought in one morning after a fall on its head:

> The . . . baby died in [the] afternoon. These Vietnamese have just no idea of how to look after the sick, they just let them

die. The baby died because it couldn't vomit and nobody sucked it out. Great fools they are and they don't want to take a hint from anybody. It is discouraging.[47]

Another role which was started by the Royal Melbourne team in 1964 and continued for most of the time that teams were in Long Xuyen was the teaching of English at the local high school. Many of the town's inhabitants were very keen to learn English, and they tested the knowledge of their teachers to the limit, as radiographer Joan Rose found:

> . . . they would ask really technical grammatical questions about different sorts of English tenses . . . I did that every week, once every week. And my family sent me some books over on English and some simple things which I used with the students and they were ever so grateful for the opportunity to practise English with you.[48]

Although the classes were often held at the end of a long and tiring day, the nurses and other female team members who conducted them enjoyed the interaction and were usually happy to carry out this 'winning hearts and minds' aspect of their duties.

While surgeons and nurses formed the core of the teams, other professionals played an important role. Despite the frustrating limitations placed on her as a radiographer, Noelle Laidlaw was able to make significant advances in that specialty at the hospital, and these were continued by her successors. A continuing problem for radiographers was the antiquated machinery they had to work with, but with ingenuity and the help of the Americans, they managed. Barbara Sutherland (née Maughan) remembers using a small American portable field unit for her X-ray work. It worked, but as she commented later, 'I'd hate to think of the amount of radiation that we were throwing around at that stage

. . . we didn't think too much about it.'[49] Radiographer Clive Bond used ingenuity to solve one supply problem. The main X-ray unit had not been working for some months because of a broken valve. He had requested a replacement from a warehouse in Saigon a number of times, but in vain. One day, he had reason to visit the warehouse in question, and saw three X-ray machines wrapped in plastic and covered in dust. They had obviously been there for some time. Refusing to pay bribe money to get the valve he needed, he simply relieved one of the three machines of the part. Back in Long Xuyen, he was soon the proud operator of a newly repaired X-ray unit.[50]

There was some debate over whether or not plastic surgeons would be sent to South Vietnam, because the DEA had some misgivings about the impact it would have on local practitioners. In a confidential memo, the Second Secretary for the Australian embassy in Saigon wrote that there was a need for plastic surgery but that 'we should take care not to overexaggerate this more sensational aspect of medical aid'.[51] That caution was not without foundation, but plastic surgery could also change the lives of patients forever.

Plastic surgeon Robert Thompson did a three-month tour with a Royal Melbourne team and performed many operations to repair cleft lips and other deformities. As word of his presence spread, more and more people appeared for treatment. Robert was able to instruct the chief Vietnamese surgeon, Dr Ban, on cleft-lip technique so that the same volume of patients could be helped after he left. Robert also demonstrated his techniques at other centres, including the Cho Ray Hospital in Saigon. Other plastic surgeons followed him, sharing their expertise among the different teams.

Bien Hoa-based paediatrician Peter Last recalls a visit from George Gunter, who operated out of Long Xuyen and specialised in repairing cleft lips and palates: 'My little ward was super saturated at that time, and George came in and did nothing but hare lips and cleft palates.'[52]

Most Australian plastic surgeons who went to South Vietnam appear to have been based in Long Xuyen, where there was a greater need for the remedial work, but they travelled regularly to Bien Hoa and other towns to conduct intensive clinics. In 1965 there were only thirty recognised plastic surgeons in Australia. To have one allocated to the aid effort was an achievement in itself.[53] Urologists, orthopaedic surgeons and pathologists also visited at various times. The need for reliable pathology testing was apparent from an early stage, and pathologists were eventually included in the surgical teams.

Children who needed surgery were treated by the teams from the first. However, those who needed specialist treatment other than operations were largely neglected until a paediatrician, Dr Bob Birrell, was included in the Prince Henry's Hospital team in February 1967. A paediatric ward existed at Long Xuyen Hospital, with thirty beds of varying sizes. It usually held around forty-five children, sometimes over fifty, with up to eight children sharing a cot on occasions. A paediatrician from a later team, Brian Kearney, commented that although this overcrowding inevitably led to cross-infection, it meant that Long Xuyen could accommodate more children in a purely paediatric ward than almost any other South Vietnamese provincial hospital.[54] One small section of the ward had an air-conditioner used for infectious cases, and another tiny room (dubbed the 'black hole of Calcutta') which was the isolation room. During Bob Birrell's tour, an average of 220 patients were admitted each month, about fifteen of whom died. The most common conditions in children were enteric infection, respiratory infection, ascaris worms, dysentery, advanced appendicitis and tuberculosis. Childhood ailments such as mumps and meningitis were also prevalent, as were diseases seen in Australia less often, such as polio, malaria and haemorrhagic fever. A few children with war injuries also ended up in the paediatric ward, often following surgery. Assisted by two Vietnamese nursing sisters, Bob was kept extremely busy and felt the deaths of his patients keenly. Described as 'indefatigable', he recalls seeing little of his fellow team members except at mealtimes, 'because my little tackers were calling'.[55] Nurse Janet Brewster was struck by the toll the work took on the paediatricians, who she thought were often traumatised by the condition of some of their patients.[56] Despite the hardships, and the frustration of having patients 'disappear' (they were often taken home by parents who did not want them dying in hospital), Bob found the work extremely satisfying:

> . . . the most rewarding time was always seeing youngsters that had come in pretty crook and went out the door with Mum . . . with big smiles. They were really a delightful people too—soft, gentle people, and the appreciation of your presence was obvious.[57]

Although team members were in no doubt that their help was needed, the form the Australian assistance should take was much debated. A symposium on medical aid in South Vietnam in May 1967 aired the various arguments. It was agreed that, ideally, medical aid should aim to improve sanitation, eradicate malaria and control communicable diseases, standard practice for helping developing countries. Vietnam, however, was not a typical case. The war and internal political discord had created an urgent need for surgery and acute medical care. By 1967, though the worst of the medical crisis had passed, it was recognised that a well-considered and sustained system of medical aid needed to be maintained.

Opinion was divided, however, about what kind of aid would be most effective in the long term. Jim Villiers doubted that the program should be expanded; instead he thought work should continue at the grassroots level, slowly building up a core of trained Vietnamese medical personnel who could eventually take over the work and allow the Australians to withdraw. Others argued that only by creating some focal point, some centre of excellence identifiable with Australia, will aid be meaningful and have impact on the future of Vietnam.'[58] The debate would continue for the remainder of the surgical teams' time in Vietnam. Members with high aspirations were often disappointed that they could not achieve more enduring results, while those who saw value in giving immediate medical help generally had a more fulfilling and enjoyable tour.

From the Australians' earliest days in Long Xuyen, it was clear that establishing good relations with the Vietnamese staff at the hospital would be critical to the teams' success. There was no doubt that the Vietnamese were glad to have help: during his 1967 visit, Alister Brass was told, 'the reason we feel so close to the Australians is that you try to understand us, you try to see how we think as a people. You don't just watch and pass judgement.'[59] Jim Villiers agreed, concluding in a 1967 paper:

> The success achieved by the Australian teams has rested not so much on any individual factor as on the overall Australian ability to accept and make friends with people as they are, on equal terms, instead of treating them as inferiors and enforcing our different outlook and way of life upon them.[60]

Despite this positive assessment, establishing and maintaining good Australian–Vietnamese relations was not always easy. The more relaxed Vietnamese standards of nursing, and what often seemed to be outright neglect, at times drove the Australians to despair. The team leader's report for October 1968 to January 1969 noted that while good relations existed with the Vietnamese surgeons, nursing standards were poor overall:

> On . . . occasions the nurse-in-charge has been found knitting whilst infusion bottles were empty, and patients needed

injections etc. On another occasion no nurse was present in
the ward, overflowing with twelve patients; when found she
was washing her hair in the theatre annex.[61]

Standards of nursing varied over time. While Susan Terry found nurses
and students receptive to her teaching and willing to try new techniques
in 1964–65, Jenny O'Neill two years later despaired: 'What can one
teach people if they don't want to help themselves?' she wrote in her
diary.[62]

From the Vietnamese perspective, the Australian system was
not always perfect either. The most common problem the local
medical staff encountered was the frequent turnover of Australian
personnel and the consequent lack of continuity in procedures and
techniques. Often there was only a very short handover period from
one team to another, leaving the newcomers unfamiliar with how
things had been done. As a result, they often instituted new procedures, confusing and distressing the Vietnamese staff. Keen to make
their mark on the hospital, new teams would sometimes make changes
seemingly for the sake of it. Médecin Chef Dr Huynh Trung Nhi
outlined some of these concerns in a speech to an Australian delegation in March 1969. Although 'deeply grateful to all Australian
team members for devoting their time and efforts to save thousands
of lives of the Vietnamese people', Dr Nhi was also concerned that
some of the physicians were not familiar with tropical diseases
when they arrived. By the time they had acquired some knowledge in
this area and were working effectively, it would be time for them to
return home. He considered the handover period between teams too
brief, noting that 'many newcomers are not aware of their mission and
must find out themselves what they have to do'. In addition, he wanted
'the new team members' arrival be notified to me so that I could greet
them properly. It looks awkward to us, being in the same hospital,
working together and not knowing each other.'[63]

Life in a war zone

The combination of language problems, frustrations on the job and misunderstandings within teams and between them and their Vietnamese counterparts could be exhausting. The start of the composite-team system only compounded the difficulties. The first such team, which took over in October 1967, was the first to have all its members sign on for a full year. However, that was not to be repeated in Long Xuyen; such a long tour was too much for most people. An *Age* correspondent touring the provincial hospitals in October 1967 noted that even with shorter tours and, in Long Xuyen, a lighter patient load, '. . . isolation and the pressures of a hostile environment have sapped the energies and undermined the morale of doctors and nurses alike'.[64] Although armed clashes did not often take place within the town, the province and those adjacent to it were by now seeing constant military action between the Viet Cong and allied forces vying for control of the delta region. The US Command imposed tight restrictions on civilian movement around the province, including a strict curfew, and areas around Long Xuyen became free-fire zones at night. Team members' excursions outside the town were now limited and heavily guarded, and travel outside the province was possible only by air.

In late January 1968, the war came to Long Xuyen in a very direct way. During the Tet (lunar New Year) holiday, the North Vietnamese launched simultaneous attacks on nearly every town and city in South Vietnam. The offensive was intended to spark an uprising among the local population and turn them to the cause of the communists. Settlements throughout An Giang province came under fire, and in the town of Chau Duc the hospital was overrun by Viet Cong, who used it as their headquarters. The first the Australian team in Long Xuyen knew of the attacks was in the early hours of 30 January. They had been out during the evening, watching movies at the American MACV unit and watching the local people set off firecrackers and dance in the streets to celebrate Tet. Although Long Xuyen itself was not attacked, the team was called into immediate action. They were woken at around 2 a.m. by knocks on their doors and calls of 'bac si, bac si'. Wounded civilians had begun to trickle into the hospital and soon there was a flood of them, which continued for many days. Back at the hospital, the team was confronted with chaos:

> . . . row upon row of patients on stretchers. Still others were in cyclos . . . Some of the patients were already dead, others had limbs missing. The injuries were horrific. Mainly shrapnel wounds from hand grenades and mortars. Most of the patients, at least as far as we could tell, were civilians.[65]

The team worked through the night and the following day. At one point they were told by American advisers from the MACV compound that the security risk in the town was extreme, and that their safety at the hospital could not be guaranteed. They were advised to go to the compound with the other American troops and be barricaded inside. Given the number of dead and injured people arriving continuously at the hospital, the team decided to stay despite the danger.

They worked almost non-stop for a week. At one stage, American soldiers arrived at the hospital with a variety of weapons, which they distributed among the Australians. Eating and sleeping was done at the hospital for the first few days, after which team members took it in turns to return to the house for showers, a meal and a few hours' rest. They distrusted the guards at the house, so one team member remained on guard on the roof with an M16 rifle while the others slept. It was a stressful and exhausting period, but things gradually stabilised as the offensive was contained and the Viet Cong were repulsed. Clive Bond recalls that they treated hundreds of patients:

> The children especially were particularly good. One little girl had had part of her arm blown off but was still able to give me

a bit of a grin when I X-rayed her . . . Somehow they seemed to accept these tremendous hardships. After a while reports began to filter through about just how widespread the war was. In fact we learnt that we were completely surrounded, but Long Xuyen, apparently, was the only town in the whole of South Vietnam that wasn't actually attacked.[66]

In a letter to his father after the offensive, Clive speculated about why Long Xuyen had been left unscathed, given that with only about sixty American soldiers in town the Viet Cong could easily have attacked it on the night of the 30th, 'annihilating us in a few hours', if they had wanted to. He was unable to come up with a reason.[67]

In early March, the DEA considered the issue of security for the Long Xuyen team in the light of the Tet Offensive. Embassy staff from Saigon had visited the town to report on conditions, and suggested that the team be withdrawn. However, such a move would have serious consequences both in Vietnam and in Australia. It would leave Australia open to criticism and damage its image in Vietnam, undoing all that the teams had achieved. After embassy officials discussed the situation with team leader Ken Doust, members were given the option of returning to Australia. No one wanted to take up the offer so it was decided to temporarily send two members to stay with the surgical team in Vung Tau and three others to work with the team in Bien Hoa. This would leave eight in Long Xuyen, a more manageable number should they need to be evacuated quickly by air or sea.[68] Janet Brewster was one of the three who travelled to Bien Hoa, where they worked for nearly a month. She remembers it as much busier than Long Xuyen, and says they worked on civilians with war wounds for the whole period. The work was very intense, and they all missed the rest of the team.[69] In Long Xuyen a twenty-four-hour curfew continued for some months, and team members began to experience 'cabin fever' from spending all their time either at the hospital or back at the house. Eventually, however, things returned to normal.

Although team members in Long Xuyen were relatively safe from Viet Cong attacks, with the sights and sounds of war all around them, working there could still be stressful. In May 1968 the wife of radiographer Clive Bond visited her husband in Long Xuyen, halfway through his twelve-month tour. She was worried about the state she found him in and wanted him to shorten his tour, but realised that he would insist on staying for the duration. Her observations of the team in general were not positive:

> Six months is long enough for most people up here. The life they lead is just so hectic . . . When it comes to getting about 4–5 hours sleep a night and trying to cope with the irritations of the work, it's not much wonder they feel dreadful most of the time.[70]

Relaxation away from the hospital took varying forms, including tennis, boating, shopping at the markets, visits to the MACV compound and socialising at the White House. Team leaders soon realised, however, that people needed to get away from Long Xuyen on a regular basis, for a change of scene as much as anything. Most had the opportunity to travel around the province at some stage, visiting orphanages, small towns and hamlets, and other medical facilities. In early 1967, Jenny O'Neill and several others travelled by boat to an orphanage in the town of Cho Moi. Because there had recently been Viet Cong action in the area, they travelled on a heavily protected US Navy vessel. After a two-and-a-half-hour journey they arrived at the orphanage, where 'we were greeted like the Queen—of course we felt like it too. Many of them have never seen white women and here we were—the central figures of the show.'[71] Visits such as these were a way of bringing medical care to outlying areas and were an important flag-waving exercise for the Australian teams.

Weekend visits from Long Xuyen were usually taken away from the local area. Team members would brave the local airport, where

Viet Cong snipers took regular pot-shots at aircraft, and fly to Saigon, Vung Tau, or further north. Most flights were on small aircraft, and they were not without their hazards. Radiographer Barbara Sutherland remembers a flight to Saigon in the last few weeks of her tour that could have ended disastrously. She was carrying some of her colleagues' passports to arrange visas for them and went in a single-engine aircraft piloted by an American. At about 14,000 feet the plane's engine cut out, and they were forced into an emergency landing. As they glided to the ground they were fired upon by Viet Cong but protected by an American helicopter gunship that had been called to their aid. Barbara kept her wits about her:

> We landed in a pineapple field . . . [and] very quickly got out of the plane . . . I grabbed my bag with all the passports in it, I grabbed the box of pathology samples . . . I was on a mission wasn't I! [Then] a Chinook picked us up and took us into Saigon.[72]

Nurse Jenny Hunter flew to Vung Tau for a few days' leave during her tour in 1967. She remembers staying in the Grand Hotel, where the Vung Tau surgical team was living at the time, in an end room near some stairs: 'There was a brothel on the top floor and we were kept awake all night by the boots going up and down.'[73] Longer and more relaxing trips could be undertaken by team members doing long tours, when they were given a week's rest and recreation leave. These visits were often outside Vietnam, to Cambodia or Hong Kong, or to South Vietnamese towns such as Dalat and Nha Trang. Joan Rose, on leave in Saigon, was invited on an impromptu overnight visit to Nha Trang in mid 1967: '. . . we had only the clothes we wore and our bathers and towel . . . Oh boy, we really roughed it, but it was lots of fun!!' In a letter home she raved about the beauty of the town, a far cry from the stresses of life in Long Xuyen:

> Beautiful, deep, clean, blue water lapping gently onto white sands, palm trees shading the nearby roads and lovely wooded, green mountains surrounding the city and running right down onto the beach. Close by—various small islands 'floating' in a glittering blue sea . . . I have *never* seen such a beautiful beach in all my life.[74]

These breaks away, although relaxing, did little to alleviate the ongoing stresses of work, and most team members, especially those on long tours, were usually ready to return to Australia at the end of their time.

The end of Long Xuyen teams

In early 1969, the leader of the Royal Perth Hospital team in Long Xuyen, Dr Leo Stubber, reported that his personnel were as busy as ever. Four medical students had been assigned to the hospital, and team surgeons were helping with their tuition. Substantial improvements had been made to the paediatric ward, and team members, especially nurses, were busy trying to educate Vietnamese parents in the principles of nutritious feeding for infants. The nurses were still giving English classes to the townspeople, and had also begun offering them to Vietnamese nursing staff. These had made communication in the wards easier and 'fostered a greater spirit of friendliness and understanding between the two groups of people who must work side by side'.[75] All in all, Stubber concluded,

> . . . most members enjoyed the opportunity to work in Vietnam. Certainly some, including myself, would have wished that they could continue to stay longer in Long Xuyen. Social and professional relationships with both Vietnamese and American have been very good . . .[76]

Stubber and his team would have been surprised, then, to read a report submitted to the DEA in March 1969. The report's author, Professor Sydney Sunderland, Dean of the Faculty of Medicine at the University of Melbourne, had spent that month visiting the four Australian civilian surgical teams in Vietnam to evaluate their future usefulness. His view on the teams in Long Xuyen was that they were no longer needed because the numbers of Vietnamese medical graduates now making their way into civilian hospitals had grown sufficiently to cover the needs of the hospital. In addition, because Australia lacked the medical manpower to continue providing suitable staff for four teams, the number should be reduced 'as soon as is practicable'. He recommended that the teams at Long Xuyen and Vung Tau be withdrawn.[77]

No action was taken on the Long Xuyen front for several months. In November, Dr John Lindell, the Victorian coordinator of Australian surgical teams in Vietnam, paid a two-day visit to Long Xuyen. He was accompanied by the Bien Hoa team leader, Dr Graeme Grove. In his report to the Australian Ambassador in Saigon, Lindell mentioned that earlier in the year in Melbourne, it had been decided to discontinue the teams at Long Xuyen from December 1969. The aim of his visit to Vietnam had been to see whether this was still necessary. He concluded that, despite pleas from the Médecin Chef, Dr Nhi, for the teams to stay, nothing had changed substantially since Sunderland's visit and the teams should be phased out.[78] Graeme Grove, on the other hand, found his views changed after this visit. He had originally agreed with Sunderland but now thought that if the teams were withdrawn,

> we will pull out at a time when Long Xuyen is on the threshold of significant advances in its medical capabilities, and this will be a disadvantage to our reputation and much of the good work that has been done by our teams since 1964.[79]

Graeme felt there were still substantial areas in which Australians could make a valuable contribution in Long Xuyen, including midwifery and paediatrics. He recommended that the Long Xuyen team should be incorporated into the main Bien Hoa team, with various members being seconded to Long Xuyen for defined periods.

The make-up of the final Long Xuyen teams largely followed Grove's recommendation. A second, smaller, Royal Perth Hospital team worked there from August to December 1969. After that time, various medical personnel were seconded from the Bien Hoa team. Surgeon Campbell Penfold and his wife, Christine, a paediatrician, transferred to Long Xuyen for five months. It was reported in June 1970 that the Penfolds were happy there, with Campbell kept busy with casualties from operations on the Cambodian border.[80] In the following months the number of surgical cases dwindled and it became apparent that Australian surgeons were no longer needed. Campbell was not replaced when he and Christine left in August.

The final Australian medical contribution to Long Xuyen was in paediatrics. The hospital was now without a Vietnamese paediatrician, so three Australians, Iain MacMillan, Bruce Hocking and James Sinclair, filled the gap until December 1970. Of the final withdrawal, Bien Hoa team leader Donald Macleish wrote:

This formally severs a most happy bond which has existed between the province of An Giang and Australian teams since October 1964. The friendships made will doubtless be renewed by occasional visits when opportunity arises to travel to Long Xuyen—a beautiful town which is a credit to its civil authorities, with an excellent hospital which is a tribute to its medical personnel.[81]

In the firing line: Bien Hoa 1966–68

The Bien Hoa provincial hospital, where Australian civilian surgical teams would serve for almost seven years, was located near the massive air base complex in Bien Hoa city, about twenty-five kilometres north-east of Saigon. The air base sat next to National Route 1, the main eastern artery into the city. In 1965 it was one of the three largest air bases in South Vietnam, the others being Tan Son Nhut and Da Nang. A mere grass strip ten years earlier, it grew to support more air combat units than any other base in the country. With the influx of United States Air Force (USAF) tactical air units in the early 1960s, Bien Hoa became a joint operating base for both the USAF and the Vietnam Air Force (VNAF). While the base belonged to the South Vietnamese, by 1966 it had some 40,000 Americans as tenants, including several infantry formations as well as Air Force units. The perimeter was ringed with barbed wire, mine fields, and concrete bunkers left by the French. Its proximity to the international airport at Saigon made Bien Hoa the easiest tactical air base for news reporters to reach, so it received the most coverage during the war.[1]

After the division of Vietnam, tens of thousands of refugees from the northern and central regions—a large portion of them Roman Catholics—had resettled in Bien Hoa city, which had a population of about 60,000. During a visit from Long Xuyen Hospital in November

1965, surgeon Peter Ryan wrote that his companion Mack Williams saw sixteen churches in one city block.[2] At that time only the main streets were sealed, and many of the side roads were made of gravel or dirt that turned to slush in the wet season. Guttering was unknown and sewerage was primitive. The poorest residents lived in shanty towns, in shacks of aluminium and steel sheeting bearing the brand names of soft drinks and beer.

The hospital where the civilian surgical team was sent stood beside the air base, overlooking the Dong Nai river. Its Vietnamese name was Pham Huu Chi, but for simplicity's sake it will be referred to as the Bien Hoa Hospital. The noise of aircraft taking off and landing and the 'thump thump' of chopper blades forcing their way through the humid tropical air were a constant backdrop to life at the French-built hospital. According to Maureen Spicer (née McLeod), who arrived in 1966:

> The architecture was French provincial style with arched colonnades, and wooden shuttered open windows to allow air flow through the wards. Around the wards were open drains and at the rear of the hospital an open rubbish dump and a large population of even larger rats.[3]

The surgical suite where the Australians would work was built by USAID in 1963 but had been unused owing to the lack of civilian surgeons in Bien Hoa. Water shortages and the partial power failures known as brown-outs were common. The city's size and closeness to Saigon made it a regular target of Viet Cong mortar bombardments and rocket attacks.

The pioneers

The first of what would eventually be ten teams to arrive in Bien Hoa came from Melbourne's Alfred Hospital in January 1966. By this time, it had become established practice for surgeons and doctors to do three-month·tours and nurses to stay for six months. Most people were given extensions if they wanted them. The Alfred had a presence in Bien Hoa until April 1967, when Royal Adelaide and then Royal Brisbane sent teams. Some members of these teams were present during the 1968 Tet Offensive. In September 1968, Brisbane's Princess Alexandra Hospital took up the baton, succeeded by Melbourne's Alfred, Royal Adelaide, Royal Melbourne, a combined Queensland team, and one from St Vincent's in Sydney. By the end of 1971, it was growing difficult to find people willing to serve in a country that seemed likely to fall into the hands of the communist enemy. The last team handed over the rebuilt hospital and left at the end of December 1972.

The first team from the Alfred comprised four doctors, four nurses and one radiographer. After being farewelled by their families and television cameras, the team transited through Jakarta for refuelling, and stayed overnight at the Raffles Hotel in Singapore. After landing in Saigon, they drove along a highway 'busy with hundreds of cars and trucks' to Bien Hoa city. Nursing sister Daphne Amos wrote of her arrival:

> A big reception from the province chief and medical chief [Médecin Chef] of the hospital greeted the team ... In Bien Hoa the war was in raucous evidence 24 hours a day. There was no equipment or surgical instruments in the surgical suite so these were obtained from Saigon. After much scrubbing and cleaning of the operating rooms and recovery room, the team performed its first two operations the day after arriving in Bien Hoa.[4]

Team leader William 'Bill' McDonald recalled a comfortable flight followed by a series of official greetings, which became standard practice for the Australian surgical teams. The team's arrival was recorded on film for television, which was just about to launch in Saigon.

The new team were not the only Australians in town. Situated at the air base was the 1st Battalion of the Royal Australian Regiment (1RAR), supported by a troop of 4th/19th Prince of Wales's Light Horse armoured personnel carriers, and 105 Battery from the 1st Field Regiment, Royal Australian Artillery. The Australian units were under the operational command of the US 173rd Airborne Brigade (Separate) until later that year, when the 1st Australian Task Force was established in Phuoc Tuy province, southeast of Saigon. The Bien Hoa teams would come to rely heavily on the Diggers for moral, social and logistical support.

Lieutenant Colonel Alex Preece, the commanding officer of 1RAR, recalled that the team's:

> ... buildings and equipment were, at best, basic. In this environment team members gave freely, generously, professionally. They gained the deep respect, admiration and gratitude of all those whose lives they touched—not the least that of their 'big brother' living nearby.
>
> Our respective roles gave us little time for socialising, but we did keep contact as far as possible. We established a liaison with our battalion medical officers, Major Mike Naughton and Captain Peter Haslam. My 2IC, Major John Hooper, arranged for members of the Surgical Team to join us for lunch occasionally. Our interpreters, Sergeant Ivan Welsh and Corporal Lex McAulay helped out at the hospital when they could.[5]

Alfred team anaesthetist Bob Gray also remarked on the rapport between the teams and 1RAR:

> We had a great relationship with 1RAR and they used to invite us over there to just go and relax, and did we ever. And they gave us Ivan Welsh, their interpreter ... [and] a

Sergeant Nanh who was a Vietnamese interpreter . . . I was tremendously impressed with the 1RAR soldiers who came and painted the kids ward inside and out, and they used to bring presents and gifts to the kids.[6]

The team's response to their first look at the hospital was disbelief, followed by dismay as they realised that things were even worse than they had thought. US Army doctor Captain John Slaughter from Bien Hoa air base witnessed their reactions:

I can still picture and hear Bill McDonald, on his second day in Vietnam, as he and Peter Mangos headed off to Saigon in notable high dudgeon to present his views of the situation, and perhaps something more beside that, to some unsuspecting and unfortunate but certainly deserving person at the Australian embassy. Bill's parting words to me were to the effect that, 'We'll be back this afternoon. We're just going to get this all sorted out and get on with it. We have talked this over last night and we are not about to just go back home . . .'

This was my first encounter with the 'stiff upper lip', and most remarkably with that unique and astonishing form of wordless communication, the 'Ummmm.' I have since learned the 'Ummmm' is imitated by many around the world but 'Ummmm' only reaches its natural true height and breadth of expressive grandeur when employed by an outraged and indignant Australian struggling against all odds to remain on her or his good behaviour. Speech and profanity may fail even the hardiest Australian, but always in reserve is the 'Ummmm.'[7]

When team leader Bill McDonald 'ummmed' his way right around the dilapidated, dirty, run-down and inadequate surgical facilities—one

DEA officer wrote in a briefing memo that the hospital 'looked ready for demolition'—he knew he had a huge challenge on his hands.[8]

Peter Mangos had been a surgeon for six years and left his practice in Melbourne because 'I thought the experience would be terrific and wanted to see what was going on in Vietnam.' Though he 'knew very little about the war',[9] he had told his parents everything would be fine. In fact, he says, he felt nervous about what lay ahead. Looking around the hospital, he found:

> A lot to clean up. A lot of the things hadn't been used for a long time and we started to clean up. The girls especially just set the pace. They were terrific and cleaned everything up and we went operational the next morning on the second day.
>
> There was no help from the locals because there was nobody there. We had one person who had been taught anaesthetics, Mr Phuoc. Mr Tho was the hospital doctor but he had his own clinic and we hardly ever saw him. Most of the medical staff had gone into the Army [ARVN]. Eighty-five per cent of Vietnamese doctors had gone straight into the Army and so the civilians didn't get much treatment at all.[10]

Maureen Spicer recalls the state of the sterilisation equipment the teams were forced to use:

> Sterilisation of instruments and stock was problematic. The only reliable autoclave was situated outside the surgical suite and was based on a design used in the Second World War. It could be described as a large drum (on its side) on stilts with a kerosene-fired barbecue flaming away underneath. Nevertheless, it worked. However, there were times when

we operated without anything sterile. No sterile gloves, packs, drapes or instruments. The question asked was, Is this patient going to die if we do not operate now because of no sterile equipment?—if the answer was yes, then we operated. We never lost any of these patients, and none showed signs of post-operative infection.[11]

For those who had not been to Asia before or served as doctors or nurses in wartime, this was the ultimate in culture shock. Jenny Leak was an experienced nurse, but even she was taken aback. Still, she recalls:

The demands of the job were such that you just focused on what had to be done and didn't really think about it. I suppose we talked about some of it when we were back in the team house. But really it wasn't something that we dwelt on at all. We just sort of grew into it and got on with the job.[12]

Surgeon Peter Mangos too struggled to adapt:

Of course, the people are different, the language is different, the smells are different, the temperature is different—it was as hot as blazes. It was so humid I was sweating all the time. It took about a month before I got used to it. I would be operating and sweat would be running down my back. But you get used to it; your body becomes accustomed to the heat somehow.[13]

Working next to the air base brought its own problems, quite apart from the ceaseless noise from one of the world's busiest airports. Maureen Spicer recalls the night at around 10.30 p.m. when the Viet

Cong blew up a massive ammunition dump that was only a kilometre or so away:

> I was at the hospital with another nurse, Sue Leyland. The explosion was so great that the patients were blown off their beds, instruments flew off trolleys, the IV stands fell and the glass IV bottles smashed, and then the night was lit with flares and the deafening din of helicopter gunships firing away. Sue and I were blown off our feet. We crashed against the theatre wall, people were screaming and running through the compound.[14]

Caroline 'Canny' Coventry (née Rigg) volunteered partly for 'excitement' but also because 'hopefully we were going to do something to make a difference with these people'. But things did not get off to a good start. Supplies that had been sent from Australia were pilfered and never seen again. The accommodation was only half finished when the team arrived, and was described as 'bloody awful'. There were no cooks, and at the hospital there were no interpreters. Their two-day Vietnamese-language course had also left them very unprepared. But 'I think we just said, "We've got to get on with it." I mean, there's no good standing around whingeing.'[15]

The team was under pressure almost from the start. Canny Coventry recalls a day soon after they arrived:

> ... the army brought in this little boy who'd been hit by a claymore mine and blew his belly out. So Bill [McDonald] said, 'We have to save this child,' because the [Viet Cong] had been going into all the villages and saying this new Australian team were coming and they're not going to be very nice people, in fact they're going to cut off your penises and sew them onto your nose ... this is what was going on.

So politically we had to start off and get the confidence of the local people. Anyway, we operated on this little boy and we stayed up for two days and two nights and saved him, and so of course the word went around in the community and it was after that we started getting a lot of the locals in for work.[16]

'We all got gastro'

The team was housed in a three-storey residence about 600 metres from the hospital. The ground floor was occupied by Americans. Theatre nurse Veronica 'Von' Clinch, who served in 1966–67, believed the CIA had people in the house because 'The people on the ground floor were always in contact with people in the country using teletype machines, sending reports and other things.'[17] In fact, they were members of the Civil Operations and Revolutionary Development Support (CORDS) organisation, whose job was to monitor enemy activities and conduct operations on behalf of the US State Department. The second floor was allocated to the dining and bar area, and the top floor contained the bedrooms. Peter Mangos recalls:

> . . . there were a lot of things that weren't finished in the house. There was only one toilet, we all got gastro and the toilet blocked up; there were nine of us all with diarrhoea! There was a lot of hammering on the door [*chuckles*]. It was awful, I had never had diarrhoea like that; it was like a tap running. A lot of the accommodation hadn't been finished; for example, the bathroom floor was on a different level and when we had a shower the water ran out into the hallway. The door lock had been put on the wrong way and when you went into the bathroom you locked yourself in.[18]

Maureen Spicer remembers that when it rained, 'water seeped through the walls in the nurses' bedrooms on the second floor, and the water-tight tiles enabled the massive cockroaches to practise breaststroke across the floors.'[19]

The property was guarded by Vietnamese police, nicknamed the White Mice for the colour of their uniforms. Armed with heavy-calibre revolvers and batons, they had a reputation for shooting first and calling 'halt' later. Peter Mangos remembers one night when the security was not all it should have been:

> ... we went to the hospital at night and when we came home and we drove up to this bloke [the guard], he was dead asleep! We even put the headlights in his face and he still didn't wake up. And here was our security![20]

But the Australians weren't about to sit on their hands. Within a day of arriving they launched themselves into work, and they soon had the operating theatres usable. A major concern was the lack of wardsmen and other staff to move patients into theatre and the recovery ward. Doctors and theatre nurses ended up carrying litters and settling patients into the recovery ward.

All this activity took place amid the constant cacophony of war. The din is burned into Maureen Spicer's memory:

> The noise of the war was constant and during the night the artillery pounded, and the F-100 fighter bombers screamed on takeoff at regular intervals, but when it was quiet it was very scary and everyone became spooked.[21]

Given that most aircraft were taking off over the house with a clearance of between fifty and 100 feet and struggling to gain altitude in the hot, humid air, it is not surprising that things became noisy.

Kay Hirst, the first radiographer to serve in Bien Hoa, described the conditions there in a letter to her former boss:

> The X-ray department consists of a room which faces onto a ditch about 2 feet deep . . . separated from the room by a veranda 5 feet wide . . . it is priceless—it is the communal male toilet. All day long I have a stream of little men with their backs to me using the ditch.[22]

Given the antiquated equipment, intermittent power supply, shortage of film and tiny darkroom (less than four metres square and with no ventilation), it was no wonder that initially Kay struggled to take twenty X-rays a day. A later radiographer, Iain Brotchie, described the Picker Machine—which he suspected of being ex-US military equipment—as 'very robust, very solid . . . the dials were actually brass . . . It was a museum piece but the beauty of it was there was very little that could go wrong with it.'[23]

Without a doubt the key figure in getting the first team started was the live-in USOM representative, Joe Trotter. He was invaluable in showing the Australians around and establishing contacts with people who would support the Bien Hoa teams for the next seven years. Unfortunately, in late May 1966, he was transferred.

After four weeks in Bien Hoa, Bill McDonald reported that 'at least 80 per cent of the patients we have operated on have been directly injured in war by either shrapnel or bullets . . . about three-fifths of remainder are the result of accidents in Lambretta taxi cabs.'[24] He noted with pleasure that their accommodation now had running water and that American Special Forces (Green Beret) medics were assisting when South Vietnamese Special Forces troops were admitted to ease the workload. In their first month, the team had performed over 160 operations. By February 1966 the monthly total would be 234. Bill McDonald wrote: 'Sometimes we start work at eight o'clock in the morning and do not finish until one or two o'clock in the morning after working right through.'[25] His summary for March tallied 189 inpatients received; 258 new outpatients seen; 260 operations; and 485 patients X-rayed. [26] He noted ruefully that they lost one patient owing to the regular brown-outs. In an attempt to save the life of a police lieutenant with multiple gunshot wounds, Bill himself had given a pint of blood, but to no avail. Many of the patients who came in for abdominal surgery had roundworm. Worms would often be found protruding from the gut or free in the abdominal cavity, evoking what one surgeon called 'most unprofessional squeamishness'.[27] Team leader McDonald also asked for a paediatrician, and the Australian government eventually sent one.

With adaptability, ingenuity and professionalism, the team quickly made its mark in Bien Hoa. The wards were full and elective cases were starting to increase. US Army physician John Slaughter was filled with admiration:

> My own experiences with the first Alfred team have remained with me throughout my entire clinical time and a military career of 32 years. To this day I have not seen another group of doctors or nurses with more unadulterated personal integrity, professional ingenuity, or conscious determination to succeed than the two surgeons, anaesthesiologist, physician, four nurses, and X-ray technician who comprised the First Alfred Team going to the Bien Hoa Province Hospital from Melbourne in 1965. I have not seen again so much successful and high-quality work turned out with so little in the way of the complex support systems and material niceties which were just as seriously considered 'absolutely necessary' for quality care in 1965 as similar equipment is today.

> From that day to this it has remained my firm and

unaltered conviction that Australian medicine and surgery, and especially Australian nursing, have much to be proud of and much to teach others, particularly about how to make do in adverse surroundings and how to help sick people get well with minimal special equipment.[28]

'What have we struck?'

Rotations of medical staff were always staggered, owing to the variation in the lengths of surgeons' and nurses' tours.

As word spread of the surgeons' work, more people came in for treatment, and the workload steadily increased. The second Alfred team, under leader Ian Ferguson, was at work within a day of arriving in country. Bob Gray, the team anaesthetist, had been a 'gas man' for almost thirteen years when he volunteered to go to Bien Hoa. He was looking forward to his tour, saying, 'I wanted to actually see if in fact what they told us was true because I am fairly cynical in regard to war and I wanted to go and have a look.'[29] When he first looked over the hospital, 'I thought, "Jesus, what have we struck?" It was a little different to what we were used to at the Alfred, but I had been to New Guinea, and so you adapt very quickly.'

There was no alternative. As Bob recalled:

We had an EMO [Epstein Macintosh Oxford brand] inhaler and it was pretty primitive. It was satisfactory, but [luckily] I was brought up in the era before all the modern techniques of anaesthesia came in. I was a student of the rag and bottle days; in fact I had given a lot of chloroform anaesthetics.[30]

Surgeon Ian 'Cas' McInnes had recently returned from working in the UK and had been married only six weeks when he volunteered. He says, 'I was as mentally prepared as you can be. I guess we weren't really prepared for what was there . . . I thought to myself, "What in the name of goodness am I doing here?"' Day to day, he recalls, the work

> was 50 per cent civilian trauma . . . people being injured in motor vehicle accidents; a lot of motorbike accidents because everybody rode motorbikes up there. There was quite a lot of war-related civilian injuries. Kiddies that were sitting on shrapnel and bombs and stuff like that, much of it inflicted by Viet Cong . . . The VC used to go in and they would shoot up a village and we would get all the civilian casualties and they would be high-velocity bullet wounds— we saw lots of them—and shrapnel wounds. The other 50 per cent was infections, basically. We took pus from virtually every cavity in the body, I am sure. Because they didn't have access to antibiotics, they didn't have anything, and there was a lot of very primitive sort of medicine for infections such as suction cups [cupping] and all that sort of thing. Witch doctors were in vogue. We saw a lot of boils, carbuncles, advanced appendicitis—which had been left for days—and all that leads to peritonitis. We saw a lot of peritonitis and a lot of pus.[31]

The power cuts continued, as the Melbourne *Sun* newspaper reported under the headline 'Our Surgeons Fighting the War, Too': 'Midway through the operation the hospital's power system failed—a common experience for the surgical team. For the next twenty minutes—until the power was restored—senior surgeon Mr Ian Ferguson operated by the light of a torch.'[32] Paul Large recalls that once he 'had a head open trying to sort out a brain injury and suddenly the light went out.'[33]

Prime Minister Harold Holt made a brief visit in April 1966, and according to Ian Ferguson's end-of-tour report, it 'seemed to go quite well'. But in the forty-five minutes that an 'extremely tired-looking' Holt was with him, Ferguson made him very aware of how critical the short-ages of supplies and equipment were at Bien Hoa.[34]

'That's not blood'

As in Long Xuyen, the team always found it difficult to get blood from the Vietnamese, yet the large number of trauma cases meant blood was always badly needed. It was a never-ending battle to convince even close relatives of injured and sick patients to donate life-saving plasma. Fortunately, the 23rd Evacuation Hospital at the air base stepped into the breach. As Bob Gray explains: 'The Yanks were very supportive and used to give us some of their outdated blood, but you then have high potassium content. So we had to be very careful with what we were doing, and the rate at which we were giving that blood.'[35]

Despite the help, the surgical teams sometimes had to improvise, he recalls:

> I remember one day Cas McInnes saying to me, 'This blood looks pretty pale, Bob,' and I said, 'Cas, that's not blood, that is 5 per cent dextrose and water,'[36] because you just couldn't use the blood because of the high potassium content, and dextrose was all we had.[37]

Helen Banff, who worked in the children's ward, at one point had in her care a pregnant woman who was bleeding profusely. Without a trans-fusion, she and her unborn child would die. But there was no blood available, and things looked dire. Helen pressed the woman's family to assist:

> I asked the accompanying relatives to be the donors. 'Yes, I'll be donor. You pay me ten American dollars.' I didn't argue. As in many instances during the six months there, I gave my

blood as other team members did, and after this I grabbed the four relatives and took a bag from each of them. No American ten dollars passed hands, either. The woman lived, and so did the baby, and so did I. The team members thought that I wouldn't . . .'[38]

As the team came to grips with a new range of injuries and illnesses, the surgeons began to operate on cases seldom encountered in Australia, such as eye diseases, and tuberculosis in bones and joints.

Conditions slowly improved as the hospital generator was rewired so it could operate independently of the town power supply, and access to a new water conduit ensured a good flow of potable water. Tom Sale, who led a twelve-month team drawn from Brisbane hospitals, said that when it came to blood, given the problems with storage and refrigeration, let alone continuous power supply, 'a transfusion would be given because it looked all right rather than [because] it had been stored efficiently'.[39]

'The day didn't end'

The major difference between the experiences of the surgical teams at Long Xuyen, Vung Tau and Ba Ria and the one at Bien Hoa was undoubtedly the workload. In Bien Hoa it was simply overwhelming, and it was little wonder that team members, especially surgeons, were exhausted after only three months. Cas McInnes describes a typical day:

We worked fairly hard, the day didn't . . . end sometimes, we would have to work on into the night. Many times we got called out at night and we weren't too keen on that because it wasn't 100 per cent secure getting around Bien Hoa at night. We always had a sneaking suspicion that people looked after us at night and didn't shoot us up . . . We started at about 7 in the morning and basically finished about 5 or 6 at night. We only worked on Saturdays for emergencies. We were virtually all on call, we didn't go anywhere, we stayed around the house at night, we were always there so we were virtually on call all the time.[40]

In April 1966 (with only two surgeons), the team performed 250 surgical procedures. The non-traumatic and elective cases were increasing by about a third each month, and often the hospital was so full people had to be put two to a bed, on army stretchers, underneath beds, and out on the verandahs.

The workload got even heavier when the Viet Cong were active in the area, particularly during the Tet Offensive in 1968. However, many of the team members believed that to some extent they were consciously ruled out as targets because of their civilian medical role. They all wore distinctive green badges indicating that they belonged to the '*uc dai loi*' surgery team, and had red crosses and red kangaroos emblazoned on their vehicles. Theatre nurse Von Clinch is certain that the Red Cross insignia saved them at least once. She and a surgeon went to fetch urgently needed blood from the US Army 93rd Evacuation Hospital, inside the air base:

[we] took it back and put it in the hospital fridge and then drove home. When we got home, everyone was up and panicking because they'd heard we'd been blown up. A jeep had been blown up at the 93rd Evac, where we'd been. And we said, 'Well, we're all right.' We were fortunately in our little jeep that had a red cross on it. The jeep after us was blown up and the driver killed and the passenger badly injured. And everyone decided, the Americans, our team and everyone else, that they probably saw our jeep with the red cross, recognised

who we were and left us alone. Now, we don't know, but we presume that probably happened . . . So we were very careful to advertise who we were.[41]

The threat of violence did not always come from the enemy. Von Clinch recalls one harrowing evening:

David Scott and I were called back to the hospital. We'd finished operating on whomever . . . put the patient back to bed and all was fine . . . [we] were about to leave and we heard an Army truck pull up. And we looked at each other, afraid of what it might bring in, and sure enough about a dozen Vietnamese Regular Army [ARVN] walked in—and they weren't supposed to come to us, you see—with about five or six stretchers, put them down on the floor and as one of them went down the man died. The soldier died. So they were furious with us. Out came the guns and I ended up against the wall with the gun here [*she points to her head*] with the Vietnamese soldier screaming at me with these battle-crazed eyes. And the thing I can remember is looking at the finger on the trigger and it was white and I was dead scared he was going to pull it. And David was in another corner in the same situation with another soldier doing it to him. Anyhow, with much waving of hands trying to imply to him—'cause our Vietnamese wasn't the best—that if they killed us the other soldiers would die too. So eventually it got through and they stood and watched us while we put drips and everything in the other fellows. But I was really scared. You know that saying, My hair stood on end? I was scared, yes, I was scared that time.[42]

The suffering of children always tugged at the heart. Von Clinch remembers:

. . . a little highland girl. She was the only person to survive in this highland village. She would have been between eight and ten, very small. And she had a bullet wound to her abdomen and she was improving and getting better. And we got some pyjamas from the orphanage nearby and she was dressed in these smart pink pyjamas and we walked into the ward from being outside one day and here she is, lying back in her smart pyjamas smoking a cigarette. And all we could do was laugh because obviously she had been smoking for years. And then of course she was ready to go home and there was nowhere to go because her village was nonexistent and no one alive. So we took her over to the local orphanage and within two seconds she was back hanging onto our frocks and wouldn't let us go. She came with us and she wouldn't stay. So weeks were going by and we were almost due to go home and she wouldn't have accepted the new team; that was the attitude. And fortunately we discovered there was a young highland man, a soldier in the paramilitary ward, so we talked to him about it and he came over and talked to her and she liked him. And he took her home with him to his highland village and his family was going to look after her.[43]

Off duty, the teams would sometimes socialise, but there were draw-backs to being hospitable. In a discreet report to the DEA, Ian Ferguson wrote: 'I would say that at least every second night that we are in the house I have to eject some either drunk or sober serviceman who is trying to make contact with the girls.'[44] Another persistent problem was theft from the 'house fund' (the cash used to buy food and supplies for the team house), as well as personal belongings such as cameras and portable radios. By the time a safe was installed, two months into the Australians' residency, losses totalled almost $1000, a considerable sum in 1966. Team leader Graeme Grove, who arrived in August, recalls that no matter what they did it was almost impossible to stop the local staff from pilfering food.

Nurse Wendy Jobberns (née Williams) was twenty-three years old and had visited Asia before, so she was prepared for the sounds and smells of a tropical city. She fitted into the bustle of life as a theatre sister very quickly, and soon came to grips with sights such as that of fourteen people lying on stretchers waiting for treatment outside the operating room: they had been in a bus and were hit by a mortar. It was so hot in the operating theatres that apart from their working clothes staff wore no gowns, only masks and gloves, and 'the perspiration used to just pour down your front'. Wendy remembers boiling instruments to sterilise them because the normal sterilising equipment was broken. In the wards there were no mattresses, and sheets were a luxury. Work became a routine of being on call every third night and having every third weekend off. Relationships with the surgeons were less formal than in Australia, and everyone used first names at work.[45]

The reports from June and July showed that the team was performing over 200 operations a month.

When plastic surgeon Leo Rosner arrived in mid 1966, he repaired fourteen cleft lips and two cleft palates in three weeks. News of his success quickly spread among the civilian population, and his list for September was booked out by the beginning of August.[46]

By then the team had finally established a blood bank, thanks in part to their relentless harassment of the Vietnamese staff and patients' relatives. US Special Forces and the 964th Mobile Laboratory supported the blood drive and helped the team maintain a good operating stock.

The Australian involvement in Vietnam drew visitors to the area, including Gough Whitlam, MP, Dr Jim Cairns, Mr Bryant, MP, and the new Australian Ambassador to Saigon, Mr L.J. Border.

Senior surgeon Paul Large volunteered to go to South Vietnam in late 1966, partly because 'there was some adventure in it', but also because he wanted to do something about the lack of medical support for Vietnamese civilians.[47] To his surprise, he was asked to be team leader for what would be the first of three tours in Vietnam. Preparation was limited, although he and some of his Alfred Hospital team attended colloquial Vietnamese courses at the RAAF School of Languages at Point Cook, outside Melbourne.

After an official welcome and a one-day handover, they were up to their armpits in work, Paul recalls:

> The first day we were swamped with casualties and cases of all sorts. A lot of our casualties were road accidents with lots of road trauma and the whole team was flat out. I got home and I thought, 'God, if it is going to be like this all the time . . .' So it was a tough introduction as we were very busy. We ran out of linen because we couldn't dry it.[48]

Things did not improve much.

> Half the time the air-conditioners weren't working, the electrical supply was all over the place. The air-conditioners would scream and then conk out. I often operated with just gloves on and no gown. It became unbearable if the air-con wasn't working.[49]

Apart from normal surgery, a large number of patients were treated for cleft lips and palates. Nursing sister Aileen Monck recalls:

> . . . it was like a miracle to the families to see this happen . . . And certainly one of the reasons that the teams were sent to Vietnam was, I suppose, propaganda to win the hearts and minds of the people, and I'm sure that that type of surgery went a long way to please and satisfy the people that we were there to help them.[50]

Burns were another common injury. They were usually caused when people used high-octane—and highly explosive—fuels in their Primus cooking stoves.

As Viet Cong activity stepped up, explosions occurred all too close to the hospital. Once, 110 rockets landed in the Bien Hoa air base in one night. When asked if that was getting a bit close, Second World War and London Blitz veteran Paul Large responds, 'Yes, it was, but they were spread around. Only two rockets came near our house, one about 150 yards away and the other about 200.'[51]

Paul, who had no administrative officer to call on, found himself poring over accounts, after a day in theatre, doing bookkeeping and checking invoices. It was frustrating:

> The Embassy supplied us with *dong* [Vietnamese currency] and also MPC (Military Payment Certificate). We had PX [Post Exchange] privileges and we bought our food off the PXs and sometimes from the markets. So I had to keep these accounts, and we used the *dong* to pay the cook, the cleaning ladies and to pay for petrol at the local garage and so on. I worked like crazy on these accounts which went via the embassy to Canberra. Then I got a letter from Canberra saying my *dong* account was something like ten *dong* [a few cents] out! I couldn't take this seriously and wrote back saying I had done my best and could they say if I was ten *dong* under or over? I got increasingly acerbic correspondence and I ended up telling them that it was bloody nonsense. I am a surgeon and I am trying to work here and I wasn't answering any more letters about it. So I have probably got a black file or black box somewhere.[52]

As in the other provincial hospitals, Bien Hoa team members received a daily allowance plus food and accommodation expenses as part of their modest salary package.[53] Clearly, nobody was doing this for the money. Before he returned to Australia, Paul Large summed up his time in Vietnam: 'I am going to leave here with very mixed feelings and will be very glad to go in many ways and . . . I am rather dreading going back to the existence one had in Melbourne after dealing with all this clinical material.'[54]

During his tour, Large visited Long Xuyen. He compared its two-month case-load of 250 cases with Bien Hoa's 592, and concluded that his southern colleagues 'had their arses in butter'. On the last night, he planned to take his team out on the town and 'make everybody intoxicated'. However, with Viet Cong activity increasing, road movement in the province after 5.30 p.m. had been banned.

Boding well for later teams, the US Air Force's 300-man 3rd Security Police Squadron had 'adopted' the hospital and was providing invaluable manpower support for minor projects.[55] Nurse Von Clinch felt that the team had made great progress, with two Vietnamese nurses working well with them in the recovery ward, freshly painted walls and rubber mattresses for the wooden beds. Things that most nursing staff would take for granted were now precious to her.[56]

If August 1966 was busy in Bien Hoa, however, it was deadly for the 1st Australian Task Force in Phuoc Tuy province. On the 18th, Delta Company, 6th Battalion, Royal Australian Regiment, fought a four-hour encounter battle in a rubber plantation at Long Tan. Paul Large had been visiting Vung Tau on weekend leave when his mate, army surgeon Bruce Fox, was called to help treat twenty-five wounded Australians. Seventeen more had been killed. Word spread fast about not only the success of the battle but the size of the enemy force that took part (over 2000 men). Unprecedented in the Australian area of operations, the battle was a crucial test for the newly arrived task force.

Nurse Suzanne 'Suzie' MacFarlane (née Leyland) had emigrated from England and become an Australian citizen so she could travel to

Vietnam as part of an Australian surgical team. 'Just before I went there was the Battle of Long Tan, and that really made me think, "Oh . . . this sounds quite sort of serious . . . this might be dangerous."' But in Bien Hoa, most of the injuries she saw in theatre were from road accidents, often involving Army trucks. The roads in Bien Hoa city were narrow, Suzie recalls, and 'all these people just [sat] on the edge of the streets' and were regularly hit by trucks and buses.[57] Like most civilian hospitals, Bien Hoa treated whoever came in to casualty. Sometimes Viet Cong would be dumped on the doorstep because the Americans would not treat them further after operating on them. Suzie recalled one such case, a Viet Cong soldier who had had a leg amputated in an accident: 'When we undid all the dressings to get to the leg which had been amputated, here were all these artery forceps that had been clamped on to stop the bleeding. So we gained all these artery forceps.'[58]

'Bring some fags with you'

Shortages were an endless problem. Von Clinch recalls the empty shelves that greeted the Alfred team when they arrived at Bien Hoa in August:

> No equipment. No drugs. We had no morphine. Two doses of pethidine [meperidine] were the only things we had for pain for the patients. Antibiotics, we only had erythromycin tablets. No other antibiotics at all. Intravenous [fluid] giving sets, we had six [sets] and about four glasses of intravenous fluid and that was all we had.[59]

Surgeon David Brownbill, who spent the last part of 1966 at Bien Hoa, recalls how the difficulties brought his team closer together:

> I think it was that idea of being under horrible circumstances in some ways professionally—no sterility, few supplies, it

was hard work, people couldn't speak the language, there
was the occasional unhappy relative out there—and then
there was the slight concern over war intervention where
you were, and the team spirit built up.[60]

The day started at around 7.30 a.m. for the nurses, who often walked to
work, playing with young children and exchanging greetings with locals
on the way. Von Clinch recalls:

> We had to reinsert all the intravenous and the Levin's tubes
> [feeding tubes] into their stomach 'cause the relatives or the
> patients would have pulled them all out. Check everyone was
> OK. And then the ones well enough to go . . . we'd carry over
> on a stretcher to the other wards to make room for those that
> were being operated on. And then we had to do all the dress-
> ings in the recovery room and as they came back from the
> operating room, do whatever was required. We might have to
> put drips in, Levin's tubes, whatever. Or connect up a Wangen-
> steen [nasogastric tube] apparatus to do suction. And then we
> always went over to the prison and did dressings over there,
> which was a bit dicey. The guard there would often be asleep
> and we'd go in, do what we had to do and then walk out.[61]

Larceny became a way of life for Von Clinch, who also had the task of pro-
curing food and medical supplies. It sometimes took all her ingenuity:

> I also went to the Vietnamese store in Saigon and you had
> to send six copies of the order a week ahead. And they'd put
> beside the drugs you'd ordered, 'not available'. Then after, say,
> two or three weeks of not being available . . . when it arrived
> in, then they'd say, 'No. Already supplied.' So I used to say,
> whichever man went down with me, I'd say, 'Bring some fags

with you. You stand and talk to the guy at the door; I'll go in and just take everything I want.' So I'd go in, take everything I wanted whether we needed it or not. And anything I thought we could barter to get what we needed elsewhere, I'd take. And then we'd barter that. And that was the way we survived.[62]

The nurses farewelled the surgeons at the end of their tour and then saw the 'new boys' come up:

> . . . the very amusing thing that we couldn't help laughing about was that the new team of men arrived and looked out the window of the house and saw fires everywhere and they said, 'Ooh, it's been bombed, it's been bombed.' So they madly clicked their photos and then we said, 'Well, they're just burning the latrines.'[63]

For twenty-five-year-old Dot Angell, arriving in April 1967, the recovery room where she would spend most of her time was a bit of a surprise: 'One of the walls . . . we'd refer to as the spitting wall. It was just covered in betel juice.' She was told that it was now her duty to insert intravenous fluids. This was not normally done by a nurse, but in at the deep end she went: 'We were in a situation where we had to quickly learn, we had to learn on the run.' The morning after her arrival, Dot found the five-bed recovery room crammed with at least thirty patients. As time went on, she and her colleagues learned that the wail of an ambulance siren was the signal to prepare for an influx of wounded or injured. Dot recalls her experience with triage:

> . . . in Australia you always took the worst injured and dealt with them first. In wartime you can't do that, because they'd take up too much time on the operating table, and a number of others may die whilst you spend your time operating

on the badly injured, and then [the badly injured] may die.
If the surgeons were tied up, then the nurses had to make
those decisions.[64]

Dot also encountered diseases she thought had been wiped out:

> ... we had cholera ... typhoid, and we had plague. We had to
> have inoculations against bubonic plague before we went, and
> that shocked us because we thought that had been eradicated.
> When we got to Vietnam and saw the rats, we realised there
> was a problem. And definitely from 1966 through, bubonic
> plague was just going through the provinces like mad.[65]

The lunar New Year (Tet) festival usually brought increased enemy
activity in Bien Hoa. In January 1967, sixty-six of the hospital's 356
operations were attributed directly to war wounds. In one case, an
unexploded shell cap had lodged against a woman's spleen; it was
successfully removed and the woman went home 'none the worse for
wear'.[66]

Professor of Surgery Hugh Dudley, the team's most senior
member at the time, complained in a letter to the DEA that 'the size
of the [operating] suite is quite unsuited to the volume of work going
through it'. He also asked for 'a clinical pathologist to come for three
to six months to implement improvements (as happened at Long
Xuyen)'.[67] The American 93rd Evacuation Hospital was an enormous
help, providing all manner of supplies, and the 44th Signals Battalion, the USAF 3rd Security Police Squadron and the 134th Maintenance Group (Engineers) also lent sterling support. Having US
liaison officer Captain 'Chuck' McDougald living in the team house
was also a boon.

Australia Day was celebrated with panache in Saigon. The Australian Ambassador's wife, who had trained as a nurse at the Alfred

Hospital in her youth, was made an honorary member of the team.[68] For Dot Angell it was a memorable trip to the party: their convoy came across a horrific road accident on the way into Saigon and they stopped to help. She wrote home later that 'we were in all our finery wading up to our ankles in blood and mud.'[69]

The first of what would be many exchanges took place in May 1967 with surgeons Owen Cole and Adrian Lowe up from Long Xuyen, and team leader Robert Lawson spending two days with the Australian 2nd Field Ambulance (a precursor of the 1st Australian Field Hospital) at Vung Tau.[70] A British doctor also worked with the Bien Hoa team.[71] The team's workload in the first few months of 1967 had increased from the previous year with 347 cases in February and 416 in March. The growing number of fractures the team was treating led to a (never fulfilled) request for an orthopaedic surgeon to accompany all future teams. Meanwhile, its work outside the hospital expanded, as it continued to support Civilian Irregular Defence Group (CIDG) militiamen, who were American-trained and not allowed treatment in Vietnamese military hospitals, as well as the National Rehabilitation Institute in Saigon and the Ben San leprosarium.

The leprosarium

The French-built leprosarium near Ben San, in western Bien Hoa province, was supported by the US military and USOM. From the time the Australian civilian surgical teams arrived in Bien Hoa they too provided assistance to the lepers. Every fortnight a nurse and a plastic surgeon made the fifteen-minute flight by helicopter (sometimes Air America or US Army) and conducted surgery, usually curettage of lesions and sometimes amputations. Nurse Von Clinch recalls:

> The leprosarium was about 80 kilometres from Bien Hoa, but in Viet Cong territory. Because of this the chopper would

not land, but hovered two metres above the ground for us to jump out. A time would be arranged to return, when we again had to jump or be lifted in with help—a rather terrifying experience.

The leprosarium was run by a French order of nuns. Sister Rose was in charge and the other nuns were Vietnamese. Sister Rose had once been kidnapped by the Viet Cong but they had only kept her for a couple of days before releasing her. When I met her I was surprised they kept her that long—she could have talked her way out of anything!

The leprosarium was well organised and clean. They grew their own vegetables and raised chickens and rabbits. Patients who were well enough worked in the laundry, kitchen and garden, and the men were busy building another ward when we visited. A very efficient organisation.[72]

(Now and then team members would also work in a hospital not far from the leprosarium where the specialty was fitting artificial glass eyes, which had been imported from India.[73])

On one flight out in 1969, the chopper that nurse Robyn Anderson was on clipped the trees, crash-landed, and was wrecked. Injuries were slight, but the door gunner had concussion, and one of the pilots was trapped in the cabin. Viet Cong showed up to investigate the crash, and Robyn and plastic surgeon Max Lovey suddenly became the rescuers:

Max and I got the [door] gunner and draped him over their shoulders [others in the helicopter] and said, 'Right, [get] back to the leprosarium.' Then we got the other two girls out and the anaesthetist who had quite literally slid across the floor on his face and was under the seat on the other side. We dragged him out on his face and draped him over their shoulders and said, 'Run.' And so they all took off to the leprosarium and Max and I went round to get the pilot out who was screaming, 'Run, run. It'll blow up, it'll blow up.' And we're all saying, 'Just shut up. We're going to get you out.' And we looked at his feet and somehow the rudder pedals had come down on the top of his feet and they were crushed to a pulp. And so Max and I just looked at one another and nodded—'swish'—and pulled a leg out each. The pilot lost consciousness, which was the best that could have happened, and so Max and I were carrying him—and he was a big man and I had the top of him. So I'm whingeing about the division of labour and Max is titting along with his legs saying, 'Hurry along there.' Anyway, we're all running and all of a sudden a tank came over the hill. Well, of course the Viet Cong immediately disappeared because of the tank and the officer in the turret is talking into his microphone and waving. Now, nobody could understand what the hell he was saying and so anybody who had a spare arm waved back and kept running. And finally he shut the thing down and said, 'Stop running, you're running in a mine field.' So everybody screeched to a halt and they brought the tanks up and we put the two injured people up on what were basically the mud guards of the tank and went back to the leprosarium.[74]

Maureen Spicer recalls another day when things at Ben San became dangerous. It was one of 'several times I thought I was about to die':

> . . . the Viet Cong suddenly appeared. The co-pilot ran into the leprosarium and screamed at us to run like hell to the helicopter. When we got to the helicopter we could see the group of VC breaking through the trees further down the hill. The helicopter pilot was trying to get the helicopter

off the ground ... and it made the most agonising noises and shuddered dreadfully as it lifted just out of the range of the Viet Cong and incoming [American] jets.[75]

Johanna Van Valen was a nurse on board an Iroquois helicopter of Air America (the airline operated by the CIA) when it clipped the tall trees surrounding the Ben San chopper pad as it tried to get airborne on a very hot and humid day. They crash-landed in a nearby rice paddy but on the 'wrong side' of a fence, which meant they were in Viet Cong territory. Van Valen recalls that their backs hurt from the crash, but what was worse was the nervous wait while the US Army came in and repaired the helicopter, an armed escort keeping a wary eye out for the enemy.[76]

Betty Lockwood's first visit to Ben San was her first ever to a leprosarium. But the presiding priest, Father Berci, soon put her nervousness to rest:

> The father there, he was just gorgeous, and after every session, every operating session you did, he'd say, 'Now come my children, come and we will get rid of the germs.' And he'd ply you full of bloomin' Scotch to kill the germs. That was amazing.[77]

The only times Australians had difficulty getting to Ben San in the entire time they supported the colony were immediately after the 1968 Tet Offensive, when visits were suspended for four months, and after the Easter Offensive of 1972, when it was impossible to venture into the area without risk of attack.

'Rock hopping'

Jenny Leak hadn't thought of volunteering to go to South Vietnam until early 1967, when she was 'accosted in the corridor' of Wakefield

Hospital in Adelaide by Mervyn Smith. Smith was about to lead a Royal Adelaide Hospital team, the first from South Australia. Jenny was a very busy Deputy Director of Nursing, but the idea of being in a hand-picked team inspired her. After a few team meetings at Smith's home, Jenny scoured the libraries for information on Vietnam and the war but without much luck. However, she did read Susan Terry's account of her tour, *House of Love*, before she left. It was Jenny's first trip overseas.

After arriving in Saigon, the team travelled directly by road to Bien Hoa, experiencing Vietnamese driving at its scariest. Like their predecessors, they began work at once after a quick orientation and handover. Jenny recalls her dismay:

> There were often two in a bed. I was in the recovery room. There were stretchers all over the floor usually, so you did a lot of sort of 'rock hopping' between stretchers . . . there was no linen on the beds, there was very short supply of basic equipment and it just looked really poor.[78]

Unfazed, Jenny mobilised her mother back in Adelaide, who started a 'linen drive', as did many other members' parents. Supported by their hospitals as well, they soon had linen sent up to Bien Hoa via the Army postal service. Getting the linen was one thing, but stopping it from leaving with the grateful patients would be a never-ending problem.

There were shortages of almost everything, including painkillers. The Americans helped out by supplying a morphine derivative called meperidine (pethidine). Jenny Leak noted that 'it made a big difference to the patients' recovery'.[79] For the team members these were eye-opening times. Not only did they have to watch a large provincial hospital with limited medical supplies struggling to cope with normal civilian surgery, but they also had to deal with being in a war zone. In Australia they were used to herding visitors out of the hospital after visiting hours. Now they found that the relatives who were often underfoot in the crowded wards were a tremendous resource, as Jenny explains:

> . . . they would run and get the ice bags to put on the head or they would run and get the tea and sterile water 'cause you couldn't drink it out of the tap . . . And help us turn people . . . once we mobilised them as a force . . . it was amazing. You could achieve twice as much.[80]

And at times things got very hectic. Jenny remembers the day fifteen patients suddenly arrived in the hospital, their litters covering the floor.

Dr Peter Last went to South Vietnam as a physician, but also served as a paediatrician and anaesthetist during his three-month tour in 1967, after being recruited by Mervyn Smith. Coming from a practice where many of his clients were ex-servicemen and -women, this was his first opportunity to serve in a war zone and discover for himself what it was like. He wanted to be able to 'look those ex-servicemen in the eye and say, I've never actually fought in combat but I have handled patients who came to us as a result of combat.'[81] Peter described the official preparation for the tour as 'grossly, flamboyantly inadequate in the sense that it didn't exist'. To this day, he rues his ignorance of the cultural aspects of his service and his dealings with the Vietnamese.

Peter's domain soon became the paediatric ward. When the team arrived,

> . . . it wasn't what I expected. It was incomparably worse . . . the paediatric ward was just across from the surgical suite [and] was established in what had originally been the hospital's rice store. It had a rough brick floor, rough cast walls, no ceiling, just the thatched roof above us, which at least was waterproof. But every now and again things fell down from that roof.[82]

The twenty-one beds often carried fifty patients, with relatives who cooked and helped with the nursing sleeping under the beds. Even though Peter himself never saw any exchange of fire, many of his patients had war injuries. They were brought in from the streets and through the American 'Dustoff' system, which evacuated wounded civilians and irregular troops from the battlefield.[83]

The workload was very demanding, with twelve-hour days in the stifling heat not uncommon. Josephine Howard (née Griffin), who worked in the demanding recovery ward, says, 'it was relentless. I was really tired ... For about a month in the middle of the six [months] I just felt I wasn't going to make it.'[84] Aileen Monck remembers:

> ... it was always crowded. Patients lying on the floor would have their drips held at the foot of the bed which they were next to with a piece of bandage, and you'd be stepping over these bodies to try to get to the beds and vice versa. So it wasn't exactly easy nursing.[85]

Although nurse Margaret Bolton felt the effort was worthwhile because the local people were 'so grateful', she recalls one particularly awful day:

> ... a little girl of six [years old came in] who was shot by friendlies [Vietnamese]. Doug [Townsend] and I worked on her for I don't know how many hours, and then she died choking on her vomit ... things like that, it was just depressing. And I'll never forget that little girl.[86]

Another night the team had sixteen emergency cases admitted at 11 p.m. following a 'drop-short' from a mortar bomb.

The mid-year report compiled by Graham Wilson showed they had performed 528 procedures of which 113 were major and the balance minor. Of these, 147 were attributed to war activity. The anaesthetist Tom Allen was kept busy administering 414 general anaesthetics.

'We didn't have any beds'

In October 1967, the Royal Brisbane Hospital dispatched to Bien Hoa a team whose members were expected to serve continuously for twelve months—a significant departure from the previous practice, and one that ignored the experience of prior team members, who were completely exhausted at the end of three- or six-month tours. This was also the first time that some wives accompanied their husbands on their tour of duty.

Carmel Hurst (née Jorgensen) signed up for a bit of adventure. As she readily admits, her motives were far from altruistic, but she was also somewhat naïve about what to expect in a war zone. After the teams' welcome in Saigon and the nerve-racking two-hour road trip to Bien Hoa, Carmel's team was soon in action. During the hospital welcome the following day, in the middle of festivities

> . . . a young man came in with a compound fracture of the femur . . . and it had broken right through the skin. Our orthopaedic surgeon just went straight off to theatre . . . Covered in dirt from the road, the lad was operated on, put into a splint—we didn't have any beds—he was nursed on a dirty stretcher on the floor.[87]

This was when Carmel made her 'mental adjustment' to the realities of South Vietnam, she says. For the next twelve months, her workload as a theatre sister would be made up of about one-third road and accident injuries, one-third war wounds and the rest 'routine stuff that we had seen at home, only it was so much more gross'. This included goitres, cleft palates and poorly treated injuries, especially burns. Some of the methods used to save lives were things she had never seen at home. One night they were called out and

> ... we found this kid bleeding through his bandages. And [his heartbeat was] flat. And the surgeon couldn't get the blood into his veins because all his veins had collapsed. So we poured the blood into just an ordinary pot and we syringed it out and forced it into his veins. And he came around, and then someone else came down and helped him and they went back in and sewed him up again and gave him antibiotics.[88]

Even though the team was managing to cope with less than perfect hygiene, they were daunted by the rats, which proliferated—and grew to enormous size—in the gardens and surrounds of the hospital. Carmel Hurst recalls seeing one little boy who had the tips of his toes nibbled off by rats when he was left on the floor of the ward overnight.[89]

Iain Brotchie was a radiographer but had also served in the Citizen Military Forces. Because of his military training he was quite prepared for what lay ahead. The toughest time he faced, he says, was when a truckload of twenty-five 'radically traumatised' workers was offloaded in casualty. The vehicle had hit a large anti-tank mine that blew it over two metres into the air. The injuries were horrific. One man's 'ankles were on his knees and just pulverized'. The overwhelming question for Iain was, 'Do you spend all your time treating a spinal case and [let] the other people die with their broken limbs?'[90]

Iain also did many chest X-rays—some 15,000 in his year at Bien Hoa—because tuberculosis was rampant.[91] Many patients developed 'big holes in their lungs—half a lung eaten away and the other half filled with fluid ... it was traumatic.'[92] It might have seemed like a conveyor-belt system at times, but every now and then something like a hand grenade in a patient's trouser pocket would ensure he was kept on his toes. Iain treated civilians, Viet Cong prisoners, and members of the South Vietnamese military who were not in the Army of the Republic of Vietnam, such as the Montagnards (Vietnamese tribal hill people) serving with the US Special Forces, Chinese Nungs (mercenaries with the American and Australian advisers), and occasionally Cambodian mercenaries, as well as Regional and Popular Force (RF and PF) soldiers, and CIDG troops.[93] His team leader, Tom Sale, reported that Iain was 'on call practically every night'.[94] A month into the tour, the team had performed 550 operations, almost one-fifth of them involving major surgery.

As 1967 drew to a close, Carmel Hurst wrote a long letter home. In a thoughtful premonition of the Agent Orange debate that would follow three decades later, she wrote:

> There is a surfeit of flora, too, but who has time to culti-
> vate or even just protect such luxuries as orchids or hibiscus?
> There is a massive programme of 'defoliation' going on, with
> the idea of flushing the enemy out of their jungle lairs, the
> side effects of which can easily be imagined.[95]

'Fire crackers going off'

The celebration of the lunar New Year in Vietnam usually starts with the detonation of fireworks to scare off evil spirits and allow the good spirits to preside over the festivities. In Bien Hoa in 1968, Elizabeth (Beth) Scott recalls, Tet

> . . . started off with people setting off fire crackers, which
> is what we expected. For three days before there were fire
> crackers going off all over the place and people were just
> saying, 'Well, that's what the Chinese people do at Tet'.[96]

Carmel Hurst was with other off-duty staff on the roof of the team house, drinking champagne and, like most other residents of Bien Hoa, watching the fireworks displays. An American pilot also on the roof terrace with the group noticed a large glow in the sky and yelled out to everyone to hit the floor, which fortunately they did. Carmel says, 'We didn't really understand what he was talking about. But then the blast hit us and if we hadn't been down on the ground we would have been knocked down.'[97]

Before long everyone realised that it was more than fireworks going off, and that a major military action was underway. The skies over the city were illuminated by red and green tracer rounds, and almost non-stop explosions from artillery shells, mortar bombs and rockets. The team house had access to a bunker through what became known as the 'Green Door'; this was the refuge when the resident Americans thought things were getting dangerous.

Peter Grant was having a drink at the air base when he noticed senior military officers disappearing from the party. An orderly approached him and said, 'I think you people ought to go back, we're expecting the Tet Offensive to start tonight.'[98] Later that evening Grant was woken by the sound of rockets and mortars hitting the air base.

One memorable night during this period there was an attack on a huge ammunition dump at Long Binh, about eight kilometres away. Beth Scott heard an enormous explosion that 'blew the sandbags off our parapets on our quarters because the whole ammunition dump went up. And that was quite dramatic.'[99] At one stage during the second or third night of the offensive the Americans warned everyone in the team house to take cover. Beth had already prepared herself, and as she looked out from her hiding place she noticed:

> There were Americans running up and down the corridor with machine-guns and you could feel their fear. They were only eighteen or nineteen or something and they were breathing heavily and one of them ran past and said, 'Get under your mattress when they start coming in through the

window.' And we said, 'We're already under our mattress.' But I remember there were three of us underneath the mattress. I just felt . . . [if] I could just get my kidneys in a little bit further, I wouldn't end up by getting a bullet through the kidney.[100]

John Scott (who would later become Beth's husband) recalled the soldiers who worked out of their building returning fire from the upper balconies. As the war thundered around them, he was called to the hospital to treat a seriously wounded boy: 'There was a kid that had stood on a mine and had his foot almost blown off and we had to amputate his foot that night.'[101] On the first day of the Tet Offensive the surgical team performed forty-two major operations. An additional operating table was set up to cope with the workload. Beth Scott remembers a scene of carnage:

> . . . the triage area was just absolutely jam-packed with people lying on stretchers. There was one woman lying in the corner with a bandage around her head. And I'd looked at her once and she seemed to be all right and when I looked at her again I could see the blood seeping through the bandage. So I thought we'd better go and have a look at her . . . so I took the bandage off . . . and she had a bullet [half an inch] long sticking straight out of her head.[102]

At Bien Hoa air base, the Viet Cong had breached the perimeter defences and a napalm strike was used to clear them off the major runway. The Scotts aren't sure how many dead were brought to the hospital but they think about seventy Viet Cong were laid out in the grounds because the morgue was full. The bodies lay in the sun for several days before being removed, making work at the hospital a sickening affair. The morning after the initial assault, at about

2 a.m., an American helicopter gunship hovered over the team house and engaged Viet Cong only 200 metres away in open ground. The spent cartridge cases from the chopper's electric Miniguns, which could fire 2000 rounds a minute, lay almost ankle-deep in the rooftop barbecue area. It was about five days before things returned to relative normalcy.

But even in the worst moments there was laughter. After one particularly scary night, when the gunfire had subsided team members looked around and realised that one of their number, Vivienne Hassett, was missing.

> Well, we couldn't find her when the crisis was over. Where's Vivienne? And we're all calling out, 'Viv, where are you? Where are you?' And she said, 'I'm down here.' And we went down to the very last room and she was hiding in the wardrobe in the very last room and she didn't even realise it was all over because she was so scared.[103]

On another occasion, pandemonium broke out after a mortar attack not far from the team house. Beth and John Scott recall:

> Barry [Smithurst] had been given two handguns by the Americans. And he had his handguns out—he was a physician—and I don't know which was more scary, the VC or Barry with his handguns. And when they said, 'Go down to the bunker,' he fell over the metal rubbish bin, so there—in the dark—there was this huge clatter and bang and everyone thought, This is it. They're coming to get us! And it was just Barry falling over the rubbish bin.[104]

The impact of the Tet Offensive affected the team's freedom of movement for the rest of the year, says Beth Scott:

... prior to that we'd been able to move around the country a fair bit. And then after Tet the roads to Vung Tau and Nui Dat, the roads pretty much anywhere were closed. We had to go to Saigon every week to get stores from the market in Cholon. And the American chopper pilot used to do a mail run on Sundays for us so we'd all take turns in going into Saigon by chopper ... [We] couldn't do any road travelling at all in the daytime.[105]

As Suzanne MacFarlane puts it, 'Every time you went on the roads you were taking your life in your hands. But, I mean, that was just something you had to do.'[106] Even more frustrating for these dedicated professionals was that they were not able to travel from their quarters to the hospital at night because of the threat of ambush or attack.

The magnitude of the 1968 Tet Offensive was not widely appreciated at the time. The fighting raged for days around Bien Hoa as the Viet Cong attempted to attack the air base and close off access to the city from Saigon. Fortunately for the allies, the attacks were relatively uncoordinated and soon driven back by the American and Vietnamese air forces. But casualties were high, and the wounded rolled into the hospital by the truckload. Wounded civilians, South Vietnamese troops and Viet Cong kept the surgical suites working constantly. The number of major surgeries in February was only slightly higher than January's total, but the number of war-related operations quadrupled, to 416. Paul Large recalls that

... it was really exciting. I wasn't there but a bunch of young Viet Cong—eighteen-year-olds—got into a paddy which covered the road across from the team house and the team was pinned down in the house and they couldn't show themselves.[107]

Team leader Tom Sale analysed the February case-load and concluded that 'the average time taken for each case, including anaesthesia, preparation, [and] carrying in of the patient was 21 minutes.' All of the X-rays done in February—1221 of them—were taken on a small mobile machine, because the static Picker Machine was out of order.[108]

The following month, the team reached a milestone of almost 3000 operations in five months. During Tet and for a short time after, USAID offered the services of three American nurses, allowing some respite for the Australian nurses, who had been run off their feet. Tom Sale's wife had returned to Australia, so the cooking and cleaning she'd overseen went back onto the shoulders of the women in the team. A night curfew meant that at least the number of traffic accident victims had dropped considerably. Sale noted in his report that 'a number of cases came in with casualty cards attached and on which the diagnosis was written as "Booby Strap".'[109]

The US CORDS organisation was now responsible for anything and everything including security of the house, and the presence of a can-do officer named John Vann ensured that the constant dramas over supplies of power and water were always quickly resolved.

In total, the Queensland-based teams that rotated through Bien Hoa in 1968 performed 15,226 operations and took 23,245 X-rays. War casualties accounted for a quarter of all surgical procedures, but Tom Sale believed this was an under-count.[110]

Prisoners of war

Australia had abided by the Geneva Conventions since they were introduced in 1950, so when Viet Cong soldiers came or were brought to the hospital for treatment there was little fuss. As Beth Scott says, 'we had a prison ward where we would treat the VC prisoners the same as any of the other Vietnamese'. Beth thought that a section of their team took decent treatment of the enemy a little 'too far', buying the prisoners such treats as chocolates from the American PX. Most of the team regarded this as 'a bit over the top', but thankfully the disagreement didn't affect the cohesion of the group.[111]

By mid 1968 daytime travel had resumed, although there were still severe restrictions on movement at night. In a letter to the DEA in July, Dr Kevin King wrote that 'our nurses showed evidence of stress in my opinion'.[112] It was becoming more and more apparent that the twelve-month-tour experiment was not succeeding: the entire team was exhausted. Tom Sale wrote that 'a lot of the camaraderie had disappeared by about the ninth month and team members existed and worked together well but not amicably'.[113] When a fresh group of Queenslanders arrived in September 1968, few were on twelve-month tours. Pat Warren, a nurse in the new team, looked at the outgoing Queensland team and recalled, 'I was surprised at how exhausted they looked . . . it was a shock to see the team in that state'.[114]

The Tet Offensive was a watershed in the war not only for military and political reasons. As the war grew increasingly unpopular in Australia, it became more and more difficult to find medical staff prepared to go to South Vietnam. Even more exhausting times lay ahead.

4

Battling on and backing up: Bien Hoa 1969–72

In January 1969 the Alfred Hospital's Brian Smith led a five-hospital team of seventeen to Bien Hoa, of whom Dr Bernard Ryan, Sister Nada Marovich and administration officer John Flynn were back for a second tour. The old team house was now the headquarters of the US CORDS program and its leader, John Vann.[1] The team's new quarters were very pleasant, and everyone had their own room and shower. Robyn Anderson was in charge of the intensive care unit, but almost needed some herself when she arrived ill with food poisoning. When she recovered she spent three days cleaning beds before she concluded that achieving Australian hospital standards would simply not be possible. She remembered that: '. . . we had to step up to a level of nursing far beyond anything we did [in Australia].'[2]

Robyn quickly had to adapt:

> There were hardships in theatre but quite different to our hardships in that if we didn't organise the right drugs, if we didn't give the blood, if we didn't put the drips in, the patient died . . . they came out of theatre and they lived or died by what we did. And so we had to be on the ball and we had to step up. And we really did.[3]

Designed for 260 patients, the hospital was catering to as many as 600 at peak times. To squeeze everyone in, Robyn says, 'we usually topped and tailed patients [lay them head to feet, side by side]. And with children we usually had them five to a bed lying sideways.' After doing rounds the nurses would venture into the waiting area, which at times resembled a charnel-house:

> Patients came in in the most incredible state. They'd all just be plonked together either on the floor of the male and female surgical wards or on the floor of the anteroom to theatre ... We used to find the most horrendous things in there ... people with legs blown off, people who were still bleeding. And in amongst it would be somebody with a sore thumb.[4]

At times the pre-operative area was a scene of mayhem. One day two patients came out of theatre dead, and Robyn knew it was because they had not been prepared properly for surgery. She confronted the surgeon and said, 'If you take one more person to theatre like that I will personally have your balls in a bucket.' This naturally got the attention of the surgeon, who agreed that there was room for greater cooperation. Before long the triage system was running like clockwork, but it also meant that the surgeons had to trust the nurses to do a lot more than was normal in Australia.

Robyn recalls the time two Montagnard women came in after walking eighty kilometres for treatment. They had been severely burnt trying to dismantle a white-phosphorous shell for its brass. When they arrived in triage they were literally smouldering:

> I got an amputation knife—which is really only a carving knife with a tarted up handle so it can go through an auto-clave—and just carved the tissue off and dropped it into a bucket full of water. And as I dropped it [it went] 'sssss' as the burning magnesium temporarily went out ... I got them

down to healthy bleeding tissue, and we then did the dressings ... But they were the most amazing people. I never heard
one of them cry out.[5]

Like most of the Australians on the surgical teams, Robyn was repeatedly struck by the fortitude and stoicism of Vietnamese people, but
these women stood out even in that courageous population. It would
take Robyn two hours a day to dress their burns, and 'sometimes I would
still be doing that at three o'clock in the morning'. The two women
did everything together, and one morning she found them in the bath
together. Back in Australia, this sort of thing was simply unheard of, but
as she looked down at them, Robyn saw that 'they'd debrided and picked
all the dead tissue off one another'.[6]

Another time Robyn treated three children, aged about eleven, eight
and four, who had been wounded in an explosion that killed both their
parents. The hospital had run out of anaesthetic, and she had to remove
shrapnel—about a cupful in all—and then suture the wounds:

I cut out dozens of pieces of shrapnel and sutured [the
eldest] without anaesthetic. She got off the table and she put
her hands together, bowed her head and said, 'Cam on bac si'
which is 'Thank you, doctor'—they called us all doctors—
and then they put the next child on the table . . . And the
same thing. And then the baby . . . and the two older girls
held her still. And although she wriggled, she didn't cry out.
She murmured . . . but she didn't cry out, and I took the
remaining shrapnel out of her.[7]

The 1969 Tet Offensive

At lunar New Year 1969, the Viet Cong launched another Tet Offensive, though it was smaller than the previous year's. The team house was

next to several villas occupied by American Psyops Corps (psychological operations) units and, being the tallest of the buildings, seemed to be a frequent target. Robyn Anderson recalls that 'about 200 Viet Cong came up out of the ground, out of the tunnel system, 200 metres in front of the house. And so we were actually attacked for three days.' Though the building was hit by small-arms fire, it was not directly assaulted, and nobody was wounded or killed. Still, the firefights nearby were frightening. In a confidential letter to former leader and colleague Graeme Grove, team leader Brian Smith described an engagement between Viet Cong and South Vietnamese troops only 500 metres away:

> At 3.30 a.m. I watched a full-scale air strike . . . At first light the [South] Vietnamese Army came in on foot with tanks, and a ground battle commenced. At this stage men were falling 100 metres away. Ricochets started bouncing off our walls.[8]

The battle left twenty-eight Viet Cong corpses rotting in the tropical sun. Elsewhere, an abortive attack on a prisoner-of-war camp saw several hundred NVA soldiers and Viet Cong caught in the open by helicopter gunships and slaughtered. By the end of the offensive, the team had taken to sharing a room, and some of the doctors carried borrowed M16 rifles. Robyn Anderson herself went about with a large revolver for a while.

At one point, a Viet Cong sniper was positioned on the top of the water tower, from where he could fire on the team house and adjoining buildings. Robyn and a surgeon set off to get drinks for people who were 'starting to lose it a bit'. To reach the bar,

> . . . we had to run, thirty metres I suppose, across the open patio. Now [the sniper] couldn't have hit a barn with a shovel full of wheat at three paces but that didn't matter. He was firing

at us as we ran across and the ricochets were going zing, zing, all around us as we ran to the bar. We made a pact before we left the shelter: don't stop. If one of us gets hit, don't stop, don't stop, just keep running and get to the bar, get the Scotch, get it down to the team 'cause we're going to have to work. We both obviously made it and so we had several stiff Scotches while we were there before we ran back. And the admonition to one another was, 'Don't drop the Scotch whatever happens'. Anyway, we got through the bullets going zip, zip, zip, all around us and we got back down and we fed them all Scotch.[9]

In the middle of this mayhem, Robyn's roommate, who was all but blind without her glasses, looked out the window one night and screamed, 'Oh, my God, there are six VC swimming across the swamp'. Robyn jumped out of bed, grabbed her own glasses and got up to the window and saw 'six ducks swimming happily on the swamp'.[10]

The offensive produced hundreds of local civilian casualties, and the team worked non-stop for almost seventy-two hours to treat them. They had to move to and from the team house in armoured personnel carriers. Even inside the house, they were forced to cook by the light of the refrigerator because turning on the light in the kitchen was too risky.

When her tour with the team ended, Robyn Anderson stayed on at the request of the Australian Ambassador to assist the Vietnamese as a chief nursing adviser. She spent her time travelling to various hospitals around the countryside—usually in CIA-provided choppers—and then set up a school of nursing attached to the Bien Hoa Hospital.

In the wake of the offensive, the American 98th Advisory Team issued a security briefing to the team and 6th Psyops Corps was assigned to guard them. The members were told what to do in the event of an attack either at the hospital or in the house. Each member had by their bed an 'emergency pack' of essentials in case they had to evacuate the building or take shelter elsewhere.

Movement around the countryside was severely curtailed and travel to Long Xuyen, Ba Ria, Vung Tau and Nui Dat could be done only by air. Even walking around Bien Hoa was advisable only in daylight, and official approval was required to travel by road to Saigon or further afield.[11]

Gavan O'Connor was transferred from Vung Tau in late February, and established a much-needed pathology service. Just as he arrived there was an attack on the village of Tam Hiep, two kilometres away, but it was suppressed with napalm and flame-throwing tanks. Gavan spent his thirtieth birthday on the terrace roof of the team house watching the battle unfold.[12] When it was over, some 280 Viet Cong bodies littered the ground.

Work now began on rebuilding the badly run-down hospital,[13] with a new recovery ward one of the main priorities. Once it was complete, it made a huge improvement in the welfare of patients coming out of surgery. However, the theatre remained without functioning air-conditioners, and Brian Smith warned that 'one should not question what a surgeon wears under his gown.'[14]

Arriving for a second tour in May with a fresh team of doctors, Professor Hugh Dudley was touched by the 'personal enthusiasm and delight' of his Vietnamese colleagues at seeing him again. Not long into the tour, a Viet Cong rocket smashed into the 'flimsy houses' near the hospital, producing 'particularly ugly blast casualties'. He wrote: 'We laboured for the whole night trying to repair the damage done to a dozen people (a further twelve having died before they reached the hospital) . . . despite these efforts we lost three more of these patients the next day.'[15] For the first five months of the year the team was averaging around 480 operations a month.

The Australian embassy had now granted approval for team members' spouses to visit for up to two weeks, and several wives made the journey.

Decorated Second World War veteran Sir Edward 'Weary' Dunlop arrived as team leader in July. Several nurses were back for a second tour, including Jenny Hunter, who had been at Long Xuyen in 1967. She would have preferred to return to the beautiful riverside town in the delta; now she found herself in a bustling city where the team's accommodation was 'next to a charming swamp'.[16]

Another reason Jenny might have preferred Long Xuyen was explained by Paul Large:

> Long Xuyen was a rest camp [by comparison]. In Bien Hoa we worked very hard and continuously. At Long Xuyen they had two Vietnamese surgeons, and we didn't have that support. In 1969 I met one of the Long Xuyen surgeons in Saigon and I asked if they would like to do an exchange with me for a couple of weeks and do you know what he said? 'No, you have to work too hard.' I couldn't believe this. We were there to work.[17]

The DEA decision to remove the teams from Long Xuyen and Vung Tau[18] meant that Australian medical assistance would now be concentrated in Bien Hoa, making the rebuilding program all the more vital.

Radiographer Joan Rose was another alumna of Long Xuyen who came to Bien Hoa on a second Vietnam tour. Driving into the city after the Tet Offensive of 1969, with clear evidence of recent street fighting, gave her a jolt. The Bien Hoa Hospital's X-ray department had been modernised, but difficulties persisted: 'I had a two-X-ray-room department . . . the equipment was fairly similar . . . we still had similar problems in terms of intermittent supplies and films out of date and so on.'[19] The workload also remained unrelenting. Joan processed 8800 patients in seven months. The team did operations from Monday to Saturday except in an emergency.

Paul Large returned in August for the second of his three tours and recalls a memorable evening with his team leader. The enemy still roamed the roads at night, conducting ambushes or small-scale attacks on 'soft' targets. He says with a chuckle:

The only chap who was shot at—you guessed right—was Weary Dunlop. It is a beautiful story. I was standing at [the team changeover] party having a glass of something and suddenly realised that Weary was talking to the interpreter and offering to run him home that night—out of Bien Hoa ... The next morning Weary said, 'You know, Paul, they shot at me,' and you know I think Weary was somewhat exhilarated by being shot at. I said to him, 'You can't do this, we worry about you.'[20]

James Don Sidey (Don) had served as a surgeon on hospital ships in the Mediterranean during the Second World War and was prepared to rough it when he arrived in Bien Hoa. Still, the heat and humidity and the frenetic pace of work were at times more than he'd bargained for: 'I think I never worked harder in my life than I did on that first tour. It was so steamy in Vietnam, I was glad to do it, but it was very hard.'[21] The climate and local conditions made sterilisation an endless challenge:

It was impossible to keep it sterile, we had of course autoclaves and we used sterilised instruments. I had learnt previously from working in adverse circumstances that the way to keep things from going septic was to keep them dry. That wasn't easy, because it was a very humid atmosphere and it was very difficult to keep things absolutely dry. If you can have your hands scrupulously washed and then dried, then you don't even need to wear gloves. You will get a good result by keeping things dry. But once you get a lot of wet about—whatever that 'wet' is—then you are much more liable to get infection.[22]

Johanna Van Valen, a theatre sister, recalls: 'It was always busy. It was never not busy.' Her worst experience was seeing and treating the horrific burns from a napalm strike. She also found it depressing that 'a lot' of patients arrived too late for the team to save them.[23]

Anaesthetist Bernard Dunn, back for his second tour, had also been at Long Xuyen in 1965 (he would return for another three months with the Army at the 1st Australian Field Hospital in Vung Tau in 1970–71). At forty-three, the father of five girls had already spent a lot of time in the tropics, so he was prepared for conditions at Bien Hoa. That was just as well, because he would soon be anaesthetising at least 1000 patients a month. Not long after he walked into the surgical suite, Neil Armstrong and Buzz Aldrin walked on the moon. His own preoccupation at the time was helping to save people who had walked on land mines. By mid 1969 he found that blood was readily available from American sources, and the bulk of his work would be with ether systems.[24]

Graeme Grove also returned, this time as team leader. The conditions at Bien Hoa had improved in some respects since his last tour, but problems with the power supply, grounds maintenance and regular cleaning of the wards persisted. Graeme recalls with relish the day Sister Gwenda Hassett was assailed by a 'cowboy' (a Vietnamese petty criminal mounted on a motorbike) who tried to snatch her handbag. It wasn't till the youth was flat on his back and dazed that he learned his intended victim had a few martial arts tricks up her short sleeves.[25]

'They didn't seem to cry'

Very early in her tour, Helen Taplin (née Perrin) saw some members of her team disappearing down a path next to the hospital. They were heading to the orphanage attached to the hospital.

What a heart-wrenching sight—a different world ... children, some so tiny, either lying or just sitting in cots and blankly staring at you ... Others were walking around or sitting on an old rusted broken swing hoping someone would give them a push. Babes of all colours, all sizes, some with almond-shaped eyes, some round eyes, and just staring ... They didn't seem to cry, they appeared mesmerised, looking with pleading eyes for someone to want them, pick them up or cuddle them.[26]

Carmel Hurst says Sister Joseph, the nun who ran the orphanage, 'was a great lady who was good at getting money out of the team members'. She was, it seems, very persuasive: 'We were forced to almost adopt an orphan, providing money and clothes for the children.'[27] Beth Scott says, 'We each adopted a Vietnamese orphan while we were there and paid for their schooling.'[28] One of the mainstays of the orphanage was Jenny Leak, who stayed in South Vietnam from 1967, when her surgical team tour ended, until the fall of Saigon in 1975, doing other work. Pat Warren too visited the orphanage attached to the hospital on a daily basis, examining and treating the children.[29]

In 1971, Matron Helen Banff, who specialised in paediatric nursing, was approached by a Catholic padre from the US Army base:

[He] called over to see how I was managing with the children, as he was particularly interested in the orphanages. He took me on rounds of the orphanages with him to witness what was happening to the orphans and it was appalling. [Vietnamese] treatment of the orphans was unbelievably bad, and the orphanages were packed out; children were sat on the floor around one little bowl of rice and all had to help themselves. If they were too weak they just missed out. We witnessed much food that was shipped into the country to Saigon, from other countries, being sold on the black market, and the money went into the pockets of those running the orphanages. The mixed-blood orphans too were also starved, so that they could use the children to play on the consciences of the American Army personnel, and get money by showing them starved half-caste children.[30]

After seeing the dreadful conditions, Helen and her associates gathered up the worst of the children and took them back to Bien Hoa Hospital to try to get them on the road to recovery:

> A number of these children were adopted by American servicemen and taken back to the United States of America. [The troops] would buy them through the black market and take them home with them. Another group were brought to Australia and adopted by Australian families.[31]

The team was doing almost 500 operations a month. The team had now been joined by a Vietnamese surgeon, Dr Duc, who was 'fully involved in the surgical roster', Graeme Grove reported. Nurse training had also stepped up considerably, giving the team hope that the standard of care would show lasting improvement. Grove declared Melbourne Cup Day a public holiday in Bien Hoa, and with a skeleton team on duty the members enjoyed a party on the rooftop (now designated 'Flynn's Roof Restaurant'). Christmas was also celebrated in style: Bernie Ryan did the ward rounds as Santa and distributed presents to all the children. The impact of the end of year rice harvest showed fewer people being injured or inclined to drive their motorcycles underneath large trucks.[32]

'A torch and a cigarette lighter'

The New Year brought a new team with the irrepressible Mervyn Smith at the helm, back after an absence of three years and delighted with the improvements. He pragmatically recommended that any new buildings should not be 'over-grand' and should be built to accommodate the Vietnamese style of care where patients' relatives lived in. The workload remained heavy: Graeme Grove noted the 'great amount of trauma' and the 'sometimes hectic' pace, which in his view precluded the use of Bien Hoa as a formal teaching hospital.[33]

Midwifery and theatre nurse Betty Lockwood, arriving in 1970 with Mervyn Smith's crew, found conditions at the hospital 'very disturbing at first'. It wasn't just the heat, the humidity and the noise of war that hit her; it was the nature of the work. Her first operation was on a young Vietnamese man who had been hit by a jeep and had a crushed chest and a ruptured liver and spleen:

> . . . if you did a chest and spleen and liver [operation] in Royal Adelaide you'd have a cast of thousands; you'd be the scrub sister, and you'd have a scrub nurse assisting, and you'd have another one or two nurses in the operating theatre, and you'd have the anaesthetist, and you'd have the surgeon's assistant. Whereas in Vietnam you just had the anaesthetist, the surgeon and yourself.[34]

Despite all the efforts and the genuine improvements the teams had made, there were still brown-outs or blackouts almost every day. Betty Lockwood recalls the evening when a child came in with diphtheria and life-threatening respiratory problems:

> . . . we had to do a [tracheotomy], with literally a torch and a cigarette lighter and mouth suction because there was no [mechanical] suction. And that was pretty hard. Of course the interpreters always left if the power went off and so you're trying to calm this mother down who's got this child who's slowly choking to death, and operate at the same time.[35]

As laboratory technician Gavan O'Connor wrote, 'there is nothing neat and tidy about a wartime death or wounding'.[36] In Bien Hoa, with its heavy traffic, road-crash injuries could be just as ugly, as Betty Lockwood recalls: 'People would be side-saddle on the Hondas and somebody would pass them and literally de-glove the whole leg [of its flesh] and so you were left sometimes with just a bit of bone'.[37] Elaine Ray (née Glenn) served with Betty for eight months in 1970. Mervyn Smith had convinced her that serving in a war zone would be 'a marvellous time' but had warned her it 'was going to be a challenge'. Elaine ended up working in triage and recovery, and the horrific suffering of war hit her hard. When she looked around the sluice room for the first time, 'I nearly died'. Cleaning it proved almost pointless: 'It always stunk. It didn't matter how much you tried to clean it and how much Lysol you poured down it, it was revolting.'[38]

Margaret Bolton was back for her second tour at Bien Hoa. 'It was different from the first time because in '70 the war was sort of easing off a bit and we didn't work as hard.' But 'sometimes things were hard when one of the doctors would say, "We can't do anything for this patient".' Still, there were joyful moments among the shocks: 'we did a caesar[ean section] one night. [The surgeon] hadn't done a caesar [before] . . . this beautiful little baby, and the mother called it Graham after Dr Graham Wilson.'[39]

Surgeon Bill Betts reported in May 1970 that Dr Duc was absent on sabbatical in Australia and this had increased the workload of the surgical team. He added that the Ben San leprosarium was still being visited and visits by the Australian Department of Works indicated more rebuilding at Bien Hoa was likely to occur.[40]

Working with Vietnamese staff remained frustrating at times, but team leader Bob Waterhouse suggested to future members that some-times going with the flow was best:

> . . . be pragmatists and be prepared to take life as it comes, because those that are fired with missionary zeal will tend

to annoy their fellow Australian team members and also the local Vietnamese. I think it is important that we endeavour to fit in to Vietnamese standards rather than forcing our standards on them.[41]

Still, he acknowledged, this could be difficult. A Vietnamese surgeon who had lately returned from a stint in Australia was, 'when confronted by a difficult orthopaedic situation, inclined to adopt a policy of amputation as an easy way out'.[42] The Australians preferred to do all they could to save limbs. Local medical services were also stunted by the sheer lack of Vietnamese doctors.

Waterhouse was told by Dr Le Van Khoa, Médecin Chef of the local military region, that 'there are only 1700 [Vietnamese] doctors to look after a population of 17 million people in [South] Vietnam and that there are approximately twice as many Vietnamese trained doctors in practice in Paris as there are in Vietnam.'[43]

The annual harvest had also made an impact on November's workload: elective surgery lists dried up because people toiled in the fields rather than go to the hospital for minor complaints. The war ground on; just before dawn on 17 November the Bien Hoa air base was attacked and rocketed leaving five Americans killed and twenty wounded.[44]

Admissions for surgery fell in January 1971, as the local people avoided being in hospital over the Tet holiday period. During the festivities, so many weapons were fired into the air that Donald Macleish thought the falling bullets would surely cut the phone lines. Matron Helen Banff arrived as Donald was leaving. She had been intrigued by the move to boost the team's work in paediatrics. Already, by late 1970, the team was dealing with more than 2000 paediatric cases a month (nearly 3000 in October).[45] Helen found that the ward where she would be working needed a 'damn good clean' from top to bottom, and that became her first priority. Before long the children's ward was overflowing. As senior nurse, Helen was asked to submit a report to the retitled

Department of Foreign Affairs (DFA). She must have raised eyebrows with her scathing comment that in the recovery ward the Vietnamese nurses were 'unresponsive, irresponsible and accept no responsibility for patient care and endeavour to do as little as possible for as long as possible'. She added that the Australian nurse in charge of that area 'has been tested to her utmost limits and will leave Vietnam a disappointed and disillusioned person'.[46]

Paediatrician Geoffrey Bourke, who had started the children's ward at Bien Hoa in 1968, left Vietnam frustrated that so many problems remained 'perennial'. Yet despite all the difficulties, he wrote:

> I have found it an interesting experience, I have enjoyed the work and the camaraderie of the medical teams and have felt that I have been able to help many of the Vietnamese people who, without the Australian presence, may otherwise have received no medical care at all.[47]

Theatre nurse Jill Storch, who did two tours at Bien Hoa, in 1971 and 1972, found working conditions equally trying in both. The air-conditioning went on the blink so often it was left off permanently and windows in the operating theatres were thrown open. Jill recalls that 'the kids were hanging in the windows watching us all the time'. Like Helen Banff, she was dismayed by the attitude of the Vietnamese nursing staff, who would work like 'public servants in the sense that they clocked on at eight o'clock or nine o'clock . . . clocked off at twelve and didn't come back till two. And then they'd work till five and that was it'.[48]

As the war dragged on and South Vietnamese morale declined, young men began coming in with fingers shot off. They had mutilated themselves to avoid being drafted into the military.

The team moved house again. This time their residence was close to the air-base perimeter—too close for comfort at times. The Viet Cong would attack the perimeter using delayed-launch rockets and explosives. Sometimes nearby houses went up. When that happened, Jill Storch says,

> . . . you'd just have to dive under your bed and wait until the sound went away . . . And you knew you'd have to go to work but we'd then run down to these houses . . . And three times I went into a house and there were people burnt to death in them. One was particularly bad where there was a woman lying in bed with her two children on her breast. Just across her . . . And they were black . . . and stiff. It was terrible.[49]

Despite the attacks the allied war effort in Bien Hoa province was being reduced. But land mines, accidental shootings and road accidents kept the workload as heavy as ever.

Berenice Dawson (née Lenze) recalls seeing road casualties arrive on Honda step-through motorcycles, three-wheeled tricycles or a Lambretta mini-cab that could hold eight Vietnamese (or four Australians). Many of the patients had chronic malaria, 'and you'd see kids in the tertiary stages of malaria, which was pretty horrible.'[50]

Soon the team digs were upgraded to the most salubrious yet—a five-storey apartment building protected by an American detachment—and the nurses were allocated a grey Willys jeep with red crosses on the sides. The surgeons had a Holden station wagon to reflect their more elevated status.[51] Arriving in late October, Reginald Lord lamented the condition of these Holdens: he thought they'd been unserviceable when they arrived from Australia.

The last six months had seen averages of 680 operations per month, 2700 paediatric attendances and 1100 surgical outpatient attendances.[52] An Australian Department of Health paper in August 1971 noted that the surgical load in Bien Hoa was 'as high as some major hospitals in the capital cities of Australia' but of course tackled with only a fraction of the manpower. It concluded that, owing in part to the difficulty of future recruitment, the teams should be gradually withdrawn and Vietnamese trained to replace them.[53]

At this time the Americans had begun a program of 'Vietnam-isation', handing over responsibilities for command and control to the South Vietnamese. US troop strength was down to 200,000 from a peak of half a million; and that number would be reduced to 134,000 by June 1972. Australia had only one rifle battalion (approximately 900 men) still in Phuoc Tuy province and the bulk would be home by Christmas. All of the former Task Force troops were home by March 1972. Only an AATTV element remained, for a further twelve months. The Republic of Korea had reduced its forces to 40,000, and most of the Thai forces had gone.

The Americans had been spending US$1 billion a year to fight the war; $500 million in aid was planned for 1972 but not thereafter. The Australian government spent about AU$300,000 a year in Bien Hoa, and an additional $900,000 on rebuilding the hospital. Australia was having trouble maintaining a supply line through the RAN and the RAAF. It was all becoming too difficult, and the continuance of the surgical teams project was in doubt.[54]

In November, the team medical store received a windfall of supplies and equipment from the 1st Australian Field Hospital, which was closing down in Vung Tau. But as the year drew to a close, Jill Storch and her fellow team members sensed that the end was near. She was afraid that the enemy would soon be on their doorstep, and says, 'there was a lot of fear around. Everyone was on their toes about whether or not [the VC] would come in.'[55]

The 1972 team lived in three separate houses, mostly in the same street, but conditions were deteriorating, as Jill Storch recalls:

I can remember the last few weeks we were there, the fear was really terrible . . . there were always gunfights out on the street

and shots being fired and all the rest of it and . . . diving for
the floor. I mean, that gives you a bit of a fright in the middle
of the day, middle of the afternoon.[56]

Surgeon Paul Large recalls one memorable night on his third tour when
'about 200 rockets [were] fired in our general direction. One of them
landed about 150 yards from the house.'[57]

In December a medical aid review team consisting of former team
leaders and DFA and Health Department officials recommended that
personnel support to Bien Hoa Hospital be phased out within a year
and replaced by other forms of aid.[58]

Jim Ellis completed a tour in Vung Tau in late 1967 as part of a
Commonwealth Repatriation Department team, and now headed back
to South Vietnam at the head of a composite team whose members
were drawn from around Australia. His 1967 tour had been unhappy, in
part owing to friction among team members. A member of the Citizen
Military Forces, Ellis knew both what life in the war zone was like and
that the continuing Australian presence in Vietnam was in doubt.

The air-conditioning still malfunctioned more often than not, and
medical stores and equipment were always in short supply. The US 24th
Evacuation Hospital had closed, and its civilian patients now came to
Bien Hoa, adding to the workload. Heightened enemy activity and the
fact that the portable anaesthetic machine was unserviceable meant
the team could no longer visit the leprosarium, and the Australians' five-
year association with the institution also came to an end.

Nursing sister Frances Byak (née Sardelich), who arrived with
Jim Ellis, found some of the patients' injuries profoundly shocking. She
recalls 'a child who was raped . . . she was ripped to shreds . . . she was
only a tiny little girl.' She adds, 'that was worse than war injuries . . . and
probably one of the worst things I saw in my whole nursing career . . . It
was awful.'[59] Frances found that lack of power affected surgery in more
ways than lights and air-conditioning: 'suction power [to keep wounds

clear of fluid] was one of the biggest problems . . . suction was never very good, it was hard [work].'[60]

At Easter 1972, during the Paris peace talks, the North Vietnamese launched a huge offensive from Cambodia towards Saigon, with three divisions supported by tanks. The offensive was halted at An Loc, a town of 15,000 people about ninety kilometres north of Saigon. If An Loc had fallen, Saigon would have been next. In the savage fighting and ensuing siege, which lasted several months, the town was reduced to rubble. The team had been warned on the American Forces radio network that casualties were on their way, but by late April only a few had arrived. The rest would take over a month to find their way south on foot. In April the team carried out 570 surgical procedures, more than a quarter of them classified as 'major'. The number of minor operations also escalated, to 419, although few of these were from An Loc.[61] By May, however, some 500 wounded An Loc refugees had arrived, and the hospital was flooded. There was a month-long waiting list for elective surgery, owing to the amount of emergency work.[62] The fact that the number of surgeons had been cut from four to two made it even more of a struggle.

By July, when Bill Bye arrived with a composite SEATO team, the Americans at the 24th Evacuation Hospital had withdrawn and a valuable source of manpower and supplies—especially blood—had gone.

The end of Bien Hoa

When Paul Large was appointed team leader in October,

> I immediately got in touch with Foreign Affairs and I asked if this was the last team [to go to Vietnam]. They said they didn't know and I replied that we had to know. I said, 'I have got to go up and deal with the Vietnamese and if they ask me questions we will have to arrange a handover.' They reiterated they didn't know. When I arrived in Saigon I arranged

to see the Ambassador, Mr Morris, and he asked if it was the last team . . . Anyway, when I got out there it was pretty obvious to me it was going to be the last team. It was getting very difficult to recruit people and the wheels were starting to come off [the aid project]. So I wrote it all out on a piece of paper and he and I decided that this would be the last team, and that is how that happened. From that moment on, a lot of my time was devoted to arranging . . . a gradual handing over to the Vietnamese doctors. It was quite complicated. We had to have contacts with the Ministry of Health and Dr Tho, the hospital superintendent. He and I and a few others arranged it, and it went very smoothly, I think.[63]

It appears that the Department of Foreign Affairs did know that the team would be the last: the Australians were to be withdrawn at the end of December, at about the time the rebuilding of the hospital was completed. The first sign for Paul was

. . . some bright spark cut off our mail. And it wasn't just ours, it was also other people's mail, and we were nineteen days without our mail . . . it was pretty galling because we had to tidy up things to get home . . . I spent three months in conjunction with the embassy and the Vietnamese people and we all worked on this—arranging a smooth changeover, for their doctors to come in and take over . . . I was actually on the way to Tan Son Nhut to leave with my colleague Don Sidey, and I heard on the radio that Gough Whitlam had recalled me. [But] it was all arranged before he was even elected.[64]

Leaving was an emotional wrench for the entire team 'because of the lot of friends we had made, particularly me because I had got to know them all having been there three times'. But at least the team was present for the handover of the rebuilt Bien Hoa Hospital, to which Australia had contributed approximately $1.7 million in aid. Australian supervisors had worked with a South Korean company to build new surgical blocks, a maternity block, a dispensary, a laboratory, private wards, an outpatients clinic and an improved water supply. Don Sidey, who was on his second tour at the time, beams when he remembers the momentous day of the handover:

> The Australian Ambassador came down and he by that time spoke very good Vietnamese, which is remarkable because it is a very difficult language. He was great and he came down to officially hand over the hospital to the South Vietnamese people and that was when we got out of Vietnam . . . I look back on that, even though it was a long time ago, with a great deal of pride.[65]

But pride was mixed with regret:

> The mood was a bit sad in many ways because we knew what the score was and we knew that any treaties that were being signed would be ignored [by the North Vietnamese]. We also knew that the South Vietnamese government was corrupt and had been virtually since its inception and it was perhaps a little bit better by that time but not much. So when it all collapsed in 1975 none of us were surprised. We were sad because we liked the Vietnamese and got on very well with them and we had very good relations with them. They knew who we were and what we were about because we had been there a very long time; there had been surgical teams in Bien Hoa for five years or more [actually seven], so on the whole it was a matter of regret that we were going.[66]

Reflecting on the end, Cas McInnes says:

> I learnt a lot about how to treat people without any equip-
> ment; we had X-rays but nothing else, nothing like CAT
> scans etc., and we had a limited number of antibiotics. And it
> is amazing just going back to basics; it was very basic medicine
> and surgery. I have no doubt that your surgical skills improve.
> Improvising a little bit maybe, we used headlights in theatre
> because the overhead electric lights used to go out frequently.
> The electricity stopped and the sewerage all got blocked, and
> the water flowed, but that became part of life after a while.[67]

Paul Large says he was exhausted by the time he finished each tour:

> I lost a lot of weight each time I went up there, and I slept
> very badly when I was there and I don't know why. The loss
> of weight—and of course we all got gastroenteritis. After the
> 1969 tour I was very washed out, I did 500 operations myself
> [in twelve weeks] in that time. When I came home I had to
> stop work for a couple of weeks because I couldn't stand up
> without fainting.[68]

Surgeon David Brownbill remembers returning home and 'I slept more
than . . . I'd ever done in my life. I'd go for a swim then go to sleep on
the beach.'[69]

Forty years later, Aileen Monck still vividly remembers many of her
experiences in Vietnam. One was

> a woman who had been in a paddy field on a water buffalo that
> trod on a mine. It exploded and she had huge chunks of flesh
> missing. Her arm had been completely de-skinned, she had
> collapsed lungs, she had big pieces missing from her buttocks.

And she was in for a long time. Her lungs responded well and then we had to prepare her for skin grafts. And she had a wonderful result really, and her relatives were so grateful. I remember them through an interpreter saying that they would remember us all their lives.[70]

As the team's work wound to a close, the enemy came ever nearer. In mid December, twenty-six rockets slammed into a house 200 metres from the team accommodation, killing eleven people and wounding several others. There was another rocket attack the following night. The last surgery was done on the 29th, the eve of the handover.[71]

The Australians in Bien Hoa left behind not only a new hospital but thousands of lives saved or transformed. Aside from the buildings, there are no monuments to their work, but their efforts, professionalism and dedication live on in the hearts of the Vietnamese people who came under their care.

5

Life in Phuoc Tuy: Vung Tau and Ba Ria

Phuoc Tuy province, home to Australian ground forces, also became the home of two Australian civilian surgical teams. The first went to the coastal city of Vung Tau, the second to the provincial capital of Ba Ria. The Ba Ria team served for only five months before it was withdrawn. The Vung Tau teams served continuously until July 1969.

By late 1966 Phuoc Tuy province, in the southeast of South Vietnam and some 130 kilometres from Saigon, had become the centre of Australia's military operations in Vietnam. The 1st Australian Task Force was located at Nui Dat, in the heart of the 2500-square-kilometre province, and its logistics base, 1st Australian Logistic Support Group (1ALSG), was positioned on what was termed 'the Back Beach', at Vung Tau. The logistics base was also the location of the Army's 2nd Field Ambulance (later 8th Field Ambulance, then 1st Australian Field Hospital), which provided soldiers with expert medical care only a short helicopter flight from most of the actions they were engaged in. Also based in Vung Tau were elements of the Royal Australian Air Force (RAAF), including 35 Squadron, flying Caribous, and 9 Squadron, flying Iroquois helicopters in support of Australian infantry. There was also a significant American presence in Vung Tau, including the US 36th Evacuation Hospital. The presence of these military units in Vung Tau was one of the principal reasons for the placement of a third surgical team there, and they would all play an important part in the life and work of team members.

Vung Tau, previously known as Cap Saint Jacques, was a port city of approximately 50,000 people located on the entrance of a narrow peninsula that jutted into the South China Sea. It was connected to Saigon by road and via the Saigon River, which entered the sea nearby. During the French colonial occupation of Vietnam, Vung Tau had been a popular seaside resort for Saigon's elite, who erected many substantial buildings there. After the French left, the city became run down, and by the mid 1960s it was also crowded with refugees from the war-torn countryside and dotted with bars and nightclubs catering to the thousands of military personnel who used the city as a rest centre. Despite its proximity to the war, though, Vung Tau remained largely free from Viet Cong attack. It was generally believed that this was because the Viet Cong used the city as a rest zone. Its geographical layout also helped: the enemy was presumably reluctant to attack a peninsula from which they would have no easy retreat.

In August 1966 an Australian embassy representative from Saigon and Bien Hoa surgical team leader Graeme Grove visited Vung Tau and Ba Ria to report on the possibility of locating a third surgical team in Vung Tau. It was, they decided, an ideal location in which to boost Australia's medical aid to South Vietnam. The French-built, government-run city hospital, Le Loi, had a surgical suite built by USAID, but as was the case throughout the country the hospital had a severe shortage of skilled surgeons and other medical personnel. Consequently, the two-man team concluded, the hospital was doing very little towards meeting the needs (both medical and surgical) of the population of Vung Tau and its environs.[1] Other than the obvious need for surgical assistance, the hospital was well located because of its proximity to a USAID office and to the Australian logistics base, especially its field hospital. The Commanding Officer of 1ALSG, Lieutenant Colonel Rouse, welcomed the idea of a civilian surgical team nearby, promising whatever limited resources he could provide to support it. Major Bruce Fox, sole surgeon at 2nd Field Ambulance, was also seen as a great potential source of support, and it was thought that the team would be able to help the Army's Medical Civic Action Program (MEDCAP) by treating patients sent to them by MEDCAP teams. The possibility that an enlarged Vung Tau team could also provide surgical assistance at the Ba Ria Hospital was raised in the report, although no definite decisions were made in that regard. In all, it was felt that although establishing a third team in Vung Tau would not be easy, it was badly needed and should be sent as soon as was practicable.[2]

The first surgical team for Vung Tau arrived in November 1966. Made up of personnel from the Prince Henry and Prince of Wales hospitals in Sydney, it was led by the head of surgery at Prince Henry, Professor Doug Tracy. He hand picked his team members, who included surgeon Tom Hugh, physician Noel Lucas, anaesthetist Judith Ross, six nurses, a pathology technician, and a radiographer. The team was administered by George Wilson. After farewelling his pregnant wife, Doug left for Vietnam a couple of weeks ahead of the others to see what work and living conditions would be like in Vung Tau. What he found there dismayed him. The hospital was, simply, 'an absolute mess'. As well, the house supposedly fixed for the team was far from ready and, as had been the case in Long Xuyen, the team would be living in a hotel for the foreseeable future.[3] The impressive-sounding Grand Hotel was anything but that, yet it became home to Vung Tau teams for several months.

At the end of November the rest of Doug's team left for South Vietnam. Two of the nurses, Dorothy Burgess and Jenny James, were interviewed a couple of weeks before their departure and conveyed a rather naïve optimism about what lay before them. Dorothy was going to Vietnam 'because it sounds fun, and will certainly be different from the usual routine work ... I don't think we'll be in any danger. Vung Tau is so big and very close to an RAAF base.' Jenny was a little more realistic:

'I'll be lecturing to untrained Vietnamese girls who are helping out at the hospital, and have been told to expect to start at rock bottom.'[4]

Team arrivals had become more commonplace by now and little fuss was made of newcomers. The Prince Henry team had an inauspicious beginning when vehicles arranged by the embassy to take the team from Saigon airport to Vung Tau failed to arrive. Half the team ended up flying down on a Royal Australian Air Force courier flight, embarrassing the Vietnamese, who had arranged an elaborate reception for the team.

There is no doubt, though, that hospital personnel and the civilian population of Vung Tau were happy to see the Australians. Their arrival was reported in several newspapers, with photos showing garlanded team members standing in front of welcome banners, being greeted by Ministry of Health officials. After being introduced as one of Australia's 'most impotent surgeons', Doug Tracy responded to the welcome, recognising the difficulties that the South Vietnamese faced in delivering medical care, and hoping 'that the small contribution that we can make will help and that this assistance will grow until it is no longer needed.'[5]

Within a short time the team had begun to face the challenges before them. The state of Le Loi Hospital was a major problem. Poorly funded, lacking even the most basic amenities and served by a skeleton staff, the hospital was, according to physician Noel Lucas, a shambles: '. . . a rat-ridden, dirty, unkempt, broken-down civilian hospital . . .'[6] Like most other provincial hospitals, it was made up of a number of pavilions linked by walkways. These comprised a medical ward, containing an outpatients clinic and casualty run by the Vietnamese, a surgical ward which the Australians would run, an ante-natal clinic, an X-ray department, and a thirty-seven-bed maternity unit. Water and electricity supplies were intermittent, and though the surgical unit contained two theatres, only one was operational when the team arrived. The hospital was run by the Médecin Chef, Dr Lam, who was very welcoming to the new team. Although the members had been expecting Third World

The first Australian civilian surgical team to South Vietnam being welcomed at Saigon's Tan Son Nhut airport on 4 October 1964. Standing with six unidentified trainee nurses from the Saigon School of Nursing are (left to right) radiographer Noelle Courtney, registrar Tim Matthew, nurse Susan Terry, nurse Jenny Jones, nurse Ann Boucher (partly obscured), Director General of Health and Hospitals Dr Truong, anaesthetist Jim Villiers, and surgeon and team leader Donald 'Scotty' Macleish. AWM P05373.003

The main entrance to the provincial hospital in Long Xuyen, where Australian civilian surgical teams worked for over six years. AWM P05283.001

Team paediatricians were known for their devotion to their young patients. Here Dr Bob Birrell, a member of the Prince Henry's Hospital team in 1967, poses in the grounds of Long Xuyen Hospital with the family of one of his patients. AWM P05282.001

Patients crowding outside the outpatients clinic in Long Xuyen. The first civilian surgical teams in Long Xuyen were very successful in building up numbers in this clinic, to the point where they sometimes had more patients than they could deal with.
AWM P04999.010

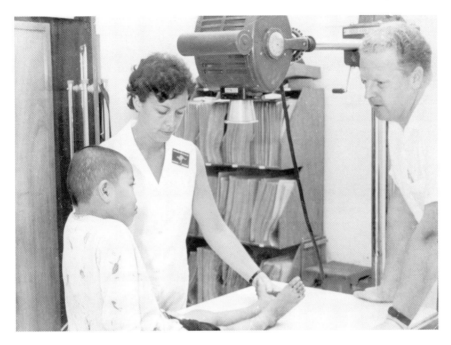

Radiographer Barbara Maughan and Dr Jim Downie, members of a Prince Henry's Hospital surgical team in Long Xuyen, prepare a young Vietnamese girl for a leg X-ray. AWM P05385.001

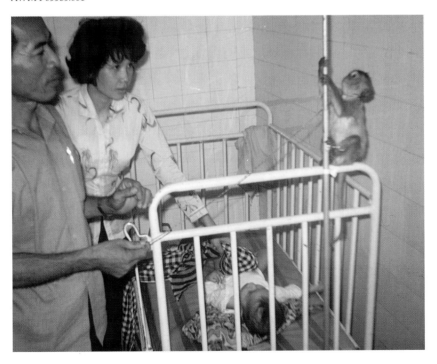

Vietnamese parents looking after their sick child in Long Xuyen Hospital. They have brought in their pet monkey, possibly to help cheer up the infant. AWM P05282.003

Right: Nurses from Melbourne's St Vincent's Hospital pose outside their living quarters, dubbed 'the White House', in Long Xuyen, April 1966. They are (standing, left to right) Aileen Crothers, Nance Keon, Margaret O'Connor; (seated, left to right) Marea Fennell, Margot Cornish. AWM P04999.032

Centre: A South Vietnamese policeman stands guard in front of the White House. AWM P04999.020

Some of the members of Melbourne's Prince Henry's Hospital surgical team who made up the Long Xuyen Cricket Club (LXCC) during their tour in 1967. Standing (left to right) are surgeon Adrian Lowe, surgeon and team leader John Kendall Francis, paediatrician Bob Birrell, and administrator Richard Papworth. Seated is anaesthetist George Robinson. AWM P05282.002

An aerial view of Bien Hoa Hospital in 1966. Buildings identified are:

1. Outpatients department
2. Private ward
3. Maternity ward
4. Laundry and prison ward
5. Surgical ward
6. Surgical suite
7. Children's ward
8. Medical storage
9. Female surgical ward
10. Military ward
11. Male surgical ward
12. Female internal diseases ward
13. X-ray department.

Photograph courtesy Von Clinch

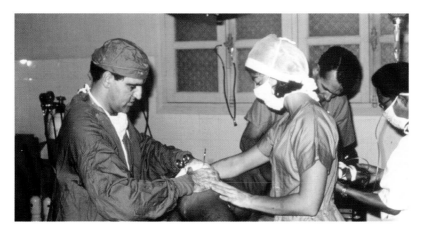

Sister Heather Beveridge (front, right) assisting Dr Peter Mangos (left) as he operates on a wounded Vietnamese in 1966. In the background Dr Chan Piercy administers the anaesthetic with the help of a Vietnamese assistant. All three Australians were from the Alfred Hospital team and were members of the first team to work in Bien Hoa Hospital. AWM P03122.003

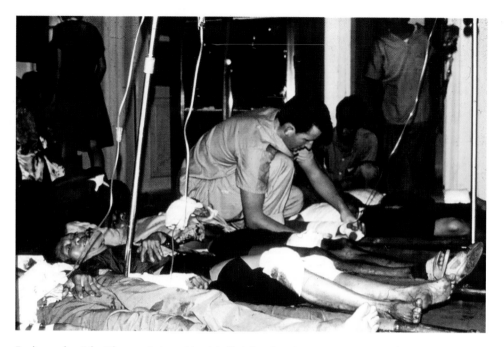

Radiographer John Flynn assisting with critically injured patients prior to surgery at Bien Hoa Hospital in 1966. Photograph courtesy Alfred Hospital Nursing Archive

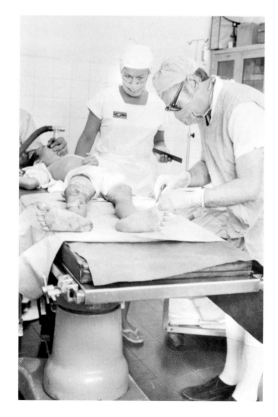

Surgeon Mervyn Smith (right) cleaning the leg wounds of a Vietnamese child at Bien Hoa Hospital in April 1970. Smith is being assisted by nurse Betty Lockwood; both were members of a Royal Adelaide Hospital team. AWM P05522.003

Nurses Dot Angell (right rear) and Pamela Matenson (right front), members of an Alfred Hospital surgical team, helping to transport a patient from the surgical suite to the recovery ward at Bien Hoa Hospital in early 1967. AWM P03122.002

Australian surgical team members found it a continual challenge to care for patients in the primitive hospital surrounds. Here nurse Von Clinch washes a young patient at Bien Hoa Hospital in 1966. Photograph courtesy Von Clinch

The human cost of war. Children injured in a bus explosion are treated in the foyer of Bien Hoa Hospital in 1966. Photograph courtesy Alfred Hospital Nursing Archive

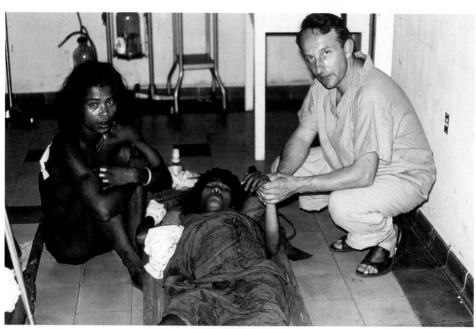

A Montagnard patient being treated by surgeon Guy Hutchinson at Bien Hoa in 1966.
Photograph courtesy Alfred Hospital Nursing Archive

Above: Nurse Jill Storch (centre) teaching Vietnamese nurses how to incise a breast abscess at Bien Hoa Hospital in early 1971. AWM P05014.015

Above left: Shown at Bien Hoa Hospital in 1966 are (left to right) nurses Miss Nguyet, Von Clinch, Mrs Bic Son and Maureen McLeod. Miss Nguyet and her family left Vietnam after the fall of Saigon in 1975 and were accepted into Australia as refugees. Photograph courtesy Von Clinch

Nurse Helen Perrin in 1970 with two children from the orphanage adjacent to Bien Hoa Hospital. Many nurses from surgical teams in Bien Hoa helped care for these orphaned children, becoming very fond of them during their tours. They found it a wrench to leave them when it was time to return to Australia. AWM P05336.015

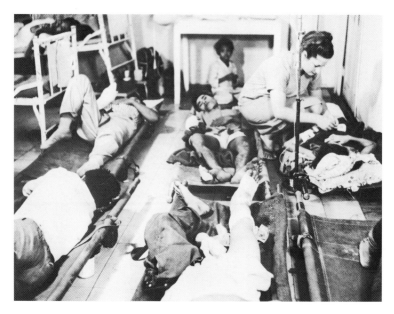

Nurse Maureen McLeod checking the intravenous drip of a wounded Vietnamese lying on the floor of the recovery room in Bien Hoa Hospital in 1966.
With only a small number of beds in the ward, patients were often either
double-bunked or accommodated on stretchers on the floor, making patient
care particularly hazardous. AWM P03122.001

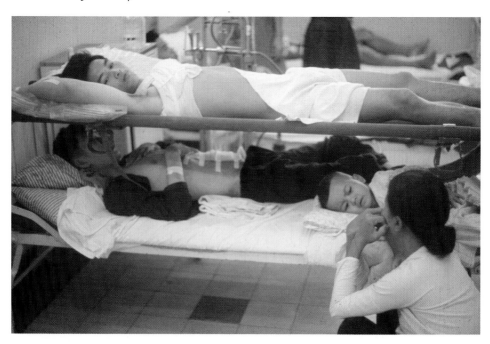

A Vietnamese mother sitting beside her young son, one of three patients in a double bunk bed
in Bien Hoa Hospital, in May 1966. The other two men are Viet Cong, and all three patients are
recovering from surgery in the recovery ward. Double bunking of beds was common, in order to
accommodate up to fifteen patients in the six bed ward. AWM P05375.001

Vietnamese locals gathered around the window of a clinic being run by an Australian surgical team in Bien Hoa Hospital in 1969. Lack of privacy for patients was quite normal for the Vietnamese, but something the Australians struggled with. AWM P05529.002

Patient care in all Vietnamese hospitals was usually provided by relatives. Here an elderly relative feeds a child in Bien Hoa Hospital in 1966. Photograph courtesy Alfred Hospital Nursing Archive

Patients at Bien Hoa's mental asylum, seen here in their yard, were kept in the most basic conditions. Australian surgical team members who visited the facility were often haunted by the hopelessness of the inmates and the conditions in which they lived. Photograph courtesy Caroline Clark

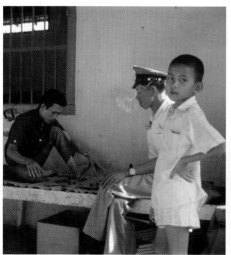
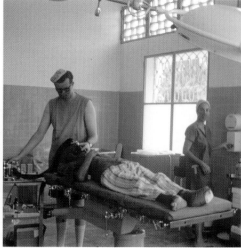

Left: A young Vietnamese boy looks at the camera while a Viet Cong prisoner and his guard play checkers in the prisoners compound at Bien Hoa Hospital in 1969. Australian civilian surgical teams treated whoever came through the hospital doors, even if they were known Viet Cong. AWM P05336.006

Right: Surgeon Brian Jordon and nurse Yvonne McLaren operating on a patient at the Ben San leprosarium outside Bien Hoa. Surgical teams made regular visits to treat patients at this facility, finding it a welcome break from the constant pressure of work at Bien Hoa Hospital. AWM P05336.001

Nurse Thelma Foxall and Ron Madden (who was working on the Bien Hoa Hospital rebuilding project) leaving the site of an Iroquois crash in early 1969. Surgical team members from Bien Hoa had just finished a day's work at the Ben San leprosarium, when the aircraft's rotor detached and they crash-landed. No one was seriously wounded. AWM P05519.001

Bien Hoa team members receiving rifle practice under the watchful eye of American soldiers at the Long Binh air base in late 1967. The Australians learning to shoot straight are nurse Therese O'Brien (lying down), surgeon Douglas Friend (kneeling), and radiographer Iain Brotchie (right rear). AWM P07264.001

American army personnel providing the Bien Hoa Hospital with drinkable water in 1966. Australian surgical teams in all areas relied heavily on the American armed services to provide them with services and supplies. Photograph courtesy Alfred Hospital Nursing Archive

Because of its close proximity to Saigon, Australian surgical teams in Bien Hoa received many visits from politicians and other dignitaries. Deputy Opposition Leader Gough Whitlam visited the hospital in August 1966, escorted by Médecin Chef Dr Tho. Photograph courtesy Alfred Hospital Nursing Archive

Members of a Royal Adelaide Hospital surgical team in their Bien Hoa accommodation in early 1970. Standing, left to right, are pathologist Erica Badman, paediatrician Gordon McKay, general practitioner Colin McLeay, surgeon and team leader Mervyn Smith, anaesthetist Tom Allen (partly obscured), and nurses Betty Lockwood and Dawn Garnaut. Front row, left to right: nurses Joan Pitcher, Olga Nichols, surgeons Jim Young and Betty Gordon, and orthopaedic surgeon Charles Shearer. AWM P05522.002

Two jeeps parked outside Bien Hoa team accommodation, named 'Australia House', in February 1970. By this time the standard of team housing had improved substantially, compared to the early days of shared sleeping quarters and bathrooms. AWM P04999.035

Time out from the hospital for Bien Hoa teams often included sunbaking on the roof of the team house. The sight of women in bikinis often resulted in a noticeable increase in American helicopter traffic above the house. Photograph courtesy Von Clinch

Christmas dinner for the Alfred Hospital team in Bien Hoa in 1966. Seated, left to right, are radiographer John Flynn, surgeon Guy Hutchinson, unidentified USAID worker, physician Ted Cordner, nurse Suzanne Leyland, plastic surgeon John Snell, surgeon and team leader Paul Large (at head of table), unidentified, anaesthetist Victor Brand, nurse Von Clinch, nurse Wendy Williams, nurse Nada Marovich and nurse Maureen McLeod. The meal consisted of turkey and chips, and Christmas pudding. Photograph courtesy Suzanne MacFarlane

RAAF Group Captain Peter Raw helps nurse Jenny James (left) and laboratory pathologist Julie Cearns raise the Australian flag at Le Loi Hospital in late 1966. RAAF members gave the first Australian surgical team to Vung Tau an enormous amount of help to prepare the hospital for its first surgical patients. AWM VN/66/0105/08

In November 1966 members of the RAAF pitched in to help the Prince Henry and Prince of Wales surgical team prepare Le Loi Hospital in Vung Tau for patients. In this image Leading Aircraftman Lewis Bock (left), Sergeant Mike Chapman and Squadron Leader Cecil Kilsby (right) paint hospital bed frames. AWM VN/66/0105/06

A group of Australian, American, Korean and Vietnamese medical and military personnel at the front entrance of Le Loi Hospital in 1968. The Australian surgical teams in Vung Tau and elsewhere relied heavily on military personnel from Australia and its allies to maintain essential supplies. Australian surgical team members in the group are orthopaedic surgeon Jim Ellis (extreme left), nurse Jan Bell (in white, fifth from left) and physician Ken Hume (in white with camera around his neck). AWM P05246.005

Members of a Commonwealth Repatriation surgical team that worked in Ba Ria between November 1967 and April 1968. They are (left to right) David Watson, Sue Quinn, team leader Bob Rayner, Pat Healey, Australian army engineer Keith Voigt, Barbara Buscombe and Don Cordner. AWM P05376.001

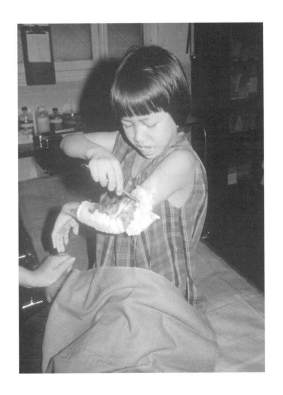

A young girl, daughter of a South Vietnamese soldier, removes a dressing from burns on her arm in a ward of Le Loi Hospital in 1968. Australian surgeons later successfully completed a skin graft to the area. AWM P05211.014

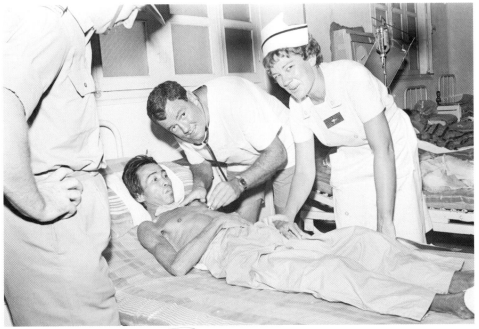

Vietnamese patient Le Van Sang at Le Loi Hospital following an amputation and treatment for tetanus. He is being cared for by surgeon Bob Perrett (centre, facing camera) and nurse Jenny James. The tetanus treatment was complicated and time-consuming, requiring a respirator borrowed from the US 36th Evacuation Hospital and cylinders of compressed air provided daily by the RAAF. AWM VN/67/0017/02

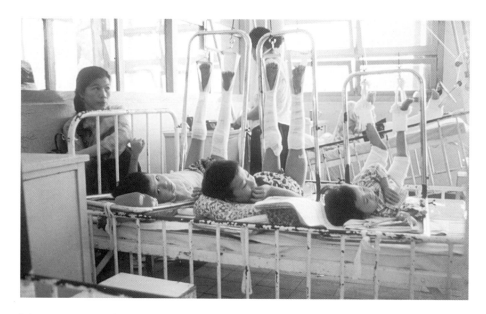

Three Vietnamese children recover from leg surgery performed by Australian surgeons at Le Loi Hospital in late 1966. The children's bandaged legs are tied to a metal frame to keep them raised. Many children seen by the teams had never had proper medical attention and often had advanced conditions that needed radical treatment. AWM P05792.009

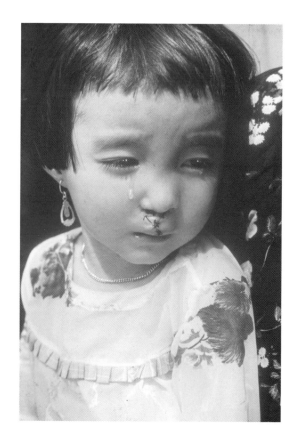

A young girl showing the results of surgery on a cleft lip and palate, performed by Australian surgeons at Le Loi Hospital in late 1966 or early 1967. AWM P05792.012

Some of the Ba Ria surgical team standing with their Vietnamese guard in the hospital's residential compound. They are (left to right) surgeon John Williams, nurse Pat Healey, Vietnamese guard (name unknown), nurse Barbara Buscombe and anaesthetist Peter Malouf. AWM P05376.002

This photo shows the living quarters for the Australian surgical team based in Ba Ria from late 1967 until April 1969. The accommodation building is on the left; the bunker in which the team hid during a Viet Cong attack in February 1969 is a small timber-clad shed on the right of the compound. AWM P05211.009

Surgeon Bob Perrett eating pineapple on Vung Tau's Back Beach during a well-earned break. He and other members of the Australian surgical team enjoyed relaxing at the sometimes dangerous beach, occasionally helping to rescue inexperienced American servicemen caught in the surf. AWM P05792.014

Nurses Barbara Buscombe (front) and Pat Healey, part of a surgical team based in Ba Ria, enjoying socialising with soldiers at the Australian task force base in Nui Dat, Phuoc Tuy province, in 1968. The Australian women were always welcome visitors to the base, to which they enjoyed travelling as a break from their nursing duties. AWM P05378.005

Marita Mulcahy, a nurse in a Repatriation hospitals team at Vung Tau in mid 1968, is picked up near the team house by an American helicopter pilot, en route for a nearby social event. AWM P05246.004

Julie Cearns, a member of the Prince Henry and Prince of Wales surgical team, joined RAAF airmen for Christmas carols at the RAAF base in Vung Tau in 1966. Pictured are (left to right) Squadron Leader Norm Lawless, Julie Cearns, Vietnamese interpreter for the surgical team Nguyen Thi Ngoc, and Leading Aircraftman Graham Bryant. AWM VN/66/0110/12

The end of the Australian surgical team commitment. Veteran of three tours Dr Paul Large (left) shakes hands with the South Vietnamese Minister for Health at the handover of Bien Hoa Hospital on 28 December 1972. AWM P04326.001

Former members of Vung Tau and Bien Hoa civilian surgical teams gather in Sydney prior to the 2004 Anzac Day march. They were to march for the first time behind their own, newly made banner. Front row, left to right: son (name unknown) of Helen Beasley, Bill Townsend, Fran Sardelich, Mair Jones, Jenny James, Jan Allen; back row, left to right: Brian Symons, Don Sheldon, Lynn Ward, Jan Bell, Jim Ellis, Reginald Lord. AWM P05377.007

conditions, Doug Tracy thought 'everyone was a bit shocked because we thought . . . we were a surgical team going to do surgery and they'd be ready for us. But they weren't.'[7]

The new team found it impossible to begin surgery immediately. Only one theatre had an operating table, most of the air-conditioning was broken, and the autoclave and refrigerator didn't work. Jenny James was horrified; there was 'no water, no electricity, no equipment, no instruments, no mattresses, no nothing . . .'[8] Sanitary conditions were appalling. For unknown reasons the Vietnamese staff had prevented patients from using toilets in the wards, most of which were not working anyway, and the hospital grounds had become a giant latrine. As a result the rat population had exploded and the team spent much of its first week getting rid of the rodents, which were 'as big as cats'. Tom Hugh remembers the help provided by the Australian forces:

> I can remember that first week . . . the Australian Army com-
> mander came in from Back Beach . . . a sergeant came up and
> said he would like to meet the team leader. I said, 'Come with
> me, he's around the back killing rats.' Noel Lucas, who was
> our general practitioner, was at one end of [a] ditch, banging
> with a stick and the rats were coming out the other end and
> Doug [Tracy] was belting them as they came out with a big
> stick . . . Well the next day the army moved in and they fogged
> the compound with insecticide, they erected a fresh water
> tank on a tower . . . did a lot to help us really.[9]

The team would have found it impossible to begin work if not for the help of Australian and allied forces. As well as two water tanks installed by Army engineers (and filled daily with potable water), a RAAF electrician worked on the burnt-out operating-theatre refrigerator, other RAAF personnel located and painted beds, and medical supplies were provided by the 2nd Field Ambulance, the US 36th Evacuation Hospital, and a nearby Korean military hospital. In addition, a Vietnamese military unit cleaned up the hospital grounds, cutting down undergrowth and sweeping up rubbish. A large pit that had been filled with water and garbage and heavily infested with rats and mosquitoes was filled in with sand. Traps and poison were set out to catch more rats, and a program of weekly spraying with insecticide was begun to try to control the insect population. The team itself scrubbed and painted the entire surgical block, including an empty ward in which six new beds were installed.

Apart from the physical state of the hospital, the other overriding problem was lack of supplies. The shortage of instruments, drugs, linen, blood supplies and other essentials made it impossible to start surgery in the short term. Jenny James found only two drugs in the hospital: vitamin K, used to control bleeding, and hypertonic saline, which would kill people if given in excess.[10] Some team members had brought small stocks of equipment and drugs with them, but these were insufficient and they put in an immediate request to Prince Henry Hospital for more. Despite having a USAID representative in Vung Tau, the team found it impossible to obtain supplies through official channels. Their requests for supplies from the USAID depot at Phu Tho in Saigon were either ignored or delayed.

Again the Australian and American armies filled the gap, supplying the team with all its essential instruments, drugs and other equipment in the first few months. By the end of Doug Tracy's tour, in early 1967, the supplies problem remained, but the Australian government was attempting to help. In March the Director General of Health, William Refshauge, recommended to the DEA that the team be allowed to draw on Army sources for urgent supplies, and that a pharmacist be appointed in Saigon to liaise with the Phu Tho depot, ensuring that orders for all surgical teams were filled. Although it does not appear that the second recommendation was acted upon, the supply system gradually improved, but the team continued to rely mostly on informal networks to obtain what it needed. Tom Hugh remembers that the Army was a major source of support, helped by the team's nurses: 'We never used to go out to the Army base without taking a couple of the girls with us, who'd dress up in their tightest things, you know, and [carry] a suitcase. And we always came away with supplies. They were terrific.'[11]

As late as 1969, laboratory technician Gavan O'Connor commented on the supply problem in a letter to colleagues in Australia:

> As far as running the lab goes there are only two problems. No supplies and no services. The only service industries here are taxis and brothels and the only supplies are in a warehouse in Saigon and that's so busy supplying the black market that we don't get much of a look in.[12]

After a couple of weeks, and having put their hands to whatever needed doing, the team was ready to start clinical work. The number of patients they dealt with was small at first. Much of the initial work involved running a general practice outpatients clinic, something that frustrated the surgeons until they began to receive more serious cases. Until the team arrived, most people in need of surgery had been taken to a Korean Army mobile hospital just outside Vung Tau, and it took some time to change this habit. Both the team and Dr Lam persistently urged Australian and American forces to send patients their way, and gradually the serious casualties, war-related and otherwise, began to arrive.

The first surgical operation took place after a couple of weeks, and it went badly. A Vietnamese man brought in his son, who had a large hernia. Doug Tracy, who operated on the boy, remembers that it must have been nearly forty degrees Celsius in the operating theatre because one of the many power outages prevented the air-conditioner from being used. The child was covered in heavy sterile drapes and the operation began. The anaesthetist, Judith Ross, administered a drug to dry up secretions, but it also prevented the boy from sweating. The operation was completed but the boy could not be woken. When Doug

Tracy felt him, his skin was burning hot, and he soon died of malignant hyperpyrexia, a condition in which patients react adversely to anaesthetics and their temperature soars. It would normally have been recognised and dealt with but because everyone was so hot it went unnoticed. The team was devastated. Knowing that their reputations rested on this first case, they dreaded breaking the news to the boy's father. Doug recalled that 'he looked at me as though I'd hit him with an axe . . . And he just turned his face away and ran away with tears [running from] his eyes.' To compound the team's anguish, the father returned the next day, apologised for crying and gave Doug a small gift, thanking him for doing all he could to try to save his son. Doug recalls: 'It was just unbelievable. The girls were crying and Judy Ross was inconsolable. They all wanted to go home.'[13]

The team recovered from the setback and soon acquired a good reputation in the area. The kinds of cases seen were the same as those treated elsewhere by Australian surgical teams. Congenital deformities such as cleft lips and palates, diseases like tuberculosis, tetanus, bubonic plague and malaria, large goitres, traffic accident injuries, burns and war wounds were all routinely dealt with. Surgeon Tom Hugh had great success with his work on cleft lips and palates, with wealthy patients coming from as far away as Saigon to make use of his services. He recalls that 'doing cleft lips was very satisfying for me. There are children walking around in Vietnam now that don't have an unsightly thing. It was worthwhile. The people were so lovely . . .'[14] Once again, the instantaneous results of operations like this helped boost the team's reputation quickly.

Fairly early in its tour the Prince Henry team had a major success with several tetanus cases. Previously, tetanus sufferers usually died because the necessary treatment was not available to them. When a man with tetanus eventually did come in, it was a major logistical exercise to treat him. Tom Hugh is still 'amazed at our boldness in taking it on, but there wasn't any alternative.'[15] The patient needed around-the-clock ventilation. This was provided by compressed air from aircraft cylinders delivered by the RAAF. The Army supplied the doctors on duty (nurses were prevented from travelling to the hospital at night at this stage) with two-way radios to allow them to let the team at the Grand Hotel know if they encountered any problems. The work was exhausting and the treatment continued for about two weeks, but the patient was cured.[16]

Initially, outpatients clinics saw between fifty and ninety people a day. By the end of the first three months, they were seeing about 200 a day. The acquisition of a second surgical table allowed more operations to be performed: forty in the first month and sixty in the second month. As at other team bases, there was a notable reduction in patient arrivals around Christmas and during the Tet holiday period in February. It was probably fortuitous that the build-up of cases was not particularly rapid or dramatic. Given the shortages of supplies, interpreters and trained Vietnamese staff, the team would have been hard-pressed to treat more patients than they actually did. With sterilising continuing to be done in the 36th Evacuation Hospital, some five miles away, and blood supplies from various sources needing to be picked up regularly, the team administrator was also kept busy ensuring that the group kept up the current moderate pace.

Although the hospital's obstetric unit was run by the Vietnamese, Australian surgeons were frequently called upon to help out with emergencies, performing many caesareans each month. Physician Noel Lucas received thanks for his obstetric work on one particular woman, Minh Hall, many years after the event. In 2002 he received a letter from Minh, who had married an American with whom she had been working at the 36th Evacuation Hospital. According to her letter, she had been taken to Le Loi Hospital close to death with a septic miscarriage. Several other doctors had seen her and apparently believed her situation was hopeless, but Noel treated her and she recovered. She remembered the 'large size of the doctor and his big hands' with enormous gratitude, saying that his optimism and treatment had saved her life.[17] Noel himself found his Vietnamese experience extremely rewarding, and the frustration of losing patients unnecessarily was partly offset by the successes he had with patients such as Minh Hall.

At the end of the first three months, the team was well established in Le Loi Hospital, although opinions varied about how much it had achieved. Tom Hugh felt that although it was good to 'do magical things—fix people's faces up and things like that', unless they left behind something lasting for the local people, their efforts were fairly fruitless. He felt they had had only enough time to get the hospital cleaned up, start surgery, establish clinics and get the logistics working. No lasting impression on the local health scene had been made.[18] In his end-of-tour report, Doug Tracy was more optimistic, noting that as well as improving the hospital's buildings and surrounds, the team had increased its surgical capacity, begun to teach Vietnamese nurses and physicians English medical terms and surgical techniques, and initiated a regular tuberculosis clinic at which more than fifty people were being treated.[19]

There is no doubt that these early months were stressful, and that good leadership was the key to the team's success:

> When things got difficult—the air-conditioner broke down or the generator wasn't working, the supplies were difficult . . . people would get short with each other . . . But we all ended up friends in the end. And the leader was a key part of that . . . Doug is a born leader and he kept us all stitched together.[20]

The Prince Henry and Prince of Wales team was succeeded in May 1967 by a team from the Royal Prince Alfred Hospital in Sydney. It served for six months, after which time teams recruited from Commonwealth Repatriation hospitals around Australia served in both Vung Tau and Ba Ria. Thanks to the first team's improvement of conditions at the hospital and supply lines, later teams were able to concentrate mainly on medical and surgical issues. Life became more routine and the number of cases dealt with continued to grow.

The daily pattern of life in Vung Tau was similar to that elsewhere, although this team's working week began differently. On Monday mornings hospital staff would gather outside for a flag-raising ceremony, with Vietnamese lined up on one side of a flag pole and Australians on the other. At the foot of the pole a transistor radio played first martial music, then the national anthem, as Vietnamese and Australian flags were slowly raised. Derek Meyers, who worked at Vung Tau in early 1968, was highly entertained by the sight of the Australian jeeps depositing team members with minutes to spare, and staff 'more or less coming to attention' as the flags were raised.[21] Nurse Marita Mulcahy also remembers the ceremony, when she would watch the flags rising, 'wondering who was going to get there first but they always made sure that they just got there at the same time'.[22]

The working day began at eight o'clock with outpatients and other clinics; these went on until the midday siesta brought everything to a halt. Surgery was carried out in the afternoons, and team members also conducted evening rounds and worked a Saturday-morning shift, leaving Sundays free for relaxation. Living in a coastal city had its advantages. The midday break was often used by team members as an opportunity to cool down with a swim at the 'Back Beach' at Vung Tau. Doug Tracy recalled that the surf could be quite dangerous, with rips and large waves that often had American servicemen in trouble. Tom Hugh and Noel Lucas, both experienced surfers, found themselves giving lifesaving tips to the Americans, for which they were grateful because at that stage nearly forty American soldiers had drowned.[23] When not swimming, team members used the break to return to their accommodation and rest. Most found the constant heat and humidity and the pace of work exhausting. While teams were still based at the Grand Hotel they became regular visitors to what was dubbed the Pink Panther Club, the officers' mess of the United States

39th Signals Battalion, located nearby. The meals were free and the Americans welcomed them warmly.

Successive teams arriving in Vung Tau continued to find the conditions primitive. Despite the work done on the hospital by his predecessors, Donald Sheldon, leader of the Royal Prince Alfred team, remarked that 'we were all appalled at our first sight of the hospital. Although the theatre block is quite comfortable and clean, the ward was reminiscent of the pre–[Florence] Nightingale era.'[24] The 120-bed hospital frequently held more than double that number of patients and the wards were, as in all provincial hospitals, full of patients' relatives—cooking, sleeping, and caring for their loved ones. Donald's team attempted to improve standards: 'By constant threatening and scolding, and by exhibiting public health posters at strategic points around the building, we have been able to greatly improve the standard of hygiene and cleanliness.'[25]

The outpatients clinic saw about 100 patients a day, and surgeons performed over seventy major operations each month. The increased number of surgical cases was partly a result of continued liaison between the team and the Australian Army surgeon Bruce Fox, who conducted medical clinics in isolated villages around the province. He arranged for more seriously ill patients to be transported to the hospital and then returned to their homes after surgery. The team found this to their advantage because the preselection of patients for operations meant they spent less time assessing non-surgical cases, and could perform more operations. It also greatly increased their sphere of influence and effectiveness around the province, giving villagers a degree of medical care they had not previously had access to.

Surgeons in Vung Tau experienced the same frustrations as their colleagues elsewhere with the Vietnamese mistrust of hospitals. They continued to deal with the effects of traditional medicine on their patients, whose conditions were usually far advanced when they arrived at the hospital. Derek Meyers recalled a typical case during his tour in early 1968, involving an eight-year-old boy:

His mother brought him in, his right arm completely covered with an old rag. 'Ask her to take it off,' I said to Hue. The arm was dead from above the elbow down to the fingertips, black, stinking and dripping pus ... It appeared that he had sustained a supracondylar [above-elbow] fracture of the humerus five days before, and the 'Chinese doctor' had advised the use of a very tight bandage. His advice had been too slavishly followed. There was nothing for it but immediate amputation.[26]

Another class of patients who often needed surgery urgently were known as Hondas. As in other Vietnamese towns and cities, the most common type of transport used in Vung Tau was the motorcycle, which often accommodated up to four people, none wearing helmets. Accidents were common, and it was enough for a team member to be told that their next patient was a Honda to know what to expect. Nurse Jan Bell remembers having a ward, known as the Honda ward, full of young men in traction from their accidents:

> . . . they'd take their tractions off on Friday night and go home and come back on Monday morning and put their tractions back on again . . . They thought this was a bit pointless and silly, staying in hospital. They were only doing it to get along with us, I suppose.[27]

Relatively few of the teams' surgical patients had war-related injuries, but people would be sent in from outlying areas with bullet, grenade or mine wounds, and as always the deaths of children were the most upsetting. Nurse Barbara Buscombe remembers a young girl killed by a piece of shrapnel through the heart during the 1968 Tet Offensive:

> I had to help [her father] carry her round to the mortuary on a stretcher and that's all he had left in this world . . . a lot

of things stick in my mind but that—no man should have to do that.[28]

Derek Meyers assisted in an operation on a twelve-year-old girl with an abdominal wound that was probably caused by a mortar fragment. The operation, though complicated, was successfully completed in an hour and a half. The girl recovered and later went home, 'a great advertisement for the Australian surgeons', although as Derek's own twelve-year-old daughter later wrote to him: 'It seems terrible that little children can get hurt by bullets and bomb shells when they're playing.'[29]

Although much of the work done by surgeons involved dealing with physical trauma, they were all well equipped to cope with the cases and situations presented to them. Some of the surgeons who completed a tour were the best in their field in Australia and if anything, their talents were under-utilised, a criticism occasionally made about the teams. Orthopaedic surgeon Jim Ellis served in Vung Tau in 1968 and Bien Hoa in 1972. He was a highly experienced surgeon who believed that all those who went were capable of managing, even in the case of the frequent caesareans many of the surgeons were called upon to perform, a procedure they had not necessarily expected to do. Ellis prepared for his tour by packing a comprehensive selection of medical books, together with a portable orthopaedic table and some specialist tools. He worked on a wide variety of cases—'appendixes, broken legs ... traffic accidents ... ruptured spleens'—but also lent his talents elsewhere, operating on wounded Australian soldiers who had been placed in the 36th Evacuation Hospital. He recalls American nurses visiting Le Loi Hospital and being shocked at the conditions the Australians worked in, with no air-conditioning in the operating theatres and teams working with sweat pouring off them. At the time, Ellis remembers thinking that 'the sweat of an honest man doesn't do anyone any harm. But when it drops on to the bone graft that you're putting in the leg, you think to yourself, Well I'm glad he's on penicillin or whatever.'[30]

Australian Army anaesthetist Marshall Barr visited Le Loi Hospital in early 1967 and was full of praise for the way anaesthesia was conducted by the Australians in such primitive conditions:

> I watched a hare-lip repair, which was done very well, but my admiration was for the anaesthesia. The patient was an undernourished child . . . he had come in 'off the street'. They were using the EMO apparatus to give ether/air, plus a trickle of oxygen from one precious cylinder, which would help cope with the anaemia. This was brave and skilful stuff in difficult circumstances.[31]

Nurses in the Australian teams faced their own difficulties. Crowded wards and poor hygiene were a constant challenge, as were the problems of dealing with Vietnamese nurses, patients, relatives and translators. Laboratory technician Gavan O'Connor noted during his tour in 1969 that the nurses had some unexpected problems: 'It is not at all unusual for them to come in and find that the patient who was flat on his back the night before with an IV [intravenous tube] in his arm—has disappeared, all that's left is a dirty bed and the drip [tube] hanging from the bottle.'[32]

On the other hand, Jenny James found that intravenous drips were so popular with the Vietnamese that precious supplies were often wasted: 'It was not uncommon for us to find the cleaning lady lying in the intensive care ward with intravenous fluid going, because she had a headache and this must be good powerful medicine, this stuff that you get in the vein.'[33]

Nurse Jan Bell, initially disenchanted with the work in Vietnam because 'being surrounded by filth, stench and misery does not appeal to me,'[34] came to love it after learning to accept the situation as it was and not trying to change things to suit Western ways. The work was demanding, stressful, and required adaptability. Jan was on hand on one occasion when surgeon Dick Cowdery came rushing for assistance. A Buddhist monk he had operated on for a urinary obstruction had had a filthy and germ-laden catheter reinserted by well-meaning relatives. Unconventional means were required to save the man's life so Jan raided the pharmacy shelves for every antibiotic they had. These were administered en masse, and one of them must have worked because the monk survived.[35] Such cases were satisfying, but at times the nurses felt that what they did was simply bandaid work. Jan felt that 'it just seemed that we weren't winning the hearts and minds of the people a lot of the time. That we were banging our heads against a brick wall.'[36]

Some of the teams' frustration stemmed from the feeling that when they left they would leave nothing of value behind. At one stage Derek Meyers casually proposed the idea of a mass immunisation program to a USAID officer but soon realised the difficulties it would entail:

> . . . one would of course have the necessary stationery printed, with advertisements and immunisation cards in Vietnamese, arrange for supplies of vaccine to be sent from the depot in Saigon, recruit suitable paramedical personnel, and start the campaign . . . With the patience of Job, the tact of a professional diplomat, and the determination of a bulldozer, one could have made a beginning.[37]

Another area where lasting benefit could have been made was in teaching Vietnamese medical staff, but the Vung Tau teams were not able to instigate any formal system for doing this. Demonstration of techniques by practical example, both in the operating theatre and the wards, was the main way team members taught Vietnamese doctors and nurses. Occasionally some of the surgeons gave guest lectures elsewhere. Doug Tracy remembers lecturing to medical students at Saigon's main medical school, with a Vietnamese neurosurgeon translating everything he said into French, the language still used for teaching at that time. He received a flowery speech of appreciation in return, delivered in English and understood only by Doug himself.[38] Such efforts, although valuable, could not alleviate the overall problem of a shortage of qualified Vietnamese medical personnel in Vung Tau.

Team cohesion was essential in dealing with the daily stresses of life in a surgical team. A team report by Donald Sheldon in mid 1967 noted that 'working amicably and effectively with the Vietnamese medical and nursing staff demands considerable effort, understanding and patience'. In order to deal with this stress, he noted that 'in recruiting team members high priority should be given to those with cheerful dispositions and a high sense of dedication. Those who envisage their tour of duty as an oriental holiday will make poor team members and do little to foster goodwill among the Vietnamese for Australia.'[39] The difference that a poor team player could make became apparent to a Vung Tau team in 1969. The leader was unhappy with the conditions he found himself in and made his feelings clear to the rest of the team and to his Vietnamese colleagues. On the job, he interfered with the work of others, insulting Vietnamese staff and abusing patients; socially, he isolated himself. A fellow team member wrote to his own wife that 'not only have I not heard anyone say a kind word about him, I haven't even heard anyone say a moderately bad thing about him, every description of him is in superlatives.'[40] In a perverse way, the poor leadership pulled the rest of the team together, but there is no doubt this individual had a negative impact on their work.

Another factor working against team cohesion in Vung Tau was accommodation. The Australians finally moved out of the Grand Hotel in early 1968. Most of them were housed in a villa overlooking the sea, a few kilometres from the hospital. The senior doctors, however, moved into a house in the town centre. The split was necessary because accommodation was at a premium in Vung Tau, and it was impossible to find a residence large enough to hold the whole team. But team leaders realised that it could militate against cohesion. At various times they instigated regular social gatherings such as weekly team meals, but these were often disrupted by emergencies at the hospital or other demands. At other times, teams living in the villa would throw parties to which everyone was invited, but some teams gathered as a unit only when they were required to represent Australia at official functions. It was unfortunate, if unavoidable, that Vung Tau teams were physically separated in this way, but it appears that good leadership could overcome this problem and was a more crucial factor in a given team's success.

Just as other surgical teams developed strong relationships with their Vietnamese counterparts, so too the Vung Tau teams worked hard at cultivating a strong Australian–Vietnamese relationship. As well as supporting the Vietnamese hospital staff in their work, they were able to offer them valuable advice, and in many cases close friendships developed. Médecin Chef Dr Lam was grateful for the teams' assistance and helped them when he could. Surgeons found they could work well with him, although they had to adopt a particular approach to new surgical cases:

> Dr Lam will come over to us and say that he has a case requiring an operation, suggesting a diagnosis but does not ask for an opinion. Our practice is to admit the case without question, thereby supporting his reputation. We then come to our own conclusion about the case. At this stage Dr Lam is quite happy for us to alter the diagnosis.[41]

Gavan O'Connor, in particular, established a solid working relationship and personal friendship with his laboratory colleague Hue. Like other team members, O'Connor had soon concluded that he was there to help and it was not his job to try to take over the laboratory. He was therefore able to work harmoniously with Hue and became good friends with her and her family. Many years later, after the death of his first wife, O'Connor visited Hue in Vietnam. It was through her that he met his second wife, Ha, Hue's niece.[42]

Although most team members were not as close to their Vietnamese colleagues as O'Connor, many of them socialised regularly together, learning much about Vietnamese food and customs in the process. These occasions and the friendships formed are some of the happiest memories now held by many team members. A Sunday lunch in early 1968 attended by Jan Bell and her colleagues at the home of the hospital's head nurse, Mr Pho, was typical. They were greeted by their host and ushered immediately to the table. Mr Pho's wife served them, starting by filling large glass tumblers with ice and whisky. A four-course meal followed: spring rolls and soup, a main course, and flans for dessert. Glasses were regularly refilled, and although Jan hardly touched hers, the men in the group indulged and, as a result, 'had a whale of a time'. They left promptly at 3 o'clock, having stayed the customary three hours. It was Jan's first Vietnamese meal in a private home and like many of her colleagues she found the food delicious and the customs fascinating.[43] Sometimes, though, the unfamiliar food produced particular challenges, as Marita Mulcahy found when she was the special guest at an official function during her tour in 1968:

> I looked at the plate and I could see this eye looking at me. And I thought, 'I've got to eat that eye. How am I going to get it down?' . . . It was a bird's eye, I think. And I remember Myra [Chenery] saying to me, 'Just eat whatever is on your plate' . . . So I just decided it was like an oyster and I let it slip down . . .[44]

Ba Ria

After a year of service and with their reputation well established, the Vung Tau teams were asked to take on a new challenge. In early 1968 the Australian government received a request from the Vietnamese Ministry of Health to provide a surgical team for Ba Ria. The provincial capital had previously been considered a suitable location for a team, and although Vung Tau was decided upon instead, Ba Ria had always been seen as a potential site for the future. In a February 1968 recommendation to the External Affairs minister, the Australian embassy in Saigon strongly supported the establishment of a new team, because it would allow a coordinated Australian effort in the area where Australian troops were operating. A Korean team then working in the Ba Ria Hospital would be moved to an area where Korean troops were engaged. Ba Ria Hospital would be used as a district hospital and for emergency cases, and Le Loi Hospital at Vung Tau would act as a base hospital. Major Bruce Fox, by then in charge of the Australian Army's civic action medical units, also supported the proposal because it would provide an Australian-staffed hospital closer to his area of operations, to which he could refer patients.[45]

It was envisaged that the Ba Ria team would be a subsidiary of the main Vung Tau team. The overall number of team personnel would not need to be increased, as Long Xuyen teams could be reduced in size, thanks to a lighter workload, and the extra personnel used to fill positions for Ba Ria. The Ba Ria team would have only three doctors and three nurses. Procedures such as X-rays and plastic surgery, and services such as pathology, would continue to be carried out in Vung Tau. The Ba Ria team would be under the control of the Vung Tau team's leader and administered by its administrator. In assessing the security situation for Ba Ria, it was realised that the town was more vulnerable to enemy attack than Vung Tau and that extra precautions would need to be taken to protect team members. A security report recognised that 'the threat to a medical team could easily arise from a ground attack which may or may not be capable of overrunning the hospital. This could occur with very little warning.' It was not thought that such an attack was likely to occur in the near future, and to protect the team its living quarters would be surrounded by a high cyclone-wire fence, within which a bunker would be erected to protect the inhabitants from a possible attack.[46] No one could have foreseen how important this structure was soon to become to the Ba Ria team.

By late September arrangements were in place for the Ba Ria team to begin work. Initially it was made up of doctors Douglas Blake, who was put in charge of the team, and John Williams, and nurses Pat Healey, Barbara Buscombe and Geraldine 'Estelle' Gladstone. A third doctor later joined the team and its number remained at six from then on. For the first few days, the team worked by day in Ba Ria but returned to Vung Tau each night, waiting for security measures at their living compound to be finished. Before long, though, they moved to Ba Ria and settled into their new home.

Ba Ria was a town of approximately 16,000 people on the main highway from Vung Tau to Saigon. Its main street was typically crowded with traffic travelling through, as well as people making their way to and from the marketplace and shopping centre. The hospital was of typical French colonial construction, made up of five ward buildings used as a medical ward, storeroom, laboratory, outpatients clinic and pharmacy. A more recent addition was the surgical ward, in which the Australians worked. Vietnamese staff also maintained an obstetrics and a children's ward, and there was a basic X-ray machine available. The adjacent accommodation compound, built in 1967 by the Americans for the Korean team, consisted of a concrete brick building containing bedrooms and bathrooms, a large living–dining room, kitchen and pantry. It was comfortable but not luxurious.

During the 1968 Tet Offensive a large battle had been fought in Ba Ria, and its effects on the town and on the hospital could still be seen by the first Australian team. Both Sue Quinn and Barbara Buscombe remember seeing mortar holes in town buildings and in the walls of some of the hospital pavilions. The team found the surgical ward filthy and uncared for, with blood caked so hard on the operating table 'that you really had to get a chisel to chisel it off'.[47] Sue Quinn also recalled the lack of glass in the theatre windows, the work of a New Zealand mortar position whose shelling of nearby hills would cause ceiling fans to fall and glass to shatter. The open windows, she remembers, were 'all right for air conditioning and that but . . . everybody could peer in through the windows while surgery was going on . . .'[48]

The nurses in the team were initially kept busy trying to obtain sufficient stocks of drugs, instruments and other essentials to enable surgery to start. Aided by two Vietnamese nurses and an interpreter, the team ran two operating theatres as well as the outpatients clinic, and also attended to the twenty-one-bed men's and women's wards. Dr Donald Cordner, who worked at the hospital in 1969, felt that 'the standards of our facilities would have equated those in pre–World War I Melbourne'[49]—they were similar, in other words, to the conditions experienced by the Vung Tau teams.

By early 1969 the Ba Ria team had its full complement of staff and was hard at work. Donald Cordner was proud of the fact that though it was the only Australian surgical team composed entirely of general practitioners, during its tenure only a small number of difficult cases had to be sent to Vung Tau. The three doctors divided their duties, with one carrying out morning ward rounds, another conducting the outpatients clinic, and the third on duty in the surgical suite, taking care of cases referred from outpatients and the wards. The nurses shared their time between the operating theatre and the wards. Donald found the surgical workload intermittent. The outpatients clinic was consistently full, with doctors performing three or four minor operations a day and an occasional major elective operation. More than half of the surgical work was on war-related trauma, with another third from frequent traffic accidents. Of the war-related work Donald wrote:

> Most war injuries came in groups, nearly always caused by the explosion of a land mine, usually, but not always, of Viet Cong origin. Sometimes children strayed onto a marked allied mine field, with tragic results. On one terrible occasion

ten people were killed and twenty-four injured in a double mine explosion outside a high school some twelve kilometres distant.[50]

Other conditions dealt with by the Ba Ria team were diseases such as scabies, tuberculosis, pneumonia and tetanus, burns, ruptured appendixes and broken bones. In three months Donald's team dealt with 649 cases in theatre, and he felt that 'the fact that our rate of work, particularly in outpatients, increased almost explosively during our stay, is an indication that we were accepted and trusted by the local inhabitants . . .'[51]

The nurses in the Ba Ria team found the work both demanding and fulfilling. The Vietnamese nurses were accustomed to suturing wounds and soon demonstrated the procedure to the Australian nurses, who had not been allowed to do it in Australia. Sue Quinn also remembers doing a procedure unheard-of for nurses back home: a leg amputation on a war victim. Donald talked her through the operation, which she wanted to do because 'it was certainly something that I knew I was never going to get to do at home and I wanted to see what it felt like to do it'.[52] This event was the most memorable of her Vietnam tour, but Sue also clearly remembers the Honda victims and the children burnt by aviation-fuel explosions. As elsewhere, the Australian nurses tried to train their Vietnamese counterparts by example, with mixed results. Sue found that they were resistant to the idea of counting instruments and swabs, giving her baleful looks when she made the suggestion, but 'they were good technicians. And they knew all about scrubbing, gloving and gowning so the only thing was that their tolerance for theatre cleanliness was different to ours.'[53] Like their colleagues in Vung Tau, the Ba Ria nurses adjusted their expectations of hygiene and procedure to fit in more readily with their Vietnamese colleagues.

Given the relative isolation of the Ba Ria Hospital and the limitations on travel owing to security concerns, Ba Ria team members relied heavily on each other for entertainment. On the whole the team worked and socialised well together, organising various activities to keep themselves amused. They entertained a constant stream of visitors, mostly American and Australian servicemen, who were happy to be entertained by Western women. Christmas 1968 was celebrated in style, with Sue Quinn and an American visitor driving around Ba Ria in the early hours of Christmas Day hunting for loaves of bread to make stuffing for an enormous turkey. They succeeded, and had the bird in the oven by 4 a.m. Sue remembers it as 'a lovely, lovely Christmas dinner'.[54] Another notable occasion involved Sue having her feet blackened with shoe polish and being 'walked' up the walls of the living room. She was small in stature so two doctors found it easy to lift her, and after several reapplications of polish she had left a trail of black footprints up the wall, across the ceiling (between the blades of the ceiling fan) and down the other side. She remembers that 'Gough Whitlam [then Leader of the Opposition] came the next day, didn't he. And there's these footprints up there. He was not amused.'[55] Weekly trips to visit the Vung Tau team, as well as occasional trips around the province, also helped to relieve the pressure.

Being in the heart of Phuoc Tuy province and surrounded by both allied and enemy positions, they soon became accustomed to the sounds of war. As the 1969 Tet festival period approached, the team was given the usual warnings about possible increases in enemy activity. There was some mild apprehension, but life continued smoothly. Donald Cordner reflected:

Here at Ba Ria I was very happy—we had a pleasant group of people living together—we had repeatedly been assured that our security was 100 per cent, and that we would be evacuated by the Australian Task Force at the first sign of any real trouble. We were well housed and well fed, and reasonably free to come and go in our spare time during the day . . .[56]

The team's sense of security was shattered in the early hours of 23 February. They had retired to bed at about midnight to the usual sounds of distant artillery and mortar fire, as well as some occasional small-arms fire. Donald was woken just before 3 a.m. by what sounded like louder, closer and more frequent explosions. He wondered 'why we were firing so many more mortars . . . it never crossed my mind that these might be incoming shells'.[57] Team members were hurried out of their rooms by an American colonel and into the compound's bunker a short distance away. Donald was not alarmed at this stage, because 'had we not been repeatedly assured that we would be whisked away to a nebulous somewhere if ever real danger threatened?'[58] It soon became apparent that the hospital compound was under heavy enemy fire and that it would be impossible to evacuate anybody. The compound yard, which should have been kept clear in case of an emergency, had become cluttered with vehicles and through the bunker's slits Americans could be seen firing back at the Viet Cong, who were directing small-arms fire at them and at the bunker from outside the compound fence. At one point a shout was heard, followed by a large explosion and a sheet of flame as a grenade blew up one of the trucks. An American soldier called out, injured, and was dragged to safety inside the bunker. Team doctor David Watson had had the foresight to bring his medical bag, and he attended to the wounded man. Barbara Buscombe remembers that he was cool under fire, he 'just did his thing as though he did it every other day'.[59] For about one and a half hours the battle continued, American and Vietnamese soldiers inside the bunker exchanging small-arms fire and grenades with the Viet Cong. Team members felt a sense of unreality about the situation they were in, as Donald recalled: '. . . it was extraordinary to think that men 50 feet away wanted to kill me and were trying their best to do so'.[60]

As dawn broke the attack subsided and everyone in the bunker cautiously emerged, 'dirty, dishevelled and sweaty'. They were able to have a hot shower before spending the day dealing with the many casualties created by the attack. Word of the attack quickly spread to the Vung Tau team and reinforcements were sent to help deal with the large number of wounded, and to give the Ba Ria team a much-needed rest. Donald Cordner remembered the evening after the attack as one of his worst times: another attack was expected.[61] It did not come, but Donald's apprehension remained for the duration of his time in Ba Ria. As well as taking care of the wounded, the team spent several days boosting security at the hospital and the accommodation compound, but its time in Ba Ria was coming to an end.

A few days after the attack, team members travelled to Saigon to report their version of events to the Australian Ambassador, Ralph Harry. On 28 February Harry was optimistic, reporting to the DEA that 'the situation [in Ba Ria] has been restored and that after two days of relaxation in Vung Tau the team will be able to carry on normally'.[62] Two weeks later, however, he had changed his mind. In a new report to the DEA he noted that a recent intelligence analysis had revealed that the attacking force was the local Viet Cong battalion, *D445*, which had deliberately attacked what it called the 'Australian hospital'. He concluded that 'since the attack on the Australian team was apparently planned rather than accidental my view is strengthened that the civilian team should be withdrawn'.[63] Throughout the rest of March, discussions on the future of the team were held between the DEA, the Australian embassy in Saigon and the Australian Army. The Army was asked, but declined, to provide a replacement team with its medical personnel. During this period, too, Professor Sydney Sunderland visited the Ba Ria and Vung Tau teams on his mission to report on the future of Australian civilian medical aid to Vietnam. His report, submitted at the end of the month, concurred with the decision to withdraw the Ba Ria team for safety reasons, but recommended that medical aid should continue in the hospital if possible. On 31 March a Korean team arrived to take over from the Australians, who rejoined their colleagues in Vung Tau.

Ba Ria team members experienced mixed feelings about their withdrawal. Bob Rayner objected to the move, believing that withdrawal on safety grounds was unjustified and that there was a definite need for an Australian team in Ba Ria. Sue Quinn also disagreed with the decision and, having been given the choice of working with the Vung Tau team until the end of her tour or going home, she opted to leave. Donald Cordner, on the other hand, was happy to leave Ba Ria because he felt insecure there. He found that 'it was wonderful sleeping in the peace and quiet of Vung Tau without fear of VC'.[64] Despite the dangers and the early end to his tour, Donald had no regrets, describing his three months in Vietnam as 'a fascinating experience':

> I met wonderful people and made many friends. I had a glimpse into a world that previously I had only heard about, and, albeit rather belatedly, I had a small taste of warfare, and was at times quite scared. I embarked on many surgical ventures which would never otherwise have been my responsibility ... I am glad that I went.[65]

Back to Vung Tau

Donald Cordner was justified in feeling safe in Vung Tau, because the city was never seriously attacked while Australian surgical teams were stationed there. Despite the sounds of distant bombing and the sight of flares and tracer fire at night, the war seemed very distant to most team members. A lack of information on the progress of the war was partly responsible for this feeling: it was not uncommon for relatives at home to know of events in Vietnam before team members did. The one occasion when a Vung Tau team felt the full impact of the war was during the 1968 Tet Offensive, which affected everybody throughout South Vietnam. Like teams in Bien Hoa and Long Xuyen, the Vung Tau team had heard rumours of an enemy attack before the 1968 Tet holiday but they were generally ignored. Nurse Marita Mulcahy flew to Saigon for a much-needed rest, and soon found herself in a deadly war zone. Other team members had also planned a break during Tet as the hospital emptied out, with relatives taking their sick family members home for this important holiday. On the first morning of Tet, Jan Bell and others drove to the airport at Vung Tau hoping to catch a flight to Saigon. They found the airport gates closed and manned by armed American guards, who told them to return to the hospital because Saigon was being bombed. Even as the wounded began to flood into the hospital, information was scarce. Jan Bell wrote to her family of the bombing of Saigon, the night-time curfew in Vung Tau, and of the 'wild rumours' flying around the town. She only felt 'a little apprehensive', clearly unaware of the widespread nature of the attacks around the rest of the country.[66]

The full impact of the Tet attacks was brought home to the team when they arrived at the hospital. As Jan Bell remembers, 'all hell had broken loose'. Injured people were lying or sitting wherever they could find room, both theatres were in constant use and the team's nurses found themselves making difficult decisions about which patients needed urgent attention. The surgeons preferred working on people they knew they could save, rather than operating for hours on someone who inevitably died. As teams elsewhere found, the injuries they treated were horrific and those most affected seemed to be women and children. Jan Bell set down her impressions in a letter to her worried family:

> I've never seen so much devastation to the human race. Little children shockingly injured bewildered, crying, poor little devils who just don't know what's going on. Our hospital is bursting at the seams and we're all just about ready to drop. God, I've had just about all the experience I could ever want, but I guess it won't stop for a while.[67]

The team worked constantly for about a week, treating what 'seemed like hundreds' of people. Some of them were Viet Cong, one of them a fifteen-year-old boy soldier who Jan Bell felt sure did not know what the fighting was all about.[68]

The team's situation was not helped by the absence of Marita Mulcahy, who was stuck in Saigon for several days and probably wished she had stayed in Vung Tau, despite the heavy workload. When she tried to return by plane, she found Tan Son Nhut airport closed and surrounded by guards and barbed wire. Forced to return to the city, she spent the next few days moving between locations with embassy staff, attempting to stay out of danger. She later recalled:

> At one stage we were staying in a hotel opposite a police station. Then one morning we looked out and saw about 100 people milling round the station. We found out that they were captured Viet Cong, and we knew that if they escaped they would come straight for us, so we got out of there.[69]

She feared she would not survive the attacks and wrote a diary of her experiences as a memento for her mother, to let her know what had happened if she was killed. The airport finally opened and Marita flew back to Vung Tau to find that the team had relocated to the Australian logistics base for security.

After several days of constant work and little sleep, Vung Tau team members were exhausted. Five days after the initial attacks Jan Bell wrote to her family that their letters to her were the only things keeping her sane. They were still bound by a strict curfew and receiving regular alerts of potential Viet Cong attacks, with the hospital apparently high on their target list. She wrote, 'everyone has the jitters at the moment and the doctors have all been issued with weapons'.[70] Making matters worse, casualties were still coming in and the unrefrigerated bodies of the dead were piled high in the hospital's mortuary, causing an appalling stench.

A reprieve came a week after the attacks began, when casualty numbers dropped and the Vietnamese staff took over the hospital completely. The Australian team moved temporarily to the Army's 8th Field Ambulance at the logistics base for a rest. After a few days they made daily visits to the hospital to check on patients, but they continued to reside at the base until the security situation stabilised. As life began to return to normal, the team returned to regular work, but instead of moving back to the Grand Hotel they finally moved into their team house, a villa on the beach.

Once established there, they were able to relax more easily. They returned the hospitality they had received elsewhere and held regular social gatherings. The women were in particular demand to attend parties and other social occasions, and although some found this lifestyle too demanding, others relished it. Marita Mulcahy remembers American pilots landing their helicopters on the road below the villa and flying her off to various social events. Sue Quinn also remembers doing what she called 'aerial hitchhiking' whenever she had a couple of days off. Regular destinations were the Australian task force base at Nui Dat and visits to other surgical teams in Ba Ria, Bien Hoa and Long Xuyen. The latter was a popular destination because of its attractive location, and Sue and her colleagues enjoyed waterskiing on the Bassac River, a pastime not without risk from Viet Cong snipers along the river bank. Team members on longer tours took their half-tour rest and recreation break overseas, with Thailand, Hong Kong and Cambodia popular destinations. Vung Tau was a popular weekend destination for other surgical team members and the Vung Tau team were regular hosts to them. Doug Tracy found the constant stream of visitors a strain at times, since he had to set aside valuable time to show them around the hospital and then entertain them. Some of the nurses, too, occasionally lacked the energy or will to social-ise, but they were required to dress up and go out in order to obtain the supplies necessary for their work. Gavan O'Connor found this kind of socialising an essential part of keeping the team functioning:

We can't just walk up to a stranger and say, 'Please can we have a starter motor so our jeep will go?' We would just get laughed at, but if we call around to a Mess where we know there are people who can help us, have a few drinks with them and then mention that if they hear of any starter motors going to let us know—and we will have it within twelve hours. It is a crazy system but it is the only one which works.[71]

The end of the Vung Tau teams

As previously mentioned, the Vung Tau team hosted a visit by Professor Sunderland and Dr Boxall in early March 1969. By then all the major problems of supply, communication and accommodation had been solved and the teams were running smoothly. Although some members felt that they had not achieved any lasting changes in local health care, it was generally agreed that the population's immediate medical needs had been met at a time when those needs were greatest. In his report to the DEA, Sydney Sunderland concurred that achieving major change through the education of Vietnamese medical personnel would be almost impossible in the short term:

> . . . though some staff and students will be receptive to new ideas and change . . . these represent only a small minority. By far the majority will continue to resist our system of medical education and training, this opposition being deeply and firmly rooted in tradition and aggravated by a language barrier which allows no room for useful dialogue and discussion. I believe that enthusiastic and well-meaning Australians often underestimate the magnitude of those forces which combine to defeat our task as teachers.[72]

Vung Tau team administrator in 1969, Bill Townsend, believed that the teams suffered from a lack of clear objectives, and Sunderland agreed, reporting that 'though the emphasis on surgery remains, too many splinter groups in non-surgical fields have appeared to complicate our programmes and to offend the Vietnamese'.[73] Because some team members were the leaders of their field in Australia, they felt a natural desire to extend their expertise to the Vietnamese. However, their efforts to effect lasting changes were inevitably disappointed. The teams had their greatest success in the modest sphere for which they were originally intended, the basic provision of surgical services.

As well as clarifying the objectives for prospective surgical teams in Vietnam, Sunderland's report commented on the future of the team in Vung Tau. As in Long Xuyen, Sunderland felt that the declining workload and increased number of local civilian doctors there meant that the team was no longer needed. He recommended a gradual phasing-out, to be completed by the end of 1969, with all future medical aid to be concentrated at Bien Hoa. As a result of these recommendations, embassy staff in Saigon held discussions with team members and a strategy for the team withdrawal was established. It was decided that the team would leave for good by the end of June, with a staff of one surgeon, a physician, a radiographer, two nurses and an administrative officer to finalise the withdrawal in the last six weeks.[74]

News of the withdrawal was generally greeted with disappointment by Vung Tau team members. Bill Townsend did not agree with the suggestion that Vietnamese medical staff would be able to carry the load by themselves. He was also disappointed that team members had not been consulted by the Sunderland–Boxall team. Several members felt there was still much work to be done, and they were left with a sense of unfinished business. Bill echoed the feelings of others in expressing doubt about how the hospital would continue in their absence:

It was up to this Dr Lam how they managed. And he'd done very well out of us. And we certainly wouldn't be replaced but maybe . . . they'd have to organise themselves a little better.[75]

As part of the last group remaining in Vung Tau, Bill found the scaling back and final withdrawal a sad process: 'gradually there were more and more people going. And the servants were always very upset when people left and there'd be tears and little presents given out, and fare-wells.'[76] He did not feel ready to leave and indeed was one of the last to do so, clearing out the team residence and returning team vehicles to the embassy in Saigon. His term as administrator ended on 14 July.

There is no doubt that the surgical teams in Vung Tau and Ba Ria achieved a great deal. Men, women and children disfigured by facial deformities, suffering from horrific diseases such as tetanus and plague, or ill with cancers, goitres or ruptured appendixes benefited greatly from the expert care they received from the teams' surgeons, nurses and other personnel. As well, the teams' close links with the Australian Army and its MEDCAP programs meant that their expertise was made available to more people within the province than had ever had access to such care. Undoubtedly teams cultivated close links with Australian and American forces in order to obtain the goods and services they needed to survive, but they repaid the favour by providing surgical assistance for allied soldiers at the 36th Evacuation Hospital and at the 1st Australian Field Hospital.[77] Some team members undoubtedly had high ambitions and were unable to fulfil their wishes of establishing province-wide immuni-sation programs or formal teaching for Vietnamese doctors and nurses. Despite these disappointments, most were proud of their service. Gavan O'Connor's philosophical conclusion reflected the satisfaction most team members felt about their Vung Tau experience:

I think it had long-lasting benefit to those who were directly affected, you know, people who are living now who otherwise would have died of fairly simple things like meningitis or loss of blood or burns or whatever ... For those people ... I'm not sure that you could expect much more than that really. I don't think we changed history or anything ... but we changed it for many people, probably hundreds of people. So in that sense it was worthwhile.[78]

Mixing it: interaction with the allies

When the surgical teams first went to Bien Hoa, it didn't take long for 1RAR to find out that there were fellow Australians in town. Peter Mangos fondly recalls the hospitality offered by the soldiers: 'We went to a lunch in the 1RAR Sergeants' Mess in Bien Hoa one day; they put on a beautiful lunch . . . seafood and everything.'[1] As well as having the team to Sunday lunch several times, Ian Ferguson reported, the infantrymen would service their cars a week before members were due to rotate back to Australia. The team was all the more grateful for this when the battalion's mechanics found that the Holden had no oil in its differential case, and the Landrover had none in the differential or the gearbox.[2]

The first surgical team to work in Bien Hoa initially had to struggle without interpreters. Canny Coventry recalls how 1RAR's commander stepped into the breach:

> Colonel Preece got us one of the men from 1RAR who was on sick leave and he became one of our interpreters. And this little [Vietnamese] boy who was about ten years old became our other interpreter.[3]

Surgeon Cas McInnes also has affectionate memories of the Diggers:

They were great fellows; they didn't overstay their welcome. Our doors were always open to them and they would come across in their twos or threes. There was a fellow called Bruce Fox who we had known at the Alfred and I think at one stage he was their [regimental medical officer]. And he came over and stayed a night with us at one stage. We did get on pretty well with them.[4]

The personnel at 1ALSG also made the nurses especially welcome. Barbara Sutherland remembers the time

we stayed for a couple of days with the military people [at 1ALSG]. The colonel actually very kindly gave up his tent for a couple of nights so we could sleep in his tent, and two of us went over [to Vung Tau] at a time.[5]

There were occasions, however, when civilian nurses who visited the Australian Army field hospital felt that the Army nurses were less than welcoming. Jan Bell thought relations between Army and civilian nurses weren't very cordial—'stand-offish' was her term—because 'they were locked up [with a curfew] and we weren't. Although we were supposed to be locked up.'[6] Janet Brewster visited Vung Tau for a couple of days on a break from Long Xuyen in 1968, and says the atmosphere at 1AFH 'was rather strange. We preferred to be with the conscript guys [male nurses] because they did want to be there [in South Vietnam]'.[7]

Pat Warren agrees, saying, 'the civilian nurses had more personal freedom, and more freedom with what they could do with the patients. They could explore the town on foot, or get on aircraft to go somewhere.'[8] As well, she notes, the Army nurses might have underestimated the scale of their civilian counterparts' duties: 'The civilian nurses also had a much greater exposure to the effects of war on civilians than the

Army nurses ... the Army nurses were quite protected from that side of the war, [and] they wouldn't realise just how much the war affected the civilian population.'[9]

But relationships with other Australian units in Vung Tau were very good, as Jan Bell recalls:

> The RAAF had the best Mess. They had a wonderful Mess because they could fly food in from Butterworth . . . It was great. But also 17 Construction Squadron [Royal Australian Engineers] and some of the RAAF ground forces used to come and work at the hospital on their days off. Not with patients, but they'd come and build things. They'd maintain stuff. They'd keep our autoclaves going, they'd keep our generator going.[10]

The American military units also made life easier, Jan says:

> We used their commissaries to buy our food, the American commissaries, and the Australian Army guys gave us food as well. We used their PXs all the time as well but we certainly used them to keep things going at the hospital.[11]

Jan will never forget Anzac Day 1968. After a very interesting six months in country, she and the rest of the surgical team from Vung Tau were invited to the Australian logistics base:

> We all went down to 1ALSG to the dawn service . . . We were on the chopper pad and all the guys were drawn up in a U shape and they all had their weapons. It was fascinating . . . the sun rising behind them over the South China Sea, and the lone bugler. That to me was quite the most extraordinary thing . . . I had been to dawn services of course, but this was just amazing.[12]

Jan's friend and colleague Sue Quinn was also there. 'It was the real thing,' she says.

Betty Lockwood spent time in Vung Tau during her tour in Bien Hoa in 1970 and visited the Australian base, but most of her interactions in the town seemed to be with the American nurses. Her focus was on socialising, 'having a barbecue, and a sail in the lovely warm sea.'[13]

The Americans

With vastly more troops, matériel, machinery and political commitment, the Americans were the mainstay not only of the war effort as a whole but of the civilian surgical teams. Bob Gray believed that without the support of the US military, things in Bien Hoa would have been quite difficult:

> We got our support from the Alfred [Hospital]. 1RAR supported us ... [but] the Yanks were tremendous; when they knew we were short of blood, a lot of the American soldiers came over and voluntarily gave blood ... I was impressed with the way they handled civilians over there. Sometimes some of their surgeons would come over and help us out when we had difficult problems because they had the facilities we didn't have, and they would bring the facilities with them.[14]

Paul Large arrived in Bien Hoa just as the Australian soldiers of 1RAR were leaving. The vacuum of support they left was soon filled:

> The American 93rd Evacuation Hospital people were very helpful to us. In 1969 [on his second tour] we were having problems getting the Vietnamese people to donate blood. That changed eventually. But we used to get groups of Americans to come over and give blood; they were very

generous. The effort supporting the Vietnamese community was enormous through CORDS and USAID. They
were terrific; they put endless effort and time and money
in.[15]

As well as the 93rd Evacuation Hospital, the 3rd Surgical Hospital,
the 44th Signals Battalion and the USAF 3rd Security (Air) Police
Squadron in Bien Hoa provided support. And the USAF 90th Tactical
Fighter Squadron made the whole Bien Hoa team honorary members.

In Maureen Spicer's view:

It would be fair to say that without the support of the Americans we could not have achieved what we did. At times they
kept the teams in food and certainly in surgical supplies. Later
on, they even supplied rat-catching cages and tested the rats
for plague—the results were mostly positive.[16]

Surgeon Don Sidey also found the Americans extraordinarily generous,
giving support with no strings attached. Their relationships with the
Australians 'centred around grog', he says with a chuckle:

On the whole, I think we got on with the Americans very
well, but their system of medical records and triage and all
that sort of thing was quite different from ours . . . they had
more facilities, of course, they always have had more. The
funny thing I remember is the American Red Cross, who
when welcoming [receiving] American casualties gave them
two things: doughnuts and a dressing gown.[17]

Betty Lockwood never really took to Vietnamese food, so she jumped at
any chance to visit the American base in Bien Hoa and 'have their great
big steaks and salads and cook-outs'.[18]

Occasionally the nursing sisters would date American servicemen, but only a few such relationships ended in marriage. Wendy Jobberns explains:

> . . . it was just nice to have a break from your work and everything . . . to have the companionship of the opposite sex, because there was no way you'd be having a relationship with any of the men in your own team.[19]

Betty Lockwood readily admits that the girls on her team were 'party animals', but says they never played harder than they worked. Visiting the American base was not without risk, however:

> I used to go to Mass every Sunday, to try and cleanse my soul or something. We were at Mass one day, at the [US] air base, and the next thing the odd rocket lobbed over and everybody just dived underneath the pews. I thought, my God, it would be typical—me to meet the Almighty here in His church. Very unfair, I thought that was.[20]

On a visit to the enormous American hospital in Long Binh, on the outskirts of Bien Hoa, Gavan O'Connor glimpsed the scale of the US operation—and sacrifice. The 24th Evacuation Hospital, which specialised in neurosurgery, had 320 beds. Of 15,135 patients (all military personnel) admitted in 1969, 302 died. O'Connor remembers that:

> I . . . was a bit distressed at what I saw there, particularly . . . There was this ward of about thirty or forty guys with head injuries . . . and this hospital only held people who were going to be [in country] less than twelve days . . . And then they were shipped out to Japan. And I remember just seeing all

these . . . fellows, comatose with head injuries and I thought, God, this is only twelve days' supply.[21]

During Robyn Anderson's tour in Bien Hoa in 1969, a dead baby was brought in with the large black nodes in the groin that indicated bubonic plague. When Robyn asked the hospital pharmacy for the drug chloramphenicol to vaccinate the staff, she was told that supplies would take at least three months to arrive. Without hesitation,

> I went to the Americans and said, 'We've got a plague outbreak.' And I had more chloramphenicol—I could have swum in the chloramphenicol . . . and I remember that on that particular occasion they said, 'Is there anything else you want?' And at that time all our surgeons had size seven-and-a-half hands and I said, 'Yes. We need gloves. We need seven-and-a-half gloves. We're desperate for them.' He said, 'Oh, well, we'll bring you some stuff down . . . anything else?' I said, 'Yes, I've got to get some blood.' And he said, 'Oh, I'll bring you some stuff this afternoon.' And they arrived with a two-and-a-half-tonne truck full of medical equipment.[22]

Cas McInnes met many Americans while working at Bien Hoa. Occasionally Cas would have to brave the road trip into Saigon for supplies. Just driving on Highway 1 without getting into trouble was a challenge in itself:

> . . . We had a Holden and one of the cooks used to act as a driver. Sometimes he wasn't available and we had to drive ourselves in, but it was a dangerous road between Bien Hoa and Saigon. I mean, the Americans used to go in and they would have a tank up the front and a tank up the back and all

that sort of thing. We were told, 'Don't stop, don't get out and keep moving,' so that was always a bit of a worry, but nothing ever happened to us.

The Americans at the 93rd Evacuation Hospital [in Bien Hoa] were very good to us and sometimes gave us equipment or some antibiotics . . . We got in touch with two of their doctors . . . they were very good, young, keen and enthusiastic, and they would sometimes come over with a whole lot of sutures or something. In fact, they gave us a [Special Forces] green beret each as a souvenir, and I have still got mine.[23]

The Australian embassy staff found it difficult supporting the surgical team efforts around the country. They were often able to provide little more than consular support, apart from the trickle of supplies that came through the Departments of Health and External/Foreign Affairs. It was probably the worst aspect of the program. Surgeon Paul Large comments on the teams' dependence on the Americans:

[If] we suddenly had a lot of casualties, the Americans came to the rescue in the emergency. We formed lots of friendships; they were great people, and they were happy to assist in any way, and often went out of their way to do it. And CORDS helped us quite a lot with some of our equipment shortages. Not often, but our instruments were not that fancy.[24]

US military doctors also provided some unconventional help at the Ben San leprosarium, as Maureen Spicer explains:

. . . the [Bien Hoa] nurses were in charge of delivering frozen placentas to the nuns [at Ben San]. The placentas were from the maternity section of the hospital, and had been bathed in antibiotics by the US Air Force public health doctors before being frozen and then kept in our food freezer at the house. The nuns at the leprosarium were convinced that when a piece of placenta was sewn on the abdomen of a person with leprosy—or, as we now term the disease, Hansen's disease— it would halt the progression of the disease.[25]

Surgeon Kendall Francis remembers one night when the American advisers came down for a party at the team's villa in Long Xuyen, and an issue of etiquette arose:

> . . . we asked them for their guns when they came in and they said, 'We never give our guns away.' And we said, 'Well, you can't come in. The party's here.' And in the end we were fortunate; we took their guns and put them away. Then they got into a few drinks and one fellow tried to drown another fellow in an ice bucket. It's hardly the way to go about things. So we were glad we'd confiscated their guns.[26]

The Iroquois helicopter revolutionised the way in which the Vietnam War was fought. It allowed troops to be inserted rapidly where they were needed and forever changed casualty evacuation from the battlefield. The US Army and Air Force had hundreds of choppers on the go in South Vietnam at any given time, and it was seldom a problem to hitch a ride to anywhere in the country, especially if you were a woman—or had something like a slouch hat to swap for the favour.

Maureen Spicer recalls being flown to various locations, saying, 'the Americans were extremely generous and choppered team members to most places, including an A [advisory team] camp, and Tay Ninh on the Cambodian border, where a Philippine civilian surgical team worked.'

The Americans also provided land transport, especially in Long Xuyen. They would take sections of the team out to small villages and hamlets around the delta to conduct outpatients clinics. Jenny Hunter formed some close relationships with the USAID personnel who came down to Long Xuyen in 1967: 'I got invited to a whole lot of village openings and things like that, and I'd go off on an Air America helicopter. So that was fun. And I did a few trips out with one guy in a vehicle visiting projects out in the country.'[27]

Nurse Marita Mulcahy, who worked in the Le Loi Hospital at Vung Tau, spoke glowingly of the immense support her team received from the Americans, especially the 36th Evacuation Hospital. This hospital also assisted the 1st Australian Field Hospital, particularly with pharmaceuticals and other supplies. The town was spread out, and the team's accommodation was quite a hike from the hospital. To help, Mulcahy says, 'Originally somebody stole or gave us jeeps. They just appeared, and they put red crosses on them . . . Then if you wanted a tyre, we would get in touch with the Americans, and they'd bring over a tyre.'[28]

Bill Townsend, the team administrator in Vung Tau in 1968–69, admits that without the Americans things would have been difficult. 'The Americans were very generous and they did have a huge warehouse, and they were really bankrolling the whole of the hospital services in Vietnam.' In fact, the Australian government did supply vehicles for the teams, but keeping them on the road was always a challenge. Townsend was frequently across at the 36th Evacuation Hospital picking up stores, and sometimes the Australians' mail, which would be delivered to the base. He also picked up blood, which always seemed to be in short supply.[29]

In 1972, as the Americans began scaling back their hospital work as well as their military effort, the Australians in the Bien Hoa Hospital had more contact with the local Americans, as surgeon Jim Ellis recalls:

Some of the American sisters came over to look at the work
we were doing. Because at one time we were doing much

more work than the nearby American hospital. They were downgrading and we were catching all the trade.[30]

Socialising

Jenny Hunter, who served in Long Xuyen and Bien Hoa, saw both kinds of socialising: the official and the unofficial. She thought the diplomatic type was a waste of time:

> [The bureaucrats] were not at all interested. We would get marched out if there was something big or for an Australia Day party, but that's diplomatic life. [The diplomats] were not interested in the work we were doing. They didn't understand the work we were doing or why we were doing it or how we did it or anything like that.[31]

Unofficially, the Australians frequently got together with the Americans who gave them so much help. Keeping the relationship cordial was important to the teams' survival (especially in Bien Hoa), so they often felt obliged to offer hospitality. Some of the nurses thought this was 'enforced' socialising. But surgeon David Brownbill says he saw no signs of enforced pairing up, despite the huge disparity in numbers between women and men:

> . . . the [team] leaders, in our case Paul [Large]—it was an unwritten rule—would not allow nurses to go out with males like myself. You were a team; there was no fraternisation of that sort. And the girls were not to go out one to one with the Americans; they could be there, but we as a team were [there] together. The team provided a lot of protection for those girls.[32]

But Dot Angell was one who resented having to party when she wasn't in the mood just to keep in good with the Americans:

> ... in one of my letters to my sister I describe it as almost like 'white slavery'. After sixteen hours in the hospital you'd get back to the house and it would be full of Americans waiting to party. We'd be expected to smile and all that sort of thing, because they might fix the tap in the scrub-up room, or they might get some supplies for us. There was one evening when I was relaxing in the kitchen doing some cooking. And this American came to the door and said, 'Where's your leader?' and I said, 'He's upstairs'. So off he went and the next minute I hear this absolute raging, roaring Professor [Hugh Dudley] and this scuffle down the stairs and the professor has got this American by the scruff of his neck and seat of his pants and threw him out. I asked, 'What on earth is going on?' He said, 'Do you know what he wanted?' and I said, 'No'. He said, 'He came upstairs and said, "I've got the drugs, you've got the girls, let's do a swap." He was serious!'[33]

Sister Suzie MacFarlane saw the socialising as part of the team's quasi-diplomatic role:

> ... it was all PR stuff. And [visitors] would come in and have a beer with the guys or the girls or whoever was there. And have a chat. And they'd be people who might help us with supplies and things. And then they'd say, 'We're having a dinner. Would you like to come?' And you had to say yes. And of course it was expected that the girls would go too. I mean, it was fun and really there wasn't ever a feeling of 'Oh, I don't feel comfortable'. Because we always had these really nice guys [the Australian doctors] who looked after us.[34]

Beth Scott also understood the need to maintain relationships, especially when scrounging for stores, but says there were times when the Americans would descend on the team house in Bien Hoa and

> ... the scroungers met them and they would bring them to the Mess and because we were the only round-eyes [Caucasians] within cooee, the Mess was like bees to a honey pot ... socially we had a lot to do with the American servicemen because we had Australian females, single females.[35]

Margaret Bolton, who served in Bien Hoa, didn't see the socialising as 'enforced'. She thinks the Americans liked coming to the Australian team house to mix with Caucasian women. Josephine Howard thinks New Zealand roast lamb might also have had something to do with it. That was the usual 'thank you' to the American engineering unit that helped with providing water and doing repairs. Jill Storch agrees that 'they didn't really want anything in return. They just wanted company most of the time ... some of them would try it on, but it was really company that they wanted. They just wanted somebody to talk to.'[36] Joan Rose says, 'I don't ever remember being treated in an inappropriate kind of way.'[37] Pathologist Berenice Dawson, who formed attachments to several US servicemen, says, 'You became pretty close friends, and there were times when these guys would just want to sit and talk to you. They were either homesick or frightened or whatever.'[38]

Team leaders had a big impact on the way their groups interacted with outsiders. Though the stricter ones had no problem on their watch, John Scott observed the effect of poor and negligent leadership: 'There didn't seem to be any rules at all really for us,' he recalls. 'The blokes [Americans] used to come and sleep with [nurses] in their rooms.'[39]

Bob Gray says the presence of women on the Bien Hoa team and their proximity to the air base sometimes seemed to affect flight paths:

We were protective 'brothers' because the Yanks were hanging around like vultures ... [The nurses] used to sunbake on the rooftop balcony, and we often wondered why these bloody helicopters were always flying overhead. I thought, 'Gee there's a lot of activity around the place!' The others said, 'Don't be silly.'[40]

But the Americans' appreciation of the Australian nurses wasn't solely aesthetic. Barbara Buscombe, who served in Vung Tau and Ba Ria, recalls working with the Americans at provincial refugee camps: 'The American doctors loved it when the Australian nurses went there because we could do more—not that we did much—but we could do more [than American nurses] as far as practical experience [was concerned].'[41]

'A bit cushy'

While it would be fatuous to compare the work done or the results achieved by the various teams, even their members acknowledged that they operated in starkly different settings. Bien Hoa and Long Xuyen were as different as it was possible for two hospitals in South Vietnam to be. Bien Hoa was in the middle of a major provincial city, next to a huge air base teeming with tens of thousands of people. Firefights were a daily occurrence in and around the town. Long Xuyen was in a remote rural area, and most of the provincial population supported the South Vietnamese government. On the other hand, Long Xuyen had limited logistical support, and its supply lines were long. Some Bien Hoa veterans referred to Long Xuyen as the 'country club',[42] but for the team in Long Xuyen there were more than enough challenges, especially during the wet season. Not only did they have swollen rivers quite close to their quarters to deal with, but when the waters subsided they were often up to their necks in snakes. The teams exchanged personnel to give them a break and a look at the way their counterparts worked. Barbara Sutherland says, 'We often used to swap our doctors, particularly specialists . . . they used to come down to us for a week and we'd send a doctor up to them for a week.'[43] Plastic surgeons' success with repairing cleft lips and palates made them much in demand throughout the Australian area of operations. After the 1968 Tet Offensive, some Long Xuyen personnel were sent to work in Bien Hoa for a period of three or four weeks. Janet Brewster explains:

> . . . the government decided we really were too sheltered, too isolated to have the whole team at Long Xuyen, so they sent Clive [Bond], Beryl [Nicholls] and myself. And one of the doctors, I think . . . It was more intense [work] . . . more war related.[44]

Suzie MacFarlane made the reverse trip, visiting Long Xuyen from Bien Hoa in December 1966 and finding it 'a bit cushy':

> I went with John Snell, who was the plastic surgeon, and Victor Brown, the anaesthetist. And John was going to do work there. I wasn't supposed to do work . . . because they didn't need anyone to work. They didn't reciprocate . . . They didn't think going to Bien Hoa would be much fun. Whereas for us, going to Long Xuyen was nice. And it really was a little holiday.[45]

The Vietnamese

Robyn Anderson was one nurse who took pains to involve her Vietnamese counterparts—in her case, from the hard-pressed recovery ward—in the Australians' social events. Intercultural bonding, she felt, could only improve teamwork on the job.

> It was important to invite the nucleus of the people at the hospital that we worked with. We had our two nurse anaesthetists

who did an absolutely amazing job. They anaesthetised for almost everything that was done. We had two nurses in the recovery room, one of whom was fantastic: Miss Diep. She used do anything and everything. She was like us. She was up to her elbows in it.[46]

In Long Xuyen, the Australians had more interaction with South Vietnamese than with Americans, because there was no large allied facility close by. Barbara Sutherland says this involved:

. . . a lot of formal socialising . . . the province chief would put on something, and then the head of medicine at the hospital would have a reception for us, and this sort of thing. And we were all expected to attend. It was virtually demanded of us that we attend. And sometimes it was difficult at the end of a working day. But it was almost part of our duties.[47]

Leaving Bien Hoa in 1972, team leader Paul Large reported that 'social contact with the hosts [Vietnamese] is important and no opportunity should be missed to make them in the interests of cooperation at all levels.'[48]

The Vietnamese in return showed a hospitality towards the Australian surgical teams that, given the hardship they had lived under for so long, was humbling. Dr Tho, the Médecin Chef at Bien Hoa, had by late 1967 lost three homes destroyed by fighting since 1962.[49] But cultural and culinary differences sometimes made it difficult to show the right degree of enthusiasm. Helen Banff recalls that on her first night in Bien Hoa in 1971

. . . the team members were invited to the [Vietnamese] medical superintendent's house for dinner. We all arrived and the dining room was very dimly lit, and we were welcomed, and we were served hot beer with ice added, and a variety of local food. The room seemed to me at the time to be crowded with people and dogs. When we sat down at the table—we weren't there for long—I had a shocking itch up and down my legs, and when I noticed other people scratching I discreetly had a peep under the table, and my legs were covered in fleas. I've never seen so many fleas, they were everywhere. Naturally, we couldn't finish our meal quickly enough.[50]

Robyn Anderson looked after a severely injured woman who turned out to be a Montagnard princess. She was later the guest of honour at a feast held in the grounds of the hospital. The 'King' insisted that Anderson eat first. She dipped her hand into the ceremonial bowl looking for something small to swallow:

I put my fingers in and I could feel little long things and little round fat things . . . everybody was watching me—and I knew that whatever happened I couldn't vomit. And I picked up the little long thing and I lifted it out of the bowl, and it was a neonatal mouse without any fur on it. It had been pickled in honey, and I thought, there is no way I can eat this, but I knew I had to. So I literally swallowed it like a big pill. I could feel its tongue run over the back of my throat as I swallowed it—there was no way I could crunch it. I could no more put my teeth into it than fly out the window . . . [I was] hoping I wouldn't obstruct on the bloody thing, and then I just sat there thinking, 'Please don't vomit, don't make a fool of yourself, don't vomit, don't vomit,' and I just smiled.[51]

Von Clinch was not normally adept with her chopsticks, but one event saw her rise to the occasion:

. . . we went out to dinner with some of the Vietnamese from the hospital to a local restaurant. And we're sitting around having our meal and they would give the chicken's head to the honoured guests. And the chicken head has the beak and the eyes in situ. Never have I been so adept with my chopsticks as I was then. So I waited for no one to be looking, and out the window it went.[52]

Surgeon Don Sidey found his two tours gave him an insight into another culture he had never been aware of:

I learnt a lot of things: I learnt to respect and like the Vietnamese people of whom I had previously had no experience whatsoever. Until I went to Vietnam, I really didn't know much about it, in common with most other people that I knew. But that stimulated my interest and I became extremely interested in Vietnam. I like them and I get on well with them. I also got a great liking for their arts and crafts and the things that they do so beautifully. I also got a liking for their food; I think Vietnamese cooking is superb.[53]

Janet Brewster recalled many social activities during her 1967–68 tour at Long Xuyen. At the Moon Festival, 'we were all invited to attend with them and that was quite a great honour. They had moon cakes, and the men had to eat duck's blood.'[54]

Another difference at Long Xuyen was the teaching of English by the nursing staff. There was no shortage of willing students. Barbara Sutherland recalls that the demand was sometimes overwhelming:

We went to the local high school and we had an American textbook, which made it very difficult for us. They were learning sort of American-cum-Australian English . . . But when we first went, they were teaching three nights a week. Now that became far too much for us on top of [our work], so we cut it down to once a week.[55]

Joan Rose was unable to teach her assistant anything new about her specialty, radiography, on the antiquated machines they were using, but she too became involved in teaching English. 'I guess it actually made you feel really humble that there they wanted to practise English with you, and in some aspects you probably knew less about English than they did.'[56]

Elaine Ray was surprised that there were staff to do her laundry in Bien Hoa, and she and the other nurses on the team became quite friendly with the housemaids and cooks and the Vietnamese nurses in the wards. When one nurse got married in Saigon, 'three or four of us went up to her wedding.'[57]

Putting a continuous strain on relations was the endless problem of petty (and not-so-petty) theft. The Vietnamese staff had access to all areas of the hospitals, and to the vacant team accommodation during the day, so rightly or wrongly, they were always the immediate suspects. Occasionally thieves on the staff were identified and sacked. The stealing was seen as nothing personal: times were tough and everyone had to make ends meet. But reactions weren't quite so muted when essential drugs disappeared from the shelves. After such thefts, Von Clinch recalls:

You could get [the stolen items] on the black market for money. I met a sergeant of the [US] Air Force police at the [Post Exchange] in Bien Hoa. And he was very keen to come and help us. So he came and helped us ... I'd give anything we could barter to him and he'd go off and he'd have a list of what we needed: X-ray fixer and suture scissors and all this sort of thing, and get them with the goods I'd got to barter with.[58]

Frustrations also arose from cultural misunderstandings. At times the Australians would be perplexed by Vietnamese reactions. 'Where we would cry at something sad [like a death], they would laugh,' Aileen Monck recalls. 'And we never could quite understand that.'[59] Peter Last learned much later that the Vietnamese predilection to laugh at lameness or deformity 'was a manifestation of insecurity and embarrassment.'[60] But overall, their Vietnamese hosts 'were very kind to us,' Jill Storch says. 'Very kind . . . they would spend a week's pay or a month's pay just to give us a function.'[61]

When Sir Edward 'Weary' Dunlop took over as team leader in Bien Hoa, he wrote of the 'real joy with which [the Vietnamese staff] greet members of the team who return for further tours of duty'. He added, 'Their pleasure in welcoming back old friends like Hugh Dudley, Paul Large, Barb Phillips and Judy McCormack is utterly spontaneous and warm.'[62]

Visitors

Doug Tracy, who was at Vung Tau in late 1966, says the Americans at the time were supporting the South Vietnamese medical system to the tune of about US$150 million a year. But there were also about fifty foreign medical teams in the country. 'We met a British team, Dutch team, New Zealand,' but it was a strain, especially if their reason for visiting Vung Tau was a seaside break:

> . . . we were trying to get work done and there were visitors coming through all the time and you had to sort of set aside time and show them around . . . And then they were interested in recreation, you know, they wanted to knock off a few beers and things like that so it was a disruption to our work.[63]

Bien Hoa and Vung Tau were constantly hosting visitors. Long Xuyen had its share, but the relative isolation kept the numbers manageable.

Medical training

When the Australian teams were first mooted, it was thought that there might be an opportunity for them to educate Vietnamese medical staff, especially nurses. The leader of the second Alfred team, Ian Ferguson, went into the major teaching hospital in Saigon, Cho Ray. After speaking with the Médecin Chef and an orthopaedic surgeon, Ferguson agreed that the Australians would supply a lecturer every Tuesday between 9.30 and 10.30 a.m. Sadly, this rarely happened, in part owing to the heavy workload in Bien Hoa Hospital. However, Mervyn Smith and other senior surgeons did deliver lectures at Saigon University, to which Cho Ray Hospital was linked.

Peter Last says lecturing to the medical students was 'my first experience of sentence-by-sentence translation'. Apart from the tediousness of delivering material in that way, 'it was interesting because they took all their notes in French'. And though he didn't speak French himself, he could see 'they were a very enthusiastic and attentive audience. I enjoyed those lectures immensely.'[64] The main reason Peter Last was lecturing was that as a physician he was less frantically busy than the surgeons, so could afford the travelling time to and from Saigon.

Surgeon Jim Ellis says some teaching also took place on the job. In Bien Hoa, for example,

> . . . we taught [the Vietnamese doctors] to do things like caesarean sections. I mean, here's [me,] an orthopaedic surgeon . . . teaching a Vietnamese obstetrician in a hospital that has as many births as Crown Street [Women's Hospital in Sydney] every year, 5000 a year, teaching him to do caesarean sections. And, once he sort of learned not to go at it like a bull at a gate, he could do it well.[65]

Tutoring the nurses also proved difficult. Not only was the workload too heavy to allow for systematic lectures other than in Long Xuyen, but the language and cultural barriers could be formidable. Helen Banff recalls that in Bien Hoa:

> What impression I made is questionable. I lectured the local nurses, but our cultural differences were great, and I believe even though we became quite fond of each other, the gap remained unbridged. But I don't believe the things that I endeavoured to teach them would have remained with them after I left. For instance, I could spend hours, and sometimes days, on one child, or several patients, only to find if I went away for a cup of tea, or lunch, or went home to sleep, the intravenous lines would be removed from my sick patients, and placed into the veins of locals. The reason they did this was because the locals were 'tired' . . . One day I came back and found a whole room, I'd say about twelve people, perfectly healthy, sitting up having intravenous therapy with drugs—all different kinds—and having a party and playing cards while they were all sitting there having their intravenouses. I said, 'What on earth is going on?' 'Oh, we're all tired.' I was upset and furious. I walked out and went for a quick walk around the block but there was nothing really that I could do about it. The children were dying but nobody seemed to really care what was happening.[66]

In his final report, in December 1972, Paul Large wrote, in language as diplomatic as he could muster, 'Enthusiasm should not be allowed to outrun capacity.' Six years earlier, he had said training could be undertaken if proper planning were done and sufficient posts made available, but he diplomatically suggested that to do so might give the impression that the allies thought Vietnamese schools 'inadequate— which they are not'. The only time in the teams' seven years in Bien

Hoa that junior medical officers were 'sent to the hospital in sufficient numbers to be effective', Large wrote, was at the end, in 1972, a case of too little too late.[67]

While some training was done where possible (and mainly nursing training in Long Xuyen), the simple fact was that the case-load was so heavy and resources so limited that a formal teaching program in either surgical techniques and procedures or intensive nursing care was out of the question.[68]

7

Staying sane

Living in a war zone, far from family and friends, was stressful for the teams. Those with young families at home missed them, while others felt the strain of their families' concern for their welfare. The fact that there was no 'front line' in Vietnam and that the pace of work was relentless only added to the stress. It often took considerable effort to keep exhaustion, anxiety and depression at bay.

Paul Large argued for tours of no longer than six months, separated by breaks of at least three to six months, mainly for health and morale reasons. He thought that the pressure of work, together with 'isolation, restrictions and a confined life', led to a condition he called 'Vietnam happy'. It was characterised by 'irritability, deterioration in manner, abruptness in dealing with people, loss of sympathy for patients—in fact a general falling off of standards of practice and behaviour'. Large believed the victims suffered from persistent 'strain and anxiety', irregular sleep, and the constant background of the war. In short, they were exposed to traumatic stress.[1]

In Australian military parlance the condition is unofficially referred to as 'going troppo'. To overcome it, commanders in Vietnam mandated in-country R and C (rest and convalescence), or out-of-country R and R (rest and recuperation) leave to provide a release from the pressures of combat, and allow troops to recharge their batteries and regain their sense of perspective. The civilian surgical teams did a version of this by allowing their members to travel elsewhere in Vietnam to sightsee and relax. Most team leaders saw such leave as essential. They also came up with a variety of ways, sometimes involving medication (prescription and otherwise), to keep their charges on an even keel. Thanks in part to this watchfulness, very few of the team members left prematurely, and only one or two were asked to leave or resign from a team.[2] Nursing sister Josephine Howard believes the teams in Bien Hoa were more or less rostered to take breaks.[3]

Team members also devised their own 'stay sane' methods. Peter Mangos recalled that in Bien Hoa:

> We were looked after by people around us; sometimes by Australians, mostly by Americans because there were so many of them. We were invited to so many different camps to do things and really we had a great social life. So we worked hard and we played hard, and we drank hard. There was always a bit of a party going on every night at the house, and various people would call in.[4]

As well as being given shopping concessions in the Americans' PX and commissary system, the Australians were free to visit US officer and non-commissioned officer clubs, which had good food and swimming pools. Some of the Bien Hoa nurses were reluctant to swim, however, because they felt less than comfortable in bathing suits surrounded by crowds of lonely men.[5]

Paul Large recalls that:

> . . . our Mess was friendly, and we always had a few Americans over checking out our pretty nurses. The Americans at the evacuation hospitals would always have us over. In Bien Hoa [air] base itself there was a swimming pool, which was

like swimming in warm treacle. If someone had a day off they could go into Saigon, and we could [also] get down to Vung Tau. So we were able to unwind, and I made sure that people got away. There were driving trips to Saigon, but the road to Vung Tau was not secure, so people went by chopper, as the Americans were very kind.[6]

Betty Lockwood thought the socialising was a therapy of sorts for working experiences that could be 'dreadful' and 'horrendous':

... that's probably why we all partied so hard, I know I did anyway ... I think that was your coping mechanism ... I think probably we all coped that way—even the docs. They were into the partying. I think that's basically how you did [cope].[7]

In their time off from performing several hundred operations a month, anaesthetist Bob Gray recalls that he and his colleagues:

... played darts and well, we grogged a bit ... you just had to have a few drinks. We played tennis with the Yanks, we went for swims at the pool the Yanks had in Bien Hoa base ... the CO of the American unit used to say it was good for the men's morale when the girls dived in, and I reckon it was good for his [morale] the way he responded, too! Sometimes I would take an interpreter and go for a drive around the countryside and sightsee ... I went on a few chopper flights; the Yanks were very good, they took us to Tay Ninh and places like that, and we saw some [people from] the other countries that had teams.[8]

Having been up to his elbows in gore all day, Cas McInnes often didn't feel like partying. He says, 'We didn't go out much at night because there wasn't a lot to do at night . . . we played plenty of games and sang songs. It sounds silly now, but that's what we did.'[9]

Suzie MacFarlane says dancing helped:

I think the way we de-stressed in the house was [that] we had lots of impromptu parties. I got some music sent out, some really good reels of music, and we'd just say, 'Let's have a bit of a party.' And we'd put on the Beatles or whatever and we'd just dance. And I think that was quite important . . . because there were a lot of parties that were sort of for the Vietnamese and they were more formal. But this was just our own way of letting off a bit of steam, I think. We were also very [much] into photography . . . everybody had cameras and everybody was taking photos. Everybody compared their photos. And I did a lot of letter writing too, so I think that was another way of debriefing myself.[10]

Getting away

Taking leave breaks outside Vietnam was a common pressure-release device. Janet Brewster, who served in Long Xuyen, met her sister in Hong Kong and took her ten-day R and R period in Japan.[11] Marita Mulcahy, from Vung Tau, went to Cambodia and then Hong Kong on her leave.[12] Frances Byak jumped on a plane in Bien Hoa and headed off with a nurse friend to Hong Kong and Bangkok.[13] Even on short breaks, theatre nurse Jill Storch managed to visit neighbouring Cambodia: 'I went to Phnom Penh for a weekend once . . . More buddhas than you could poke a stick at.'[14]

Those too busy to escape the country would sometimes travel to another city in Vietnam. Most days, says Don Sidey, 'you were pretty tired, you went back [to the house], had dinner and a few drinks and you tended to just go to bed and wait for the next day.'

Weekend duty also kept people close to the base. 'You were on full call one weekend and then second call the next weekend, so you didn't go away because it was very likely that you would be needed.' But every third weekend was completely free:

> We went to a particular hotel in Saigon. I think it was the Caravelle. Anyway, that was ... where we had a place more or less segregated for us. The Americans were very good to us ... I went up to all sorts of places; the Americans took us in helicopters and whatever and we went all over the place, and I enjoyed that very much indeed.[15]

The nursing sisters also had an on-call roster, as Von Clinch explains:

> ... we were on call every second night and we assisted with operating or whatever needed to be done. And the other night you usually ended up going to somewhere to represent the team. And you got one weekend in three off and you tried to get away if you could.[16]

One weekend when Suzie MacFarlane was rostered off, she was taken down to the seaside at Vung Tau, which she and her fellow nurses saw as 'like going away on a holiday.'[17] After a month working flat out at Bien Hoa in 1967, Dot Angell was given some badly needed R and C leave. After a flight in an Air America Beechcraft, she spent four days during the Tet holiday lazing in the sun at Vung Tau. She wrote home, 'It's unbelievable that such a place should exist in the middle of a war-torn country ... [it] is a dilapidated version of Cannes or Nice on the Riviera.' Dot lamented the sight of teenage Vietnamese bar girls, and wondered what the fate of their bastard half-caste children would be after the war.[18] Nurse Frances Byak's fondest memory of a daytrip to Vung Tau was of dining on lobster; the sumptuous meal cost her her entire daily allowance of $8.[19]

After visiting the former French hillside retreat of Dalat, some 400 kilometres from Saigon, team leader Graeme Grove arranged for his team to rotate through the area on their mid-tour R and C breaks. The beautiful resort town had swimming and recreational facilities that had been kept up despite the war. In 1967, Josephine Howard and several of her fellow nurses from the Royal Adelaide Hospital team visited the military installation at Phan Rang, thirty-five kilometres south of the enormous naval base at Cam Ranh Bay, where RAAF Canberra jet bombers were based as part of the American 7th Air Force.[20]

Carmel Hurst, who was at Bien Hoa in 1967–68, recalls day-tripping the twenty-five kilometres to Saigon with her female interpreter: 'We'd go to the pictures and we'd have lunch somewhere, and then she and I would go into the bazaars and go shopping. And it doesn't matter who you're with, you know, women love to shop.' Carmel's group had great contacts with the nearby Americans, and she and the team were able to travel extensively on weekends off, going to Nha Trang, Dalat, Phuoc Tuy province and Vung Tau.[21]

One of Elaine Ray's trips to Vung Tau was made more exciting when 'we got shot at on the way'. After that adrenaline rush and then a swim in the South China Sea, Elaine's group turned around to see a group of Australian soldiers standing behind them, no doubt taking in the rare but stimulating sight of white women in swimsuits. 'They had a barbecue lunch organised so they fed us. And they also gave us cold drinks . . . so it was really nice.'[22]

Paul Large says with a chuckle that he went 'down to the rest camp at Long Xuyen for a couple of weeks'. He also visited Vung Tau, but 'I didn't swim in the South China Sea; I saw a sea snake and thought better of it.'[23]

'Rest camp' Long Xuyen might have seemed, but its location meant the staff there found it difficult to get away. Since the main air bases were too far away for helicopters to reach Long Xuyen easily, most air travel was by plane, often Air America (CIA) aircraft provided by USAID or US Civil Operations support teams. Still, says Barbara Sutherland,

> . . . we were fortunate in that [the authorities] did get us out of the area reasonably frequently. Like getting us to Saigon. We also went to Vung Tau . . . I only went on one occasion, but a couple of the nurses went to Vung Tau and worked for a few days at the [civilian] hospital there [usually] . . . with the help of the Americans, they were virtually our armed escort wherever we went.[24]

The Vietnamese provincial authorities were always welcoming towards the Long Xuyen teams, and many members took up their invitations. Barbara recalls:

> We played tennis . . . the province chief had a magnificent house, [with] a tennis court by the river. And he was extremely hospitable to us, and every Sunday we tried to [play]. Sunday was our only complete day off . . . the Americans flew a chaplain in every Sunday for a church service, and I was often part of that and we'd go out to the airport to pick up the chaplain, bring him in and then return him again. He used to do a 'milk run' around the delta every Sunday.[25]

Jenny Hunter says the American troops at the US advisers' compound would sometimes help with recreational travel, and, 'We were taken out by the US Navy a few times with people who had landing craft.'[26]

Dot Angell took a break at 'Vungers', leaving behind the constant clatter of helicopters and the roar of fighters and bombers:

> I went down to Vung Tau with three of the doctors for a weekend of R and R, so we thought, and we had five hours

on the beach, a delightful meal that night, and then it was so quiet that none of us could sleep.[27]

Gavan O'Connor broke the rules once and ventured across a river in Vung Tau to show his visiting wife the sights. As he climbed Nui Nho hill with Dolores, Gavan looked around and saw 'three little rocks one on top of the other, and I knew that was a Viet Cong signal for a mine'.[28]

Paediatrician Peter Last had some great contacts in Bien Hoa, and thanks largely to CORDS official John Vann and his pilot, he went to Vung Tau, Nui Dat, Long Xuyen and Nha Trang.

Mail

For anyone serving in a war zone, a letter from home is always a huge boost to morale. Most of the team members got into a regular letter-writing routine. Jenny Leak made a practice of sending something off almost every morning. Peter Last wrote a plethora of letters to his wife. For a short time Gavan O'Connor divided his work between Vung Tau and Bien Hoa, and despite the constant travel still found time to write 140 letters to his wife in his six-month tour in 1969. Radiographer Iain Brotchie sent many letters and parcels home from Bien Hoa and notes that nothing was ever censored.[29] The prime reason for that would have been that the Australians used diplomatic bags to send most of their mail home.

Suzie MacFarlane says:

All our mail went in the diplomatic bag. And it was very quick. I'm amazed how it went. We didn't seem to use the phone. Nobody phoned anybody. I think I had one phone call the whole time I was there. It just wasn't something you did. And any parcels that needed to be sent or received, the avenues for those seemed to be very good.[30]

Morale dropped when the Australian Postal Workers Union decided that it would not send mail to South Vietnam as part of its general strike for better pay and working conditions. Apart from this brief hold-up, mail in late 1968 seemed to take an inordinately long time to travel between Vietnam and Australia, a source of frustration for all concerned.

Joan Rose, on her first trip outside Australia, used her letters and photos

> . . . to try and share with my family . . . the experience I was having, because they were the people I could tell what I really thought about, what I really felt, what I saw and so on.[31]

Frances Byak says:

> I wrote all the time. We didn't phone at all, we just wrote letters. Everybody wrote to me and I wrote to everybody else . . . That was all we had to do, really, we didn't have to wash, iron or clean. So we went to work, went out or wrote letters . . . half a dozen letters a week at least.[32]

Bob Gray, who had left a wife and young children at home, says:

> It was bloody hard. I would take a series of slides of what I was doing and send them home to [my wife] and then write her a letter explaining all about the slides. I used to write to her four nights a week, I was very virtuous, honestly, my halo was showing when I came home! . . . that plus the slides kept her going.[33]

Because servicemen and -women with access to the PX system could buy very cheap alcohol (a forty-ounce bottle of gin cost about US$1.50

in 1971), many people sent liquor home in discarded 81-mm mortar round containers, into which a bottle fitted quite snugly. The problem was getting it through Customs, but Betty Lockwood found a solution. Accompanying one bottle she sent home was a note that read:

> Dear Mr Customs, this little bottle is for my dear, sick mother who needs it. She hadn't enough money to buy it herself and so I thought I might send it as I am unable to bring it home in my normal rations. If you feel in need of a nip or sip, be my guest, but please save her a drop.[34]

Lockwood says, 'I used to get letters by the tonne from Mum and the hospital board of management, and all the other nurses at Gumeracha [near Adelaide], they'd all write.' It made an enormous difference, she adds: 'The mail was . . . just so important and you'd see people, if they didn't get a letter when the mail came in, they were really crestfallen and found it pretty hard.'[35]

Don Sidey recalls the time when the mail stopped completely:

> Australian forces got out at the beginning of 1972 [the last combat troops left in March], leaving a skeleton behind. All our girls who stayed there for a year depended very much on the postal system . . . But the postal support went out, and the poor girls nearly went around the bend because they didn't get any mail for a month and morale sagged very badly then.[36]

Another popular form of correspondence was 'letter tapes': messages were recorded and played back on reel-to-reel tape recorders, which could be bought cheaply at US PXs and were highly sought after. Some American radio stations in South Vietnam served up large chunks of music uninterrupted to allow servicemen and -women to tape entire albums without a break.

Cas McInnes had been married for only six weeks when he went to Bien Hoa. 'It was tough,' he recalls,

> probably tougher on my wife, Anne, I think. It is usually the women who do it harder. It was a sort of an adventure for a fellow and there was always something to do, and we were kept busy the whole time. I did a lot of letter writing, and tapes had just come in. The [wives at home] got together and sent us a parcel every couple of weeks and there was always a tape there.[37]

Family members in Australia would gather at someone's house to record their messages, and when the tape arrived in Vietnam the whole team would rush to listen—though team members also used small personal recorders for more intimate messages.

Listening to 'letter tapes' together was part of the family solidarity within the teams, Von Clinch says:

> . . . the fun of it all was that [when] you got letters or tapes from home everyone would listen. The guys with young families, their drawings were up on the wall and all that sort of thing . . . which was just great. And if someone had a birthday, we made a little cake. And if we could get candles we had them on them and then they had to make a speech and we all clapped. And it was really great fun and really very, very much a family attitude. We're stuck here, we've got to make the best of it, let's do it together.[38]

Cas McInnes recalls that the team at Bien Hoa 'got mail I think two or three times a week and tapes', though 'we didn't have tapes to send back'.

Their colleagues in Australia would also stay in touch, he says: 'The Alfred hospital would send a tape every couple of weeks to the team members.'[39]

Party time

Whether or not you were being shot at, serving in Vietnam in any capacity was risky. There were no front lines, and most of the enemy did not wear a uniform. Bombings, indiscriminate rocket attacks, ambushes and murder were part and parcel of the war. Tension inevitably built up, and had to find an outlet. Sometimes it was in drinking. Says Suzie MacFarlane: 'We had this little bar in the end of the dining room and always after a big day's work we'd go up there and drink, and debrief about things.'[40] Jill Storch says matter-of-factly, 'Alcohol was a big crutch. Everybody drank. Very few people didn't drink.'[41] While the teams all indulged in 'self-medicating', no leader's report mentions alcohol problems, and most members interviewed say none were evident. Jill Storch recalls a cautionary arrangement in one Mess bar: 'all the drinks were kept in a lead-lined coffin because the ice didn't melt.'[42]

The team house usually doubled as a 'mess' and became the centre of socialising for off-duty team members. It also attracted visiting allied servicemen and -women, especially from the nearby Bien Hoa air base.

Some Australian surgeons and doctors in the Bien Hoa team admitted that they sometimes became a little upset when American pilots and other officers would walk into the team house and head straight for the nursing sisters without even a hello as they strode past. But there were other advantages to the intrusions, as John Scott explains:

> I remember in the week of Christmas/New Year, we had ten parties that we were invited to. We didn't make them all but we made quite a few. And they [the Americans] used to send a Chinook over and we'd all pile in and they'd fly us back home at night.[43]

And the partying was done with gusto, says Beth Scott: 'I tell you, it was mad at work and it was mad in the Mess. It was totally mad.' Her husband, John, adds, 'We had a huge social life. We had very cheap booze, from the PX. You could get French and German wine very cheaply.'[44]

The Brisbane-based Bien Hoa team that John Scott later served with had a quite different perspective from the Adelaide team. For a start, restrictions on travel around Saigon and Bien Hoa imposed after the Tet Offensive had been relaxed. As well, Beth Scott notes:

> . . . because the [Brisbane] team was younger, it wasn't as constrained because of the team leadership. The girls were pretty much allowed to do what they wanted to do. I mean they could take a scooter off and drive themselves out to the air base when they wanted to. They could go anywhere they wanted to on their own, which we were never allowed to do with the South Australian team, and I doubt that the Victorian teams would have been allowed to do [it]. I think as the time went on everybody got more and more out of touch with reality . . . socially it was, I mean it was hedonistic, really, with the Queensland team. It was way out of control.[45]

The Royal Brisbane team's twelve-month tour obviously took a toll on some members, Beth Scott adds: 'I mean, one of the girls had a praying mantis as a pet. She used to keep it in her top drawer. Now, if that's not, you know, kooky . . .'[46]

Marita Mulcahy recalled her time at Le Loi Hospital in Vung Tau:

> Socialising was pretty full on . . . we were young. I couldn't do it now . . . we used to have barbecues at our villa and they became very famous and very well known and everyone

wanted to go to the 'cook-out' that the Aussies had at the villa.[47]

Jan Bell, who served at Vung Tau in 1968, found that being able to go to the beach and mixing with Australian Army personnel helped her retain her sanity:

> We used to go to happy hour up at [1ALSG] in the Officers' Mess . . . [I] found it a bit stuffy after a while, so I started going to the Sergeants' Mess, and I got into trouble because we were deemed to be officers, and we weren't supposed to go to the Sergeants' Mess.[48]

It was at Vung Tau that Jan Bell and colleague Sue Quinn attended a concert party put on for the Australian troops. It was 'just before Tet', she recalls. The Australian Broadcasting Commission staged it, with Lorrae Desmond and Jim Gussey.[49]

Going to the beach was something the team members always looked forward to. Surgeon Jim Ellis gave the nurses a bamboo-and-cane coracle as a present when he left South Vietnam. Jan Bell recalls their adventures in the circular fishing boat:

> We'd get it out in the middle of the night . . . jeeps lined up on the headland beaming down on French Beach . . . trying to row a coracle. And it'd just go round and round and round and then it'd tip over. It was only supposed to take three people and we'd have about a dozen. And everyone would land on their heads in the surf . . . They were great fun times.[50]

Jenny Hunter went to Vung Tau for a weekend off from Long Xuyen and stayed with the Australians at the logistics base. It was a welcome break, but things weren't that cosy, as she explained:

... we didn't like [it] because we had to abide by their restrictions ... they were all clumping around in boots and fatigues, wearing guns, and we were pottering around in thongs and a light dress.[51]

Carmel Hurst spent a year in Bien Hoa in 1967–68, at the height of the war. She says, 'very often we were very busy and very stressed by what was happening to us. And we just used to get drunk, go to bed.'[52] But non-stop debauchery it was not. On many a night, team members would simply listen to music, play cards, or write letters home.

Black humour

Despite what many war movies and novels would have us believe, the experience of war is often filled with humour, though of a kind that to outsiders may seem black or grotesque. Amid the stresses, there was much absurdity, inanity and plain nonsense, which could seem intolerable one minute and hilarious the next. Bob Gray recalls an event that became known as 'Holt's Operation'. Harold Holt, the Australian prime minister, paid an official visit to the Australians in Bien Hoa in 1966. At the 1st Battalion, Royal Australian Regiment, the mess members had coached their Vietnamese barman in a special greeting:

> ... he was to say, 'Mr Prime Minister, *uc dai loi* number one Australian, how are they hanging?' [When he said this,] Holt begged his pardon, and he said, 'How are they hanging?' and Holt replied, 'My dear friend, I have been so busy I haven't had time to look.'[53]

Holt was then to visit the Bien Hoa Hospital, where Bob was the anaesthetist on duty, and the team were supposed to put on a surgical demonstration for him to show how they worked on a daily basis.

I think Holt was due to come about 2 o'clock, and at about 1 o'clock an accident victim came in, very seriously injured. We had no blood, and I had great difficulty in persuading Cas McInnes [the surgeon] and Canny [Coventry, theatre nurse] that in fact they were doing a post-mortem. So we stopped and the patient was dead. We had a meeting and [Ian Ferguson, the team leader] said, 'We better have a tic tac [warning] system and when Holt is coming then we can fly into action'. So we got an old bottle of worn-out blood and we put that on the far side of the table and drained it into a bucket, and we splashed a bit around so that it would look realistic. One of the tic tac fellows said, 'They're coming!' Fergy opened the door and said [to the visitors], 'I think they are quite worried about the patient's condition'. The poor bugger had been dead for an hour! And then off they went to visit somewhere else, and they seemed very happy and impressed with what they saw. We got back to the house quick smart because we were frightened that they would drink all of our grog because there were quite a number of them in the entourage; there were oodles of hangers on. We rushed back about twenty minutes later and they said, 'Ooh you were quick,' and we said, 'Oh yes, unfortunately he died very quickly'. And then we got stuck into it.[54]

Don Sidey worked with Edward 'Weary' Dunlop during his time at Bien Hoa and recalls, 'He was a party man; he would stay up all night drinking and then go straight into the operating room. We thought he had hollow legs.'[55]

Helen Banff said her Bien Hoa team's best outlet was 'laughter. There were three of us in particular, we could sit down and have a laugh and have a talk . . . we just made the best of each other's company and we survived.'[56]

8

Coming home

Leaving Vietnam was a time of mixed emotions for most surgical team members. Whether they were there for a long period or only a few months, the country and its people left a lasting impression. Close friendships that had formed between team members and their Vietnamese colleagues made it hard for many to say goodbye. For a number of people, though, sadness was mixed with relief at leaving a difficult and demanding working environment and an enervating climate. Most welcomed the prospect of returning to a calm and orderly hospital environment, and of seeing family and friends again.

The length of time team members had spent in Vietnam often coloured their feelings about leaving. Many of those who were there for three to four months felt they had only just learnt the job, had begun to enjoy themselves, and wanted to stay longer. Surgeon Tom Hugh, as a member of the first surgical team to work in Le Loi Hospital in Vung Tau, felt that three months was not long enough for the team to make a lasting impression. In that time they had been able to clean up the surgical suite enough to begin operating, and had begun to gain the trust of the local people. It was left to later teams to build on these accomplishments. Hugh's colleague and team leader Doug Tracy was proud of his group's achievements but after three months was keen to return home. His wife had given birth during his absence and he was well aware of the sacrifice she had made in supporting his decision to go to Vietnam. Peter Last, a paediatrician and anaesthetist in Bien Hoa, formed the view that a tour of between three and six months would be better for surgeons and other specialists. In that time they could achieve a great deal while avoiding the burnout that affected those who spent longer periods in Vietnam.[1]

Burnout was a real issue. Peter Last noted that one of the surgeons on his team, Douglas Townsend, had 'had it' when he returned home after a tour of six months. Team members on twelve-month tours became increasingly tired and prone to illness, making management more difficult. John Scott, who was in Bien Hoa from 1967 to 1968, was one who found the intensity too great and returned home early. His team had been the first to spend a full year in Bien Hoa, and those that followed it had shorter tours. Organisers seem to have recognised the strain the teams worked under and modified the length of later tours accordingly.

Nurses and other female team members reacted in various ways to leaving Vietnam, although almost all felt some degree of sadness. Joan Rose was typical of those unready to leave after a tour:

> I guess even at that stage . . . most of us felt that we were really doing something that was very, very useful and that if we stayed there a bit longer we would be able to help the Vietnamese . . . and they could progress so much.[2]

Marita Mulcahy was one of many nurses who made strong connections with their patients while helping them cope with often difficult treatments. After a year in Vietnam she would have been happy to spend another year there, she says, because 'You were greeted with lovely smiles each morning. You couldn't do a thing wrong even if you tried, I don't think. They just loved us and we loved them. It was rewarding.'[3]

Other women, though, were happy to be heading back to Australia. Often they were worn out and suffering from anxiety or nervous tension. After twelve months, Carmel Hurst noticed that she and her fellow team members had become 'very scratchy and bad tempered, and little fights erupted'. On the plane out of Saigon she realised she had been away too long when she began to shake: 'I went to a nice hotel in . . . Singapore, and locked the door and turned on the air-conditioning and stayed there for twenty-four hours in bed.'[4] Von Clinch was another who was 'very tired. I loved the people. I was in tears when I left. Terribly upset about leaving. But physically I was at the stage where I needed to go home and I knew it.'[5] Nurse Betty Lockwood found that after 'six months in the one house with half a dozen females you start to think, maybe it's time to move out.'[6]

Much as they needed a rest, however, many felt ambivalent about going home. They cherished the sense of comradeship with their fellow team members and the relationships they'd formed with Vietnamese colleagues. Noelle Laidlaw and her interpreter in Long Xuyen 'were very, very friendly. She wrote me a beautiful letter when I left and she cried, and I cried . . . it was sad leaving.'[7] Also tugging at team members' hearts was the feeling that the job was unfinished, that much remained to be done to help Vietnamese civilians, and doubts about what would happen at the hospitals once the teams left for good. Tempering those concerns were the desire to see family and friends again, to resume jobs back home, and a general war-weariness common to both civilians and soldiers after time spent in a conflict zone.

For a small number of team members who wanted to do more for the Vietnamese, taking part in a second or even third tour with a surgical team, or working in Vietnam in some other capacity, was a way to sustain ties with Vietnam. Jill Storch, who left Bien Hoa in 1971 and returned the following year, was typical of those who felt they needed to do more. 'It was one thing to sort of be against something [the war],' she explains, 'but I also had an opportunity to go and help the local people and . . .

nurses are a bit like that ... social justice and all that sort of thing.'[8] A large number of casualties were still being treated at the hospital in Bien Hoa, and she knew her previous experience made her particularly valuable.

Anaesthetist Jim Villiers was another whose Vietnam experience, in Long Xuyen, inclined him to go back. After returning home, he was asked to advise the replacement team to Long Xuyen on the hospital's anaesthetic set-up, and then to advise the first team sent to Bien Hoa by the Alfred Hospital in January 1966. Although he was not part of this team, he felt that with his experience and the assistance he had given in organising it, 'it seemed inevitable I would end up there'. He spent three months in Bien Hoa in the latter part of 1966 and found it extremely busy, involving a great deal of trauma work.[9] Bernard Dunn was another anaesthetist who returned to Vietnam. After being on the first Royal Melbourne Hospital team to work in Long Xuyen, he completed a three-month tour in Bien Hoa in 1969. He undertook a third tour as a temporary major in the Australian Army, working as an anaesthetist at the 1st Australian Field Hospital at Vung Tau. He was interested in the revolution in care for wounded soldiers that had been made possible by the use of helicopters to evacuate casualties in record time.[10] Although his career shift was uncommon, Dunn was not the only member of a civilian team to temporarily join the Army in order to continue their Vietnam experience.

Rather than join the Army or sign on for a second tour, a small number of surgical team members opted to stay in Vietnam as charity workers. One of these was nurse Jenny Leak, who had served in Bien Hoa in 1967. At the end of her tour she arranged to work with the Asian Christian Service at a refugee camp north of Saigon, mainly because she loved the people and felt she had more to offer them. She liked the idea of working with refugees because they were the most disadvantaged civilians in the country, and found she enjoyed the work very much. The 1968 Tet Offensive forced her to abandon refugee work because her camp was overrun by the Viet Cong and was later deemed too unsafe to return to. Rather than return to Australia, Leak stayed on in Saigon, teaching children in a boarding school and establishing a registered Australian charity, the Vietnam Christian School Program. She became very close to a boy named Ching, and was heartbroken when she was forced to leave Vietnam in April 1975 before the arrival of North Vietnamese forces. She lost touch with her Vietnamese friends for many years and worried about their fate, but was eventually able to welcome Ching to Australia as a refugee in the mid 1980s.[11] Although Leak's involvement with Vietnam was unusually close and enduring, it was common for team members to maintain some contact with their Vietnamese friends. Some sponsored Vietnamese medical personnel to work at Australian hospitals, and others sponsored Vietnamese families to migrate as refugees after the fall of South Vietnam.

For those who returned home after their tour, an interim period of travel in Southeast Asia was a popular choice. Just as the ten- to twelve-day trip home on HMAS *Sydney* gave Australian soldiers a valuable period of adjustment, travel in countries such as Thailand, Cambodia and Hong Kong gave surgical team members a chance to shift gears as they made their way home. In many cases it was also too good an opportunity to pass up. Nurse Betty Lockwood was sad to leave Vietnam, but she found the prospect of travelling through Hong Kong and Kuala Lumpur an exciting distraction. Bill Townsend and Gavan O'Connor had become friends in Vung Tau in 1969 and decided to travel home through Cambodia. A visit to a North Vietnamese embassy in Phnom Penh brought to a head the disillusionment with the war that had set in during their tour. As O'Connor explained:

At this stage we were pretty pissed off with the Vietnamese government. We could see the corruption and the incompetence and everything else . . . And we were beginning to think . . . maybe the communists have got something because the present mob is bloody hopeless.

At the embassy they told an official that, while they disliked the South Vietnamese government, they understood its hatred of the Viet Cong for its violence against civilians. The man replied, 'All the people want us to win. The only ones who don't are the lackeys of the US imperialists.' At that, says O'Connor, 'I threw my hands up . . . I thought, bugger it, I'm going home and forgetting it all.'[12]

Back home

It is well documented that Australia's Vietnam veterans received a mixed, often hostile reception on their return home. Their emotions ranged from joy at being home and alive to shame or anger at the treatment they received. Civilian surgical team members were spared such abuse, but they too had difficulty settling in. Just as most received no formal briefing before they left for Vietnam, now they also received no debriefing from the DEA. Like their military counterparts (particularly conscripts), they returned to their old jobs after a short break and were expected simply to put their Vietnam experience behind them.

The lack of a formal debrief session by the DEA was unfortunate, though not surprising. At that time it was not understood that some team members would have suffered considerable trauma as a result of their tours, and people were not yet widely encouraged to air their feelings in counselling sessions. In hindsight, some team members think a formal debrief would have been useful, particularly for those who lost touch with fellow team members or were not asked to speak formally about their experience. Canny Coventry says she returned from Vietnam very angry and is critical of the lack of a formal debrief. Her turmoil boiled over in small ways after her return: overhearing a woman in a fruit shop complaining about the produce, she issued the rebuke, 'Madam, don't complain. You're darned lucky to have it.' She was left with some 'awful' memories from Vietnam and suffers from post-traumatic stress disorder.[13] Dot Angell met with some negative reactions on her return, which did nothing to help her readjust: 'I started back at work in May, and the attitude was almost that we'd been on holiday in sunny Vietnam. Nobody wanted to know, nobody wanted to hear about it. We weren't debriefed at all.'[14]

Several team members say they found themselves increasingly—and vocally—intolerant of trivial concerns after returning from Vietnam. Paediatrician Bob Birrell got into strife when dealing with the mother of an infant patient in his Victorian practice. Seeing how out of touch with her child the woman was, he couldn't help comparing her to the many impoverished Vietnamese mothers he had seen who would do anything for their children, and made clear 'that I thought [her behaviour] was a bloody disaster . . . I'd become pretty bolshie . . . I thought, these people that have got everything, and I've left my mates up there with nothing.'[15]

Some of the nurses found it difficult to adjust to the rigid rules of Australian hospitals. Janet Brewster was reprimanded for continuing some of her Vietnam habits, such as saving the wrapping material from gowns in case it was needed. She was also stopped from carrying out procedures such as suturing, which she had practised routinely in Vietnam, because it was not part of a nurse's duties at home. Fortunately, she says, her colleagues understood: 'I had people at PA [Royal Prince Alfred Hospital] still in theatre that had been in Vietnam . . . they'd say, "Oh, Janet, you're not in Vietnam now" . . . then they'd laugh and say how they had to adjust when they got back.'[16]

Team members also reacted in varying ways to the amount of war trauma they had dealt with in Vietnam. Radiographer Barbara Sutherland found it difficult being just one of a large X-ray team again, so when she was offered a position as supervisor in a casualty department six weeks after her return, she was delighted. To her it 'just seemed so appropriate, dealing with trauma cases . . . I couldn't possibly have just stayed in a normal situation.'[17] Others, however, wanted nothing more to do with trauma work, having seen more than their fair share in Vietnam.

It was not uncommon for team members to feel unsettled once they were home, and several sought new jobs to try to deal with these feelings. Bill Townsend, administrator for the final team in Vung Tau, was keen to return to Vietnam and applied for the Saigon-based position of overall administrator for the surgical teams. When the Repatriation Department refused to release him, he eventually joined the Department of Defence and worked overseas in other areas of conflict, including Cambodia, East Timor and Bosnia. Jenny Hunter, who nursed in both Long Xuyen and Bien Hoa, was equally restless on her return. Not only did she find it hard to sleep when she first arrived home 'because it was so quiet', she found it impossible to stay in the same job for more than a few years. 'I've always gone to jobs that presented a challenge and then once the challenge has been overcome . . . then I move on to another one,' she explains. 'So I've done all sorts of things and I've travelled a lot since.'[18]

The legacy of trauma for a small number of team members was severe and life changing. Jill Storch nursed during two tours in Bien Hoa, but was 'pretty shattered' after the second trip and took six months off work. When she sought help because she still felt 'really rattled', she was told there was nothing wrong with her. She continued working, but her Vietnam experiences still continued to affect her. Although she gained much from going to Vietnam, especially from seeing the strength of the Vietnamese in the face of adversity, her one regret 'is that it left me scarred psychologically . . . having the nightmares and things like that, and a lot of it's still there and I'm sure it'll be there till the day I die. But . . . I survived and I'm OK.'[19] Suzie MacFarlane also suffered flashbacks, and like many Vietnam veterans is affected by the sound of helicopters:

> . . . for a long time I thought, Why do I feel like this? Every time I hear a helicopter . . . because I actually enjoyed going on the helicopters, but it didn't make me feel nice when I heard them. Just brought back lots of sorts of feelings really.[20]

Perhaps one of the worst-affected team members interviewed was Jenny Leak. After living in Vietnam for eight years and having to leave under stressful conditions, she found returning to Australia and going back to work 'horrendous. The first four years I don't think I adjusted. I went through the motions . . . but I just felt lost. I felt guilty I was safe. I felt behind the times in nursing here. It was horrible.'[21]

For the majority of team members, however, reactions to coming home were less extreme. They felt lucky to live in a country as well off as Australia, and found greater pleasure in daily living than before. Von Clinch gained a new appreciation for uninterrupted electric light and clean drinking water, while Pat Warren, a nurse in Bien Hoa, enjoyed her first walk along Bondi Beach because it was free of mines and she finally felt safe.[22] For surgeons, physicians and other specialists who had left their practices in the hands of locums for several months, the greatest challenge was to revive their often flagging businesses. Surgeon Kendall Francis found his practice had 'gone down a bit', and for Doug Tracy the effort required to rebuild his practice was like starting over again. For all that, none of the surgeons regretted the experience, and many were keen to do more.

Staying in touch

Like Australia's military veterans, many surgical team members found talking about their experiences the most beneficial way to come to terms with what they had seen and done in Vietnam. For a number of people, and for a variety of reasons, this was not possible, and they regretted not having the opportunity. Beth and John Scott, who met in Vietnam and married soon after their return, spent the years following their tour raising children and living overseas while John completed a fellowship. On their return home they had no opportunity to relive their Vietnam experiences:

When we came back we came to Melbourne . . . and it was as though Vietnam never happened. We never spoke to anyone about Vietnam, we never heard anything about Vietnam, we never had any contact with anyone we were there with . . . It was twelve months out of our lives and it was a big, big thing in our lives but we just . . . pushed it away.[23]

Kay Dabovich, a nurse in Long Xuyen in 1969, found public apathy about the war and the fate of Vietnamese civilians hard to tolerate:

It was nice to be home but it was frustrating too . . . I just felt that nobody cared and nobody bothered . . . it was somebody else's war happening somewhere else, and nobody stopped to think about the plight of all those poor people who were caught in the middle of it who didn't really want to be in a war either. So that was hard.[24]

Team members who had been part of combined hospital or state teams had few chances to maintain contact with fellow team members. Having been recruited from different places, they now returned to their old positions, separated from their Vietnam colleagues by distance and the pressures of work. Members of single-hospital teams fared better, and the friendships they had made in Vietnam became lasting ones. The Alfred Hospital, in Melbourne, appears to have created particularly close-knit teams, many of whose members maintain close contact today. Von Clinch was an Alfred nurse who appreciated the chance to go to annual reunions with her Vietnam colleagues. 'We loved them,' she says of the dinners, 'and we had a good old laugh. There's something special about people that you've lived through that sort of thing with. There's a special relationship . . . you could trust them with your life.'[25]

Peter Last's Royal Adelaide Hospital team in Bien Hoa had made a ritual of playing tapes of The Seekers, so in the early 1980s, when the re-formed band toured Australia, he and fellow team members went as a group, reliving many memories.

Some team members were able to discuss their Vietnam experience in a formal setting. In cases where their colleagues were interested to hear about the type of surgery performed in a war zone or about new techniques the teams had developed, they would give seminars in the months following their return. Radiographers Joan Rose and Barbara Sutherland gave regular talks to colleagues, and nurses Aileen Monck and Olga Nicholls found themselves in demand to address community groups. Aileen feels that by late 1967, when they returned, there was an increasing level of interest in what was happening in Vietnam. Several team members also wrote of their experiences; one of the earliest of these publications was Susan Terry's *House of Love*. Published in 1966, it was an account of Susan's year in Vietnam as a member of the first surgical team in Long Xuyen. It provoked great interest among fellow medical staff and was an important guide for later teams, being one of the few detailed accounts of what they were likely to face in Vietnam. Also of value was a series of articles by team members published in the August 1967 issue of the *Medical Journal of Australia*, which highlighted some of the problems and suggested solutions for later teams.

While the most common way of keeping in touch was through informal reunions, in later years team members also took part in Anzac Day marches. Identifying closely with Australia's military Vietnam veterans took time, indeed many team members have always felt awkward about describing themselves as Vietnam veterans. Barbara Sutherland had experienced rejection by the Returned and Services League, which held that only military participants in the Vietnam War were legitimate members. This sentiment was shared by some surgical team members themselves. Peter Last felt he had been a privileged spectator to the war and refused to march on Anzac Day because he thought he would be doing so under false pretences.

For other team members, though, the fact that they had taken an active part in Australia's civilian aid program in Vietnam gave them a great sense of pride and a strong sense of identity with military veterans. The decision by some team members to participate in Anzac Day marches took place during the 1980s, strengthened by the Welcome Home parade for Vietnam veterans in Sydney in 1987. This occasion, cathartic for many veterans, was also the first time many surgical team members met up with their Vietnam colleagues and were able to speak of their experiences. The day was a memorable one for Jan Bell, who had nursed in Vung Tau, and gave her a great sense of belonging. She began marching on Anzac Day in Sydney, initially with former Army nurses, but when that was discouraged, with members of the former 1st Australian Field Hospital. For inexplicable reasons the rift that had developed between some Army nurses and their civilian counterparts in Vietnam continued, and the latter were made to feel that their Vietnam service had been a type of well-paid holiday rather than the demanding and difficult experience that it often was. While feeling rejected by Army nurses on Anzac Day was hurtful for the civilian nurses, it did not stop them from taking an active part. In Melbourne, marching on Anzac Day gave Beth and John Scott the chance to finally acknowledge their Vietnam experiences—and in front of their children, who were now old enough to understand what their parents had done in Vietnam. Former team members now march under their own banner on Anzac Day.

A small number of team members have returned to Vietnam in recent years. Barbara Sutherland visited the hospital in Long Xuyen a number of times and was delighted to see changes. 'I was amazed at how civilised the hospital was,' she says. 'There was some particular training program available for doctors and it was all written in English. I couldn't believe it. So we left a legacy there.'[26]

For Beth and John Scott and former nurse Jo Howard, a visit to Bien Hoa was very beneficial. Even though the hospital had changed substantially, they found it worthwhile seeing the area, and for Jo the visit reinforced her feelings about the Vietnamese people:

I think going back to Vietnam was important for me. I had even more admiration for those people having seen them a second time. They're still living under the yoke, really. Conditions haven't improved. The only new building going on seems to be government buildings . . . And people save to give their children an education. I think they're wonderful, the Vietnamese people.[27]

Was it worth it?

Although all of the team members interviewed for this book responded positively to this question, there were undoubtedly negative aspects to their service. Many of those who had believed strongly in the Australian military commitment to Vietnam became disillusioned after their experience of the war, and returned home convinced that Australia should end its involvement. Peter Last was one whose views changed as a result of his service, although he recognised the complexities at stake. 'It made me think about politics more than I ever had before,' he says. 'I came back feeling that we were in the wrong war for the wrong reasons at the wrong time. But since we were in it, well then we couldn't easily get out of it.'[28]

Others were disappointed with what they felt the teams had achieved. The frustration at not being able to establish permanent teaching facilities and courses in all areas of Australian influence has already been noted. The feeling among nurses convinced they were only practising 'bandaid' medicine also persisted after their return home. Carmel Hurst felt that 'while we were there and doing stuff for people who were there and needed it, it was great. But it was ephemera. We were there because we were the conscience of the Australian government. It was essentially a waste of time.'[29]

Joan Rose, although disappointed in some ways, was more optimistic. She felt it would have been impossible for the teams to have achieved major changes in Vietnamese practices and standards of health care, something many team members wanted to do. But, she concluded, 'it doesn't mean that what we did wasn't appreciated. And it doesn't mean that we didn't influence them in some way.'[30]

At a personal level, much of the negative legacy of the war hinged on the nature of war itself. Seeing the inhuman brutality and horror of war at first hand was deeply disturbing for some. Canny Coventry's bad memories centred on 'what mankind does to people. It is just appalling. You can't understand the futility of it.' Jill Storch was aghast at how cruel people could be, 'even when they had a choice. They still felt obliged to do it . . . People being bombed and people being killed and burnt bodies and . . . just people being dumped . . . man's inhumanity to man.'[31]

Others, like Carmel Hurst, felt deeply the plight of the children they treated, the innocent victims of war; Hurst also found that 'the prostitution and the exploitation of women was very, very sad.'[32]

Some team members suffered from the effects of their war service for years. Those who were later diagnosed with cancer or post-traumatic stress disorder were convinced their time in Vietnam was the cause even though they were unable to prove a direct link. Jenny Hunter suffered from a number of physical complaints in the years after her service and, like many veterans, believes the defoliants sprayed in Vietnam may have affected her. She always ate local food and drank the water as it came, and is sure that these habits are at least partly to blame for the state of her health. Marita Mulcahy had a mild stroke and three different cancers. She does not attribute these to her Vietnam service but concedes that there may be a link. Others, like Jill Storch and Canny Coventry, have no doubt that the stresses of working and living in a war zone, combined with a lack of debriefing afterwards, contributed to their post-traumatic stress disorder.

Despite these negatives, the overwhelmingly positive aspects of a tour of duty in Vietnam are what the majority of former surgical team members remember today. For most, the sense of comradeship in a close-knit team was one of the greatest highlights of their tour. Joan Rose articulates feelings shared by many:

> The people you got to know, the members of the team, to leave those people was like leaving your family . . . Because you're all in the one building, you're living together, you're sharing the experiences, you got to know people so much better, so much more quickly, and relationships developed much more in depth than they normally would.[33]

They also enjoyed the work, despite the difficulties, and as Carmel Hurst puts it, 'we were all young and we were strong and fit, and absolutely impenetrable by things like bullets'. Indeed, when the question of fear was put to former team members, most dismissed it as irrelevant. Aside from crises like the 1968 Tet Offensive, when the danger was obvious, few incidents caused team members much alarm. The necessities of living in a war zone, such as requiring escorts to and from the hospital, flying between locations in all manner of aircraft, occasionally under fire, or observing war at close hand, were all taken as a matter of course.

Friendships with Vietnamese colleagues were also greatly valued. Team members usually developed a great admiration for the stoicism and patience with which the Vietnamese medical staff, and the population generally, faced life in a war zone. Many speak of the pain they felt at losing patients, especially young children, and of their admiration for the way Vietnamese people endured the suffering resulting from injury or illness. Although at times they became frustrated with the attitude of the Vietnamese medical staff to their patients, they learned to adapt and to accept that Western methods were not the only ones, or even always the best. Many learnt much from Vietnamese colleagues and found it very difficult to leave them. The Australians worried about them after the fall of the South in 1975, but it was difficult to maintain contact, and it was often many years before they found out what had happened to their Vietnamese friends.

Despite the doubts held by some team members about the overall effect of their efforts, most felt they had at least made a noticeable impact on the immediate health of the Vietnamese civilian population. Robyn Anderson, who stayed on in Bien Hoa for a second tour as a nurse adviser, has no doubt about this:

> It was an enormously valuable experience from a professional point of view and, if we did nothing else, we saved thousands of lives. Literally, thousands of lives. But we did do more than that. We were able to have an effect on little hospitals all over the place . . . I think we had a lasting effect up there.[34]

Although the physical and mental toll of a Vietnam tour was at times taxing, few who participated in Australia's eight-year-long surgical team program would disagree with the statement by Cas McInnes: 'I wouldn't have missed it for quids.'[35]

Epilogue

While researching and writing her PhD thesis in 1997 on the civilian nurses' experiences, Dot Angell started to suspect that those who had served in surgical teams had, like other Vietnam War veterans, an unusually high incidence of cancers and psychiatric ailments. Determined to bring this to the attention of the authorities and push for benefits such as a Repatriation Health Gold Card,[1] Dot formed the Civilian Nurses, Australian Surgical Teams Vietnam 1964–1972 (CN-ASTV) association in late 1998. The Gold Card, given to military veterans with disabilities or conditions related to their war service, would allow former team members to obtain medical treatment at public expense. Dot rallied former team members, at first mainly nursing sisters, and began collating and gathering evidence in support of their appeal for repatriation benefits. Surgeon David Brownbill was one of the few doctors who became involved at this early stage. 'I wanted to still be part of the team,' he explained. 'I wanted to keep telling [the nurses] how much I thought of them, because they did a fabulous job.'[2]

When several former team members sought medical assistance through the Repatriation Department they were refused because they were not 'deemed to have performed qualifying service' under the *Veterans' Entitlements Act*. Thus began a long and ongoing fight for repatriation benefits. Aside from the recording of an important part of

Australia's medical and military history, that fight is one of the prime reasons this book was written.

The Mohr Inquiry

In mid 1999 Major General Justice Mohr was appointed by the Federal Government to review service anomalies in respect of Southeast Asian service. The review included an investigation of the CN-ASTV claims. The benefits the organisation was seeking were the same as those being sought by civilians who had served during the war on Australian cargo ships, such as the crews of the *Jeparit* and *Boonaroo*,[3] and civilian entertainers who had toured Vietnam.

In September 1999, Dot Angell and Maureen Spicer, representing the association, presented a submission to the Mohr Inquiry that their claim be recognised on three grounds:

> ... they assisted the Australian Defence Force (ADF) in war-
> time. In doing so they provided assistance to, and served with,
> an allied country [principally the US]; and they 'incurred
> danger' from hostile enemy forces during hostilities.[4]

It looked momentarily as if the case had been won when Justice Mohr recommended in his report 'that Australian Civilian Surgical and Medical Teams operating in Vietnam during the Vietnam War be deemed as performing qualifying service for repatriation benefits'.[5]

A Senate Foreign Affairs, Defence and Trade Legislation Committee was formed to review the Mohr Report in 2000. The Australian Nurses Federation, in a submission to the committee, reported that, '[SEATO] nurses were found to be suffering from non-Hodgkin's lymphoma, thyroid disease, autoimmune disorders, multiple sclerosis and post-traumatic stress disorder.'[6] These diseases and conditions were found to occur at higher rates among the surgical team members than in the general community. It looked as if the nurses' case would succeed.

However, the committee recommended that the civilian surgical teams would *not* be eligible for repatriation benefits because, as it had been told by Peter Reece, head of the compensation division of the Department of Veterans' Affairs:

> We would not dispute any of the evidence contained in their [the nurses'] submissions. The critical test at the end of the day is not where they were or what they did or the risk that they involved; it is whether they were under the command of the [Australian Defence Force]—that is the law.[7]

The civilian surgical teams were, however, operating in a theatre of war against an armed and hostile enemy and in support of South Vietnam, the US and other allies of Australia. They were there as part of the war effort, under the auspices of the Department of External (later Foreign) Affairs. It is true that they were not under the direct command of an Australian headquarters of the ADF, but it is certainly arguable that they were under its indirect control and influence. The ruling also appears unduly inflexible when the nature of the war is taken into account.

The government's decision seems all the more questionable in light of the fact that in 1998 the civilian surgical team members were awarded the Australian Active Service Medal and the Vietnam Logistics Support Medal on the basis that '. . . they were employed in Vietnam and were integrated in the ADF for extended periods of time, performing the functions with their ADF counterparts.'[8]

The issue comes down to semantics. The surgical teams were not 'under command' but 'integrated', and in the eyes of the decision makers were therefore not eligible for benefits. Understandably, many of the team members felt enormous frustration with this haggling over jurisdiction. Democrat Senator Natasha Stott Despoja disputed the ruling, saying:

> We believe that the minister and the government are hiding behind a technicality. The arguments are a furphy, especially when the established history tells us that they were working not only in military-like situations but also in military hospitals and, on occasions, treating military personnel . . .
>
> These civilian doctors and nurses assisted the Australian defence forces in wartime, and they incurred danger from hostile enemy forces during that time. They have a right to apply for repatriation entitlements under the *Veterans' Entitlements Act.*[9]

Other politicians have also publicly expressed their support for the civilian surgical teams' claims. Democrat Senator Andrew Bartlett stated in Parliament:

> Those who served in the Australian civilian surgical and medical teams during the Vietnam War, and who are suffering conditions as a result of that, deserve better treatment than they are getting . . . Their conditions are as war-related as the conditions of other Vietnam veterans.[10]

MP Laurie Ferguson, addressing the decision not to include the nurses in the Act, said in Parliament:

> Most people in the general Australian population would agree that [being under command of an ADF unit] is not a good enough reason not to recognise the very real dangers and the very disturbing situation that these individuals [CN-ASTV] faced in Vietnam, and that matter will be subject to an amendment attempt . . .[11]

Senators Chris Schacht and John Hogg, who were members of the Senate Foreign Affairs, Defence and Trade Legislation Committee that reviewed the Mohr Report, stated in a dissenting report in an Amendment Bill (No. 1) submitted in August 2000:

> We therefore recommend that the Veterans' Affairs Legislation Amendment (Budget Measures) Bill 2000 be amended to enable the civilian nurses and members of civilian surgical teams, who served in Vietnam between 1962 and 1972, be deemed as performing qualifying service for repatriation benefits.[12]

After numerous complaints to parliamentarians and discussion of the issue on talkback radio, the Howard Government decided to review the recommendations of the Mohr Inquiry. The independent Review of Veterans' Entitlements, chaired by the Hon. John Clarke, QC, was established in 2002 to examine perceived anomalies in veterans' entitlements and the current level of benefits and support for veterans receiving disability pensions. What became known as the Clarke Report was felt by many ex-team members to be a waste of time, money and effort.

The review was, in Dot Angell's opinion, 'a Clayton's review' of the Mohr Report and subsequent findings—a phony review. She was unimpressed with its scope or the make-up of the review board and described the whole thing as 'a sham'. In hindsight she said, 'I wish we had never been involved with it.' The review put the Nurses Association case back where it had been before the Mohr Report, and the situation now seems to be a 'lost cause'.[13]

Granting repatriation benefits to the medical teams was not going to gouge deeply into Treasury coffers. There were only 450 individuals (205 nurses and radiographers, 240 doctors, and five other medical personnel) involved and, as of 2009, approximately one-third of these people had died.[14]

Opting to claim a sickness benefit through Comcare was also unsatisfactory owing to the limited nature of benefits payable. As the Australian Nurses Federation pointed out in an article in the *Age* in 2003, under the *Safety, Compensation and Rehabilitation Act 1988*, administered by Comcare, only 'reasonable expenses are paid, while under the *Veterans' Entitlements Act 1986*, all medical expenses associated with all accepted disabilities are totally covered'.[15] At the time of publication several of the teams' nurses had been through the Comcare claim process, and, as an article by the Australian Nurses Federation noted, 'Their experience has highlighted the practical difficulties of pursuing claims under this system'.[16] Senator Andrew Bartlett shared this view, saying, 'There is clearly an argument that Comcare is not the suitable agency ... to deal with the medical teams'.[17]

The team members did not go to South Vietnam for the money or the glory. As Cas McInnes says, 'We weren't in it for those sorts of benefits [repatriation]'. But he adds:

> A Gold Card would be nice [for the nurses]. I think the nurses probably took it harder than we did. They were there for longer ... I think there were a lot of pressures that the nurses were under that we surgeons and doctors weren't. And of course the physical living conditions were also difficult for them in many ways ...[18]

The fight is not over. The CN-ASTV continue to push for a change in policy to allow their members to gain repatriation benefits. The association is hopeful that the Rudd Government will support changes to the *Veterans' Entitlements Act*.

Recognition

Apart from the repatriation debate, there was also the issue of recognition of the teams' efforts. Nobody was seeking—or sought—this recognition, but some felt that marching on Anzac Day would be a nice way to have a reunion and meet up with old friends and colleagues. As shown earlier, the Army's nursing fraternity in Sydney and Melbourne initially wanted nothing to do with the civilian nurses, perhaps because they did not have medals, and asked them to leave the march. This situation changed in 1998, when team members were allowed to apply for the Australian Active Service Medal and the Vietnam Logistics Support Medal. When asked in interviews for this book if they had their medals, many of the members showed them with obvious pride. Bob Gray said of his service and medals:

> I was proud of it, yes, I was . . . for a few years I didn't bother marching on Anzac Day—but then I thought, Well, why not? . . . My grandkids; I am the greatest thing since sliced bread in the eyes of my grandkids on Anzac Day. I march, and I am the only bloke in step as I often point out, but I was glad to get the gong for the recognition of what we had done. It wasn't given for a long period of time. I hope that we had made an impression on the Vietnamese people, and I think we have.[19]

Cas McInnes was ambivalent about discussing his medals. He said:

> I don't care too much about that side of it. We weren't too interested in medals; it was very nice to get them and I am not knocking it at all . . . I am very proud of it, but we weren't in it for medals.[20]

Reflections

Don Sidey was a senior surgeon when he deployed. Asked how he looked back on his time in South Vietnam and what he gained from it, he said:

I learnt a lot of things: I learnt to respect and like the Vietnamese people of whom I had previously had no experience whatsoever . . . I think it improved my tolerance, which probably needed improving. I enjoyed it and I have never worked harder in my life.[21]

For Cas McInnes it was

I think probably the feeling that I was doing some good for a small number of people. Looking back on it, I don't think we really had any long-term or significant effect, but I always like to think that we were doing something for the patients . . . There was a lot of pleasure in seeing kids that had been shot up walking around in three or four days' time, and then going home . . . We didn't have any splints or anything like that. We had to make our own . . . Occasionally we did cosmetic things on children—things like [repairing] hare lips—that they weren't going to get done anywhere else. It was a sort of a pleasure to see them get out . . . At least I believe I did a few people some good.[22]

David Brownbill said his time in Vietnam was something he would never forget, mainly because of the professional teams he worked with under extreme circumstances. He added:

I was very privileged to be with some very senior, very experienced men who taught me—they taught me a lot of surgery and medical insight, but they also taught me [about] being together in adverse circumstances. It was just fantastic.[23]

Paul Large said the experiences he had in South Vietnam made him better at dealing with trauma. When asked what he learnt most from his tours, Paul said unabashedly:

It really was an education . . . and I was very pleased to have it. I am not a very confident fellow; I always have underestimated what I can do. I learnt that I could manage these teams. I was very happy doing this work, in fact I enjoyed being a team leader, most things we could overcome, but the first time I went up I thought, 'Oh, God, can I do this?' Then I realised I could.[24]

Paul had seen much in his three tours, performing amputations and a lot of grisly surgery, but there were still some things that put him off:

And then there were the everyday things; every time I opened an abdomen there were roundworms in it—these large numbers of revolting roundworms. I had occasional [patients with] bowel obstructions by great clumps of roundworms. I would open the bowel and fish them all out—it was revolting.[25]

Bob Gray said, 'I learnt a hell of a lot . . . compassion, tolerance, under-standing. I reckon I was a better fellow when I came back than when I went.'[26]

David Brownbill was impressed by the nurses he worked with. His admiration for them was clearly evident in his interview:

I watched those girls in the operating theatre and in the recovery room, and then in the ward, but particularly the recovery room and wow, you can't believe how busy it could be at times . . . Watching their resilience, their resourcefulness in getting the job done.[27]

Jill Storch learnt much from her Vietnamese patients:

. . . in the face of their adversity I was really overwhelmed by the way they dealt with their life and I was very grateful for having experienced that regardless of what it did to me. I think it made me a better person.[28]

David Brownbill heartily agreed. One of the reasons he enjoyed his time in Vietnam so much was the locals, whom he 'got to love', he said, adding, 'I thought those people were wonderful.'[29]

For Johanna Van Valen, Vietnam work 'was something that was alive . . . it was chaotic, it was awful. It was horrific at times . . . but there was something very vibrant about that place that got into my being.'[30] Jenny Hunter said, 'it was a life-changing experience, physically and mentally.'[31] Wendy Jobberns summed it up this way: 'I think we saved a lot of lives. I think we all felt that we were doing some good . . . it did give them quality of life.'[32]

Feelings about the war

Something that upset many team members on their return home were the protests against the war. While none of these were aimed at the civilian teams, the members still felt the impact of the anti-war movement. Don Sidey said:

> I thought [the movement] was irrational, quite frankly, a lot of it. I mean, the [soldiers] fighting in Vietnam had no choice about it anyway. That was the military's job, to go and do what they were told to do, so it wasn't their fault that they were there doing it. Why take it out on them? I have never really been able to understand [it].[33]

Never before had the country been so divided over the politics of a conflict. Don Sidey had strong opinions on the war and admitted they have not changed since he returned home:

I still think—and this is a matter of personal opinion, although I think there are quite a few who share it—that in fact what was done in Vietnam prevented the whole area from going communist, and I think if the whole area had gone communist, the subsequent history of this country and its relationships with the Asiatic mass in general would have been quite different. In fact, I think that it might have had an effect on the demise of Russian communism. This was a holding operation; it was an operation you couldn't win, because you can't win a war if you can't hold the enemy's territory. It was impossible, so essentially it was a holding operation and in that respect I believe it was successful.[34]

Cas McInnes said his views on the war changed after he had completed a tour:

I was probably a bit ambivalent as to whether or not Australia should have been there, and I came back with the conviction that yes, somebody had to be there and it may as well have been us. It was that sort of a war that you didn't know whose side everybody was on. We didn't really know who the patients were, whether they were [South Vietnamese Army] or whether they were Viet Cong. You never quite knew who your friends were up there. I think we got the impression that although the war probably wasn't winnable, as we were told, the whole idea was to stop communism coming down.[35]

David Brownbill had thought deeply about the war. He said:

I went believing the war was appropriate. I came back feeling the war was appropriate because of, I guess, everything I'd been told, the people I met, the people I knew. I didn't mix with people who thought deeply about the morals of the war. I believed in the domino theory. I believed tremendously that if the option was fighting offshore or fighting in Australia, then offshore was the better alternative. I didn't think deeply enough to wonder if that option was true or not. So I went believing in the war. I mixed with military people there, and of course they reinforced that view of the thing.[36]

But over time, his views changed:

It wasn't until a couple of years later . . . and I had time to sit and think; I have built up a very strong doubt as to whether we should have been there. That it wasn't our [the Australian military's] role. I try and look at it [without the benefit of hindsight] . . . and I fall out with a lot of my friends. No, it was wrong. I don't believe we should have been there . . . I think if I'd tried to put my intellectual hat on in the middle '60s, even though people exhibited doubts, on balance what was going on and the decisions that were made then, I think it would be hard under similar circumstances not to make the same decision. So I don't criticise us for being there militarily. I think now it was wrong, but looking at it at that time, I think there was enough doubt that I'd still throw my hat in with it.[37]

But should he have gone? David replied emphatically: 'As far as the medical teams going, I have never had one moment of doubt. I have no doubt whatever that we should have been there. I'm proud to have been one of the ones who went.'[38]

The members of the civilian surgical teams that deployed to South Vietnam during the war have no regrets about going. They were mostly driven by a perceived need to lend a healing hand to a country that was in dire need of professional medical help. They volunteered to serve and for the most part went with their eyes wide open. The only regret some feel today is over the Australian government's failure to accept that their work was part of the overall war effort and that as a consequence they deserve repatriation benefits.

The final words belong to the Australian Ambassador to South Vietnam, Arthur Morris. At the final handover at Bien Hoa Hospital on 28 December 1972, he said:

> Australian aid is given without strings as a grant. It is given in response to a country's needs, as seen by that country itself. It is given unconditionally; it is not a weapon to precipitate social or political changes in the recipient country. We appreciate that when our teams depart they will have made little, if any, lasting impression on Vietnamese medical practices, for that was not their role. Their greatest contribution will have been at the individual level in their contribution to the welfare of patients, and we are proud to think that their reputation remains high with their patients and their Vietnamese counterparts, that they have also taught by example while carrying out their duties.[39]

Appendix A

Dates of service of Australian civilian surgical teams in Vietnam

Long Xuyen

October 1964–October 1965	Royal Melbourne Hospital
October 1965–October 1966	St Vincent's Hospital (Melbourne)
October 1966–October 1967	Prince Henry's Hospital (Melbourne)
October 1967–October 1968	NSW state team 1
October 1968–January 1969	NSW state team 2
January 1969–August 1969	Royal Perth team 1
August 1969–January 1970	Royal Perth team 2
January 1970–August 1970	Two medical personnel detached from Bien Hoa team
August 1970–December 1970	Three medical personnel detached from Bien Hoa team

Bien Hoa

January 1966–April 1967	Alfred Hospital (Melbourne)
April 1967–October 1967	Royal Adelaide Hospital
October 1967–September 1968	Royal Brisbane Hospital
September 1968–January 1969	Princess Alexandra Hospital (Brisbane)
January 1969–January 1970	Alfred Hospital (Melbourne)

January 1970–July 1970	Royal Adelaide Hospital
July 1970–January 1971	Royal Melbourne Hospital
January 1971–July 1971	Queensland hospitals team
July 1971–January 1972	St Vincent's Hospital (Sydney)
January 1972–December 1972	SEATO composite team

Vung Tau

November 1966–May 1967	Prince Henry and Prince of Wales hospitals (Sydney)
May 1967–November 1967	Royal Prince Alfred Hospital (Sydney)
November 1967–November 1968	Commonwealth Repatriation team 1
November 1968–September 1969	Commonwealth Repatriation team 2

Ba Ria

November 1967–April 1969	Subsidiary of Commonwealth Repatriation teams based at Vung Tau

Appendix B

Members of Australian civilian surgical teams in Vietnam

Long Xuyen

October 1964	**Royal Melbourne Hospital**
	Ann Boucher–Oct 1965
	Noelle Courtney–Jan 1965
	Ida 'Jenny' Jones–May 1965
	Donald Macleish–Jan 1965
	Timothy Matthew–Jan 1965
	Susan Terry–Oct 1965
	James Villiers–Feb 1965
	Ian Russell–Feb 1965
January 1965	Norma Anderson–Oct 1965
	John K. Hogan–Apr 1965
February 1965	Anthony Carden–Nov 1965
	Kenneth Hardy–June 1965
	Herbert Newman–May 1965
April 1965	Alan Cuthbertson–July 1965
	George Jerums–July 1965
May 1965	Bernard Dunn–Aug 1965
	Graham Syme–Aug 1965
	Beth Thredgold–Nov 1965
July 1965	Margaret Burgess–Oct 1965
	Vivien Lindley–Nov 1965
	Robert Thompson–Oct 1965

August 1965	John Lane–Oct 1965
	Peter Scott–Oct 1965
October 1965	**St Vincent's Hospital (Melbourne)**
	Kathy Clarke–Mar 1966
	Joan Cooney–Mar 1966
	John Doyle–Jan 1966
	Margaret Kennedy–Mar 1966
	Judith McCormack–Apr 1966
	Peter Nelson–Feb 1966
	Patricia Reilly–Jan 1966
	Peter Ryan–Jan 1966
	Edward Tomlinson–Jan 1966
	Robert Young–Jan 1966
January 1966	H. Steven Angus–June 1966
	Peter Higgs–Apr 1966
	Ross Holland–May 1966
	Desmond Hurley–Apr 1966
	Ann Keon–June 1966
	James O'Collins–May 1966
March 1966	Margot Cornish–July 1966
	Marea Fennell–July 1966
	Margaret O'Connor–July 1966
April 1966	Aileen Crothers–Aug 1966
	Hubert De Castella–July 1966
	Paul Maher–July 1966
	Walter Scott–July 1966
May 1966	Rodney Clarke–Aug 1966
	Sue Bayley–Oct 1966
	Peter Skene–Oct 1966
June 1966	Carmel Evans–Oct 1966
	Patricia Jones–Oct 1966

	Margaret Mellan–Oct 1966
	Bernard Ryan–Oct 1966
July 1966	Hugh Butel–Oct 1966
	M.E. Finn–Oct 1966
	Kevin King–Oct 1966
	John Parer–Oct 1966
	Joseph Santamaria–Oct 1966
October 1966	**Prince Henry's Hospital (Melbourne)**
	Jenny Antons–Apr 1967
	James Downie–Jan 1967
	Graeme Griffith–Apr 1967
	Pamela Griffith–Apr 1967
	Corinne Lapham–Apr 1967
	Janice Macauley–Apr 1967
	Barbara Maughan–Apr 1967
	Marianne Nacy–Feb 1967
	Ethel Robinson–Apr 1967
	Elizabeth Schoffeld–Apr 1967
	Sidney Sewell–Jan 1967
	Thomas Wilson–Feb 1967
December 1966	Richard Papworth–Nov 1967
January 1967	Owen Cole–Apr 1967
	John Kendall Francis–Apr 1967
	Adrian Lowe–Apr 1967
	George Robinson–Apr 1967
February 1967	Robert Birrell–May 1967
	Jennifer Dyason–Oct 1967
	John Forbes–May 1967
April 1967	C. Jan Blain–Oct 1967
	Gail Donne–Oct 1967
	Dinah Gordon–Oct 1967

Harry Johnson–July 1967

Patrick Maplestone–July 1967

John McArthur–July 1967

Joan Pryor–Oct 1967

Valerie Reed–Sept 1967

Lynne Schimmelbusch–Sept 1967

Samuel Slutzki–July 1967

May 1967   Michael Parker–Aug 1967

June 1967   George Gunter–Sept 1967

July 1967   Brian Jordon–Oct 1967

Donald McMahon–Oct 1967

Richard Stanistreet–Oct 1967

Brian Walder–Oct 1967

Iain MacMillan–Oct 1967

August 1967   Noel Bennett–Oct 1967

October 1967   **NSW state team 1**

Lorraine Bingley–Oct 1968

Clive Bond–Oct 1968

Walter 'Tom' Calov–Oct 1968

Kenneth Doust–Apr 1968

Janet Glasson–Oct 1968

Malcolm Goldsmith–Jan 1968

John 'Gordon' Hudson–Apr 1968

Brian Kearney–Apr 1968

Howard Menzies–Oct 1968

Beryl Nicholls–Sept 1968

Kathleen Pannell–Oct 1968

Janice Rayner–Sept 1968

Angela Ross–Oct 1968

Edward Skinner–Jan 1968

Brenda Wilton–Oct 1968

January 1968	John Fisher–June 1968
April 1968	Thomas Furber–June 1968
July 1968	Derek Berg–Oct 1968
October 1968	**NSW state team 2**
	Patricia Deal–Jan 1969
	Bruce Harris–Feb 1969
	Keith Harris–Jan 1969
	Brian Kelly–Feb 1969
	Ingrid Little–Feb 1969
	Ronald McLerie–Jan 1969
	Edward Skinner–Feb 1969
	Elvie Stevans–Feb 1969
	Janice Wall–Feb 1969
January 1969	**Royal Perth team 1**
	John Morriss–Aug 1969
	Margaret Power–Aug 1969
	Leo Stubber–Aug 1969
February 1969	Russell Bradshaw–Aug 1969
	Kevin Cullen–Apr 1969
	John Lekias–May 1969
	Susan McDonald–Aug 1969
	Kay McNamara–Aug 1969
	Christine Stocker–Aug 1969
April 1969	John Venerys–July 1969
	Patrick Cranley–Aug 1969
August 1969	**Royal Perth team 2**
	Marlene Hansen–Dec 1969
	Carole Hunter–Dec 1969
	Ian Lishman–Nov 1969

Peter Payne–Jan 1970

Ellison Scott–Jan 1970

Susan Wallace–Dec 1969

October 1969 James Bowie–Dec 1969

March 1970 **Team medical personnel detached from Bien Hoa teams**

Campbell Penfold–Aug 1970

Christine Penfold–Aug 1970

August 1970 Iain MacMillan–Sept 1970

September 1970 Raymond Bruce Hocking–Oct 1970

October 1970 James Sinclair–Dec 1970

No Australian presence at Long Xuyen from 4 December 1970.

Bien Hoa

January 1966 **Alfred Hospital (Melbourne)**

Daphne Amos–May 1966

Heather Beveridge–May 1966

Kathleen Hirst–July 1966

Peter Mangos–Apr 1966

William McDonald–Jan 1966

Barbara Phillips–May 1966

Murray 'Chan' Piercy–Apr 1966

Mary Carolyn Rigg–July 1966

Robert Wyllie–Apr 1966

April 1966 Ian Ferguson–July 1966

Robert Gray–July 1966

Ian 'Cas' McInnes–July 1967

May 1966 Josie Champion–Aug 1966

Carolin Milne–Aug 1966

Rosalie Moy–Aug 1966

	Miriam Steer–Sept 1966
July 1966	John Flynn–Jan 1967
	Graeme Grove–Oct 1966
	Paul Maher–Aug 1966
	Nada Marovich–Apr 1967
	Leo Rosner–Oct 1966
	David Scott–Oct 1966
	James Villiers–Oct 1966 (first tour to Long Xuyen Oct 1964–Feb 1965)
	Alexander Wood–Oct 1966
August 1966	Norma Veronica 'Von' Clinch–Jan 1967
	Suzanne Leyland–Jan 1967
	Maureen McLeod–Jan 1967
	Wendy Williams–Apr 1967
October 1966	Victor Brand–Jan 1967
	David Brownbill–Jan 1967
	Edward Cordner–Jan 1967
	Guy Hutchinson–Jan 1967
	Paul Large–Jan 1967
	John Snell–Jan 1967
January 1967	Dorothy 'Dot' Angell–Apr 1967
	Hugh Dudley–Apr 1967
	Gillian Geddes–Apr 1967
	Robert John Knight–Apr 1967
	Robert Lawson–Apr 1967
	Pamela Matenson–Apr 1967
	John Clarke McNeur–Apr 1967
	Phil Nurcombe–Nov 1967
	Ruth Parker–Apr 1967
	Maxwell Robinson–Apr 1967
	David Samuel Rosengarten–Apr 1967
	Barbara Walton–Apr 1967

April 1967	**Royal Adelaide Hospital**
	Mervyn Smith–June 1967
	John Barker–July 1967
	Brian Cornish–July 1967
	Josephine Griffin–Oct 1967
	Elizabeth Harvey–Oct 1967
	Olga Nicholls–Oct 1967
	Margaret Bolton–Oct 1967
	Aileen Monck–Oct 1967
	John Quirk–Oct 1967
	Douglas Townsend–Sept 1967
	Hugh Douglas (from Royal Brisbane) –July 1967
May 1967	Jeanette 'Jenny' Leak–Oct 1967
July 1967	Thomas Allen–Oct 1967
	Peter Last–Oct 1967
	Rodney White–Sept 1967
	Graham Charles Wilson–Oct 1967
October 1967	**Royal Brisbane Hospital**
	Iain Brotchie–Sept 1968
	Brian Courtice–Jan 1968
	William Friend–Jan 1968
	Judith Hagen–Sept 1968
	Elizabeth Harvey–Apr 1968 (with Royal Adelaide Apr–Oct 1967)
	Vivienne Hassett–Sept 1968
	Margaret Howitt–Jan 1968
	Carmel Jorgensen–Sept 1968
	Susan Mack–Sept 1968
	Patricia McLay–Sept 1968
	Therese O'Brian–Sept 1968

Phillip Pozzi–Oct 1968

Thomas Sale–Sept 1968

William John Scott–Aug 1968

Barry Smithurst–Jan 1968

Richard Westmorland–Sept 1968

William Mullins–Oct 1968

January 1968   Ronald Aitken–Apr 1968

Peter Grant–Apr 1968

Daniel Hogg–Apr 1968

John Lahz–Apr 1968

John Nye–Apr 1968

April 1968   Geoffrey Bourke–July 1968

Kevin King–July 1968

John Lee–July 1968

Selim 'Sam' Mellick–July 1968

Bill Laister–July 1968

July 1968   Felix Arden–Oct 1968

John Graff–Oct 1968

Donald Leaming–Oct 1968

John Pozzi–Oct 1968

Donald Tuffley–Oct 1968

September 1968   **Princess Alexandra Hospital (Brisbane)**

Geoffrey Bourke–Feb 1969

Wilemina Buchholz–Jan 1969

Norman Scott Young–Jan 1969

Helen Fraser–Jan 1969

Raymund Godwin–Jan 1969

P. Manson–Jan 1969

Anita Patterson–Jan 1969

J. Saunders–Jan 1969

K. Simpson–Jan 1969

	Pat Warren–Jan 1969
	Marjorie Winter–Jan 1969
October 1968	William Maguire–Jan 1969
	Alan Maruff–Feb 1969
	Brian Purssey–Dec 1969
	Leslie Robert Reid–Jan 1969
	John Windsor–Jan 1969
	George Murray–Feb 1969

January 1969   **Alfred Hospital (Melbourne)**

Beverley Allan–July 1969

Robyn Anderson–Nov 1969

Joan Carter–July 1969

Margaret Clements–July 1969

John Flynn–Feb 1970 (first tour
  July 1966–Jan 1967)

Thelma Foxall–July 1969

Robert Fraser–July 1969

Eric Goulston–July 1969

Rosalind Hardman–July 1969

Max Lovie–Mar 1969

Nada Marovich–July 1969 (first tour July
  1966–Apr 1967)

Michael Martin–Apr 1969

Bernard Ryan–Aug 1969 (first tour to Long
  Xuyen June–Oct 1966)

James Sinclair–Aug 1969

February 1969   Michael Shields–Aug 1969

Brian Smith–July 1969

Johanna Van Valen–July 1969

March 1969   Gavan O'Connor–July 1969 (Jan–Mar 1969
  in Vung Tau)

May 1969	Leon Bryan–Aug 1969
	Hugh Dudley–Aug 1969 (first tour Jan–Apr 1967)
June 1969	Gwenda Hassett–Aug 1969
	Yvonne McLaren–Jan 1970
July 1969	Elizabeth Bethune–Feb 1970
	Brian Buxton–Oct 1969
	Phyllis Cameron–Feb 1970
	Edward 'Weary' Dunlop–Oct 1969
	Anthony Dwyer–Feb 1970
	Jennifer Dyason–Feb 1970 (first tour Feb–Oct 1967)
	Judith McCormack–Jan 1970
	Helen Montgarrett–Feb 1970
	Barbara Phillips–Feb 1970 (first tour Jan–May 1966)
	Joan Pryor–Feb 1970 (first tour to Long Xuyen Apr–Oct 1967)
	James Sidey–Oct 1969
August 1969	Bernard Dunn–Nov 1969 (first tour to Long Xuyen May–Aug 1965)
	John Forbes–Nov 1969
	Paul Large–Nov 1969 (first tour Oct 1966– Jan 1967)
	Iain MacMillan–Nov 1969 (first tour to Long Xuyen July–Oct 1967)
October 1969	David Cousins–Feb 1970
	Graeme Grove–Jan 1970 (first tour July–Oct 1966)
	Brian Jordon–Feb 1970
	Graeme Minifie (1 Nov)–Feb 1970
	Bruce Munday–Apr 1970

Jane Oldfield–Apr 1970

Helen Perrin–Apr 1970

David Rosengarten–Jan 1970
  (first tour Jan–Apr 1967)

Bernard Ryan–Feb 1970
  (second tour Jan–Aug 1969)

December 1969   Justin Miller–Mar 1970

January 1970   **Royal Adelaide Hospital**

Thomas Allen–Aug 1970
  (first tour July–Oct 1967)

Margaret Bolton–Aug 1970
  (first tour Apr–Oct 1967)

Dawn Garnaut–July 1970

Elaine Glenn–Aug 1970

Betty Lockwood–July 1970

Gordon McKay–date unknown

Colin McLeay–Apr 1970

Olga Nichols–Aug 1970
  (first tour Apr–Oct 1967)

Joan Pitcher–Aug 1970

Charles Shearer–May 1970

Mervyn Smith–May 1970
  (first tour Mar–June 1967)

John Watson–Aug 1970

James Young–Mar 1970

February 1970   James Campbell Penfold–Aug 1970 (seconded to
  Long Xuyen from March)

Christine Penfold–Aug 1970 (seconded to Long
  Xuyen from March)

March 1970   Elizabeth Gordon–June 1970

April 1970   Erica Badman–Aug 1970

William Betts–Aug 1970
Christine Cock–Oct 1970
Geoffrey Mellor–July 1970
Alexander Nield–July 1970
Thomas Paxon–July 1970
Anthony Slavotinek–July 1970

July 1970   **Royal Melbourne Hospital**
John Quirk–Jan 1971 (first tour
    Apr–Oct 1967)
Margaret Cooper–Jan 1971
Mariamma Daniel–Nov 1970
William Daniel–Nov 1970
Geoffrey Darby–Oct 1970
Judith Kamm–Jan 1971
Vivien Lindley–Jan 1971
Glenis Little–Jan 1971
Iain MacMillan–Dec 1970 (second tour
    Aug–Nov 1969)
Andrew Crapp–Nov 1970
Arthur Waterhouse–Oct 1970
Helen Richardson–Apr 1971
Joyce Frew (from St Vincent's Sydney)–Jan 1971

August 1970   A.G. Milson–Dec 1970
Fiona Bird–Feb 1971

September 1970   Raymond Bruce Hocking–Dec 1970
    (seconded to Long Xuyen Sept–Oct 1970)

October 1970   Richard Levy–Jan 1971
Donald Macleish–Jan 1971 (first tour to
    Long Xuyen Oct 1964–Jan 1965)
James Sinclair–Jan 1971 (seconded to
    Long Xuyen Oct–Nov 1970)

	David Wallace–Jan 1971
	Peter Wearne–Jan 1971
November 1970	Colin Richmond Climie–Feb 1971
	Ann Read–Feb 1971
January 1971	**Queensland hospitals team**
	Helen Banff–July 1971
	Geoffrey Bourke–June 1971 (first tour Apr–July 1968)
	Brian Courtice–June 1971 (first tour Oct 1967–Jan 1968)
	David Dickens–Oct 1971
	Judith Dittmer–July 1971
	Paul Manson–July 1971
	L. McGuire–July 1971
	William Parker–Apr 1971
	Janice Richardson–July 1971
	Jill Storch–July 1971
	John Thompson–date unknown
	Janice Tickner–July 1971
February 1971	Peter Verras–Sept 1971
April 1971	Ian Chenoweth–Aug 1971
	Ruth Chenoweth–Aug 1971
	Brian Sommerlad–July 1971
	Ann Stewart–Feb 1972
May 1971	Kiernan Dorney–Aug 1971
	Kevin McLachlan–Aug 1971
July 1971	**St Vincent's Hospital (Sydney)**
	Robyn Beharell–Feb 1972
	David Bennett–Feb 1972
	Timothy Bohane–Oct 1971

Frederick Collins–Oct 1971

Victor Fazio–Oct 1971

Elizabeth Harmston–date unknown

Lola Higgs–Jan 1972

Berenice Lenze–Jan 1972

Basil McNamara–Oct 1971

David Pledger–Feb 1972

Carmel Rigby–Feb 1972

Mary Michael–date unknown

Joyce Frew–date unknown (first tour July
  1970–Jan 1971)

October 1971   Brian Symons–Feb 1972

Reginald Lord–Feb 1972

David Ramsden–Feb 1972

Graham Thompson–Jan 1972

November 1971   Robert McKenzie–Feb 1972

January 1972   **SEATO composite team**

James Ellis–Mar 1972 (first tour to
  Vung Tau Dec 1967–June 1968)

Russell Williams–date unknown

John Matherson–Apr 1972

John Vandervord–Dec 1972

Britt Kinell–date unknown

Cathy Blackmore–date unknown

Frances Sardelich–July 1972

Roslyn Lockhart–Oct 1972

Ann Stewart–Dec 1972

John Spehr–Dec 1972

July 1972   Bill Bye–Oct 1972

Ian Wheatley–Oct 1972

Margaret Staff–Dec 1972

	Jill Storch–Dec 1972
October 1972	Paul Large–Dec 1972
	James Don Sidey–Dec 1972 (first tour July–Oct 1969)
	Helen Montgarrett–Dec 1972
	Robyn Beharell–Dec 1972

Hospital officially handed over to South Vietnamese on 28 December 1972. Team's last day 29 December 1972.

Vung Tau

November 1966	**Prince Henry and Prince of Wales hospitals (Sydney)**
	Dorothy Burgess–May 1967
	Julie Cearns–May 1967
	Thomas 'Tom' Hugh–Feb 1967
	Jennifer James–May 1967
	Rhonda James–May 1967
	Noel Lucas–Feb 1967
	John Martin–May 1967
	Robert Perrett–May 1967
	Ellen Prendergast–May 1967
	Julia Quinn–May 1967
	Judith Ross–Feb 1967
	Graham Douglas 'Doug' Tracy–Feb 1967
	George Wilson–Nov 1967
February 1967	Michael Aroney–May 1967
	Colin Friendship–May 1967
	Gilbert Lynch–May 1967
March 1967	Peter Miles–Dec 1967

May 1967	**Royal Prince Alfred Hospital (Sydney)**
	Douglas Baird–Aug 1967
	Helen Beasley–Nov 1967
	Bruce Clifton–Aug 1967
	Lorna Finnie–Nov 1967
	Thomas McNamara–Nov 1967
	Simone Reynolds–Nov 1967
	Charles Sharpe–Aug 1967
	Donald Sheldon–Aug 1967
	Marie Townsend–Nov 1967
	Diana Wright–Nov 1967
August 1967	Colin Andrews–Nov 1967
	Michael Bookalil–Nov 1967
	Norman Wyndham–Nov 1967
November 1967	**Commonwealth Repatriation team 1**
	Jan Bell–Dec 1968
	Myra Chenery–Dec 1968
	James Downie–Feb 1968
	Lindsay Fitzgerald–Nov 1968
	Derek Meyers–Feb 1968
	Marita Mulcahy–Dec 1968
	Bruce Munday–Jan 1969
	John O'Brian–Dec 1968
	Gerta Peham–July 1969
	Isaac Segal–Oct 1968
December 1967	James Ellis–June 1968
March 1968	Kenneth Hume–June 1968
April 1968	Brian Dickens–July 1968
June 1968	Richard Cowdery–Sept 1968
	William Law–Sept 1968
	Barry Pascoe–Sept 1968

September 1968	Kevin Orr–Dec 1968
	George Palmer–Nov 1968
	Mark Sheppard–Nov 1968
	Geraldine 'Estelle' Gladstone–date unknown
	John Williams–date unknown
November 1968	**Commonwealth Repatriation team 2**
	Rosemary Coffey–Feb 1969
	Jan Olsen–May 1969
	Jack Steel–May 1969
	Keith Sweetman–May 1969
	William 'Bill' Townsend–July 1969
	Lynn Ward–May 1969
December 1968	Clive Jones–Jan 1969
	Colin McRae–Mar 1969
	Robert Rayner–Apr 1969
January 1969	Gavan O'Connor–Mar 1969
	Robert Hodge–Apr 1969
February 1969	John Davenport–May 1969
	Susan MacDonald–July 1969
April 1969	Ronald Smith–June 1969
	David Watson–July 1969
	Elaine Evans–Sept 1969

Ba Ria

November 1967	**Subsidiary of Commonwealth Repatriation teams based at Vung Tau**
	Douglas Blake–Nov 1968
	Barbara Buscombe–Mar 1969
October 1968	Pat Healey–Mar 1969
	Peter Malouf–date unknown

Susan 'Sue' Quinn–Mar 1969

William Quirke–date unknown

January 1969   Donald Cordner–Apr 1969

Note: While every effort has been made to ensure this listing is as complete as possible, the authors recognise that some personnel may have been left out, and that there may be errors in the spelling of names and dates of service. They welcome any corrections to the listing.

Notes

Introduction

1   Indochina consisted of the colony of Cochinchina and the protectorates of Annam, Tonkin, Cambodia and Laos. Cochin and Annam became South Vietnam and Tonkin North Vietnam.

2   'Biographical Information on Prominent Nationalist Leaders in French Indochina', US Department of State Research and Intelligence Service, 25 October 1945.

3   'Memorandum from General Omar Bradley, Chairman of the Joint Chiefs of Staff, to the Secretary of Defense on the Strategic Assessment of Southeast Asia, 10 April 1950', *Pentagon Papers*, Gravel edition, Vol. 1, Document 3, pp. 363–6.

4   'Press release by President Truman announcing military assistance to Indochina, 27 June 1950', *Pentagon Papers*, Gravel Edition, Vol. 1, Document 8, pp. 372–3.

5   'News conference, 7 April 1954', *Public Papers of the Presidents of the United States: Dwight D. Eisenhower, 1954*, US Government Printing Office, 1960, pp. 382–3.

6   'Memorandum of Conference on January 19, 1961 between President Eisenhower and President-Elect Kennedy on the Subject of Laos', *Pentagon Papers*, Gravel Edition, Vol. 2, pp. 635–7.

7   Peter Chalk, 'Australian Foreign and Defense SE Asia policy in the wake of 1999–2000 East Timor Intervention', RAND Organization, Chapter 2, 2001.

8   For a full account of the AATTV, see McKay and Davies, *The Men Who Persevered*, Allen & Unwin, 2005.

Chapter 1

1   Brass, *Bleeding Earth*, p. 21.

2   Ibid.

3   Game, 'Report on the Request to Provide Surgical Teams for Viet-Nam', 21 August 1962, file 2481/5/40 part 1, A1838, NAA, p. 2.

4   Ibid, p. 3.

5   DEA paper, 'Medical Assistance: Vietnam—Future composition of medical/surgical teams', 4 October 1967, file 2481/5/40 part 9, A1838, NAA.

6   Author unknown, 'DDMS Technical Weekend 18–19 September 1965: Care of civilian population—South Vietnam'. Source unknown. Copy held by the authors.

7   DEA paper, untitled, on conditions under which team members served, 21 September 1967, p. 3. Copy supplied from Alfred Hospital archive, held by authors.

8   Interview with William Townsend.

9   Ibid.

10   Ibid.

11   Interview with Janet Brewster.

12   Last, 'Some brief initial impressions'.

13   Questionnaire response from John Morriss.

14   Kay Dabovich, Department of Veterans' Affairs (DVA) interview.

15   Interview with Dot Angell.

16   Ibid.

17   Interview with Jenny Hunter.

18   Questionnaire response from John Morriss.

19   Interview with Peter Last.

20   Letter, Gavan O'Connor to Dolores O'Connor, early January 1969. Reproduced with kind permission of Gavan O'Connor.

21   Interview with William Townsend.

22   Interview with Doug Tracy.

23   Interview with Jan Bell.

24   Interview with Doug Tracy.

25   Interview with Joan Rose.

26   Interview with Janet Brewster.

27   Interview with Dot Angell.

28   Interview with William Townsend.

29   Interview with Dot Angell.

30   Last, 'Some brief initial impressions'.

31   Interview with Tom Hugh.

32   Interview with Gavan O'Connor.

Chapter 2

1   Brass, *Bleeding*, p. 25.

2   Ibid.

3   Terry, *House of Love*, p. 2.

4   Ibid, pp. 4–5.

5   James Villiers, DVA interview.

6   Terry, *House of Love*, pp. 5–6.

7   Macleish, 'The Australian Surgical Team', p. 1.

8   Terry, *House of Love*, p. 6.

9   Macleish, 'The Australian Surgical Team', p. 3.

10   Interview with Noelle Laidlaw.

11   Macleish, 'The Australian Surgical Team', p. 4.

12   Terry, *House of Love*, pp. 16–17.

13   Interview with Noelle Laidlaw.

14   Macleish, 'The Australian Surgical Team', p. 13.

15   Ibid, pp. 6–7.

16   Terry, *House of Love*, p. 21.

17   Ibid, p. 42.

18   Macleish, 'The Australian Surgical Team', p. 16.

19   Interview with Noelle Laidlaw.

20   James Villiers, DVA interview.

21   Ibid.

22   Terry, *House of Love*, p. 69.

23   Ibid, p. 18.

24   Macleish, 'The Australian Surgical Team', pp. 18–19.

25   Report, 'Concerning the Activities of the Royal Melbourne Hospital Surgical Team in Long Xuyen at the Completion of the First Two Months in South Vietnam', PR89/49, AWM.

26   Macleish, 'The Australian Surgical Team', p. 10.

27   Hughes, 'Report on Visit to Long Xuyen, South Vietnam—December 5th and 6th 1964', 15 December 1964, file 2481/5/29 Annex, A1838, NAA.

28   Ibid.

29   Macleish, 'The Australian Surgical Team', p. 23.

30   Ryan and Hurley, 'Report upon the Australian Surgical Team'.

31   Letter, Susan Terry to Mr Marshall, 20 November 1965, file 2481/5/40 part 5, A1838, NAA.

32   Grove, 'Background', p. 7.

33   James Villiers, DVA interview.

34   Bernard Dunn, DVA interview.

35   Clive Bond, personal papers, p. 29.

36   Macleish, 'The Australian Surgical Team', p. 12.

37   Nam Phuong, *Red on Gold*, pp. 99–100.

38   Terry, *House of Love*, p. 75.

39   Brass, *Bleeding*, p. 30.

40   Interview with Noelle Laidlaw.

41   Jenny O'Neill, diary, 27 October 1966, private collection.

42   Terry, 'Nursing in Vietnam', p. 17.

43   Interview with Jan Mills.

44   Dr Brian Kearney, 'Report on Paediatric Ward, Long Xuyen, 10/10/1967–13/4/1968', author's copy.

45   Barr, *Surgery*, p. 238.

46   Terry, 'Nursing in Vietnam', p. 17.

47   Jenny O'Neill, diary, 4 February 1967.

48   Interview with Joan Rose.

49   Interview with Barbara Sutherland.

50   Clive Bond, personal papers, p. 13.

51   Thompson, 'Vietnam: Medical Aid'.

52   Interview with Peter Last.

53   Thompson, 'Vietnam: Medical Aid'.

54   Dr Brian Kearney, 'Report on Paediatric Ward, Long Xuyen, 10/10/1967–13/4/1968', author's copy.

55   Interview with Robert Birrell.

56   Interview with Janet Brewster.

57   Interview with Robert Birrell.

58   Author unknown, *Medical Journal of Australia*, Vol. 2, No. 8, 19 August 1967. This issue of the *MJA* published a series of articles that were presented at a symposium on the Australian surgical teams in South Vietnam at a meeting of the Australian Medical Association (Victorian Branch) on 3 May 1967.

59   Brass, *Bleeding*, p. 28.

60   Villiers, 'A Second Look', p. 24.

61   Report of the team leader, Australian Surgical Team, Long Xuyen, October 1968–January 1969, PR00926, AWM.

62   Jenny O'Neill, diary, 25 October 1966.

63   Dr Huynh Trung Nhi, speech to Australian delegation, Long Xuyen, 3 March 1969, file 2481/5/45/14, A1838, NAA.

64   Bennetts, 'Medical Battle', in the *Age*, 18 October 1967.

65   Clive Bond, personal papers, p. 17.

66   Clive Bond, letter tape to his children, personal papers.

67   Clive Bond, letter to his father, personal papers.

68   Cablegram, Australian Embassy Saigon to Department of External Affairs, 5 March 1968, file 2481/5/41/1, A1838, NAA.

69   Interview with Janet Brewster.

70   Letter, Coral Bond to her parents, 14 May 1968, in Clive Bond personal papers.

71   Jenny O'Neill, diary, 17 January 1967.

72   Interview with Barbara Sutherland.

73   Interview with Jenny Hunter.

74   Joan Rose, letter, 21 June 1967.

75   Stubber, 'Final Report', p. 6.

76   Ibid, p. 10.

77   Sunderland, *Australian Civilian Medical Aid*.

78   Lindell, 'Report to His Excellency', file 2481/5/45/14, A1838, NAA.

79   Grove, 'Report to His Excellency', file 2481/5/40/10, A1838, NAA.

80   Team leader's report, Australian Surgical Team Bien Hoa, June 1970, file 2481/5/42/12 part 1, A1838, NAA.

81   Team leader's bulletin, Australian Surgical Team Bien Hoa, November 1970, file 2481/5/42/12 part 1, A1838, NAA.

Chapter 3

1   Wikipedia and Mesko, *VNAF*.

2   Ryan, 'Visit to Bien Hoa Hospital'.

3   Maureen Spicer, personal memoir, 11 August 2007.

4   Letter by Daphne Amos, January 1966.

5   Alfred Hospital, 'Faces and Places'.

6   Interview with Bob Gray.

7   Alfred Hospital, 'Faces and Places'.

8   Game, 'Report on the Request to Provide Surgical Teams', 21 August 1962, file 2481/5/40 part 1, A1838, NAA.

9   Interview with Peter Mangos.

10   Ibid.

11   Maureen Spicer, personal memoir.

12   Interview with Jenny Leak.

13   Interview with Peter Mangos.

14   Maureen Spicer, personal memoir.

15   Interview with Canny Coventry.

16   Ibid.

17   Interview with Von Clinch.

18   Interview with Peter Mangos.

19   Maureen Spicer, personal memoir.

20   Interview with Peter Mangos.

21   Maureen Spicer, personal memoir.

22   Letter, Kathleen Hirst, 6 February 1966.

23   Iain Brotchie, DVA interview, p. 102.

24   W. McDonald, second report, January 1966, file 2481/5/42/5 part 1, A1838, NAA.

25   W. McDonald, third Bien Hoa report, February 1966, file 2481/5/42/5 part 1, A1838, NAA.

26   W. McDonald, fourth Bien Hoa report, 8 April 1966, file 2481/5/42/5 part 1, A1838, NAA.

27   Large, 'Bizarre and Unusual Aspects of Surgery in South Vietnam'.

28   Alfred Hospital, 'Faces and Places'.

29   Interview with Bob Gray.

30   Ibid.

31   Interview with Ian McInnes.

32   *Sun*, article by Geoff Murray, 12 May 1966.

33   Paul Large, DVA interview, p. 41.

34   Ian Ferguson, sixth report, 18 May 1966, file 2481/5/42/5 part 1, A1838, NAA.

35   Interview with Bob Gray.

36   Dextrose was a mixture of sugar and water.

37   Interview with Bob Gray.

38   Interview with Helen Banff.

39   Tom Sale, monthly Bien Hoa report, April 1969, file 2481/5/42/5 part 2, A1838, NAA.

40   Interview with Ian McInnes.

41   Interview with Von Clinch.

42   Ibid.

43   Ibid.

44   Ian Ferguson, team report, Bien Hoa, 3 June 1966, NAA Series A1838.

45   Wendy Jobberns, DVA interview.

46   Graeme Grove, Bien Hoa report, 11 August 1966, file 2481/5/42/5 part 1, A1838, NAA.

47   Interview with Paul Large.

48   Ibid.

49   Ibid.

50   Interview with Aileen Monck.

51   Interview with Paul Large.

52   Ibid.

53   Director General of Health, Memo 66/1542, 16 November 1966.

54   Paul Large, Bien Hoa report, 19 December 1966, file 2481/5/42/5 part 1, A1838, NAA.

55   Ibid.

56   Letter, Von Clinch to Director of Nursing at Alfred Hospital, 24 December 1966, private collection, copy held by authors.

57   Interview with Suzanne MacFarlane.

58   Ibid.

59   Interview with Von Clinch.

60   Interview with David Brownbill.

61   Interview with Von Clinch.

62   Ibid.

63   Ibid.

64   Interview with Dot Angell.

65   Ibid.

66   Robert Lawson, January Bien Hoa report, 5 February 1967, file 2481/5/42/5 part 1, A1838, NAA.

67   Letter, Hugh Dudley, 19 June 1967, file 2481/5/42/5 part 1, A1838, NAA.

68   Robert Lawson, February Bien Hoa report, 2 March 1967, file 2481/5/42/5 part 1, A1838, NAA.

69   Letter, Dot Angell, 27 January 1967, private collection.

70   Robert Lawson, February Bien Hoa report, 2 March 1967, file 2481/5/42/5 part 1, A1838, NAA.

71   Robert Lawson, March Bien Hoa report, 3 April 1967, file 2481/5/42/5 part 1, A1838, NAA.

72   Alfred Hospital, 'Faces and Places'.

73   Interview with Elizabeth and John Scott.

74   Interview with Robyn Anderson.

75   Maureen Spicer, personal memoir.

76   Johanna Van Valen, DVA interview.

77   Interview with Betty Lockwood.

78   Interview with Jenny Leak.

79   Ibid.

80   Ibid.

81   Interview with Peter Last.

82   Ibid.

83   Helicopter battlefield evacuation of casualties. Dustoff was termed by some an acronym for 'dedicated and untiring service to our fighting forces'.

84   Interview with Josephine Howard.

85   Interview with Aileen Monck.

86   Interview with Margaret Bolton.

87   Interview with Carmel Hurst.

88   Ibid.

89   Ibid.

90   Iain Brotchie, DVA interview.

91   Tom Sale, monthly Bien Hoa report, April 1969, file 2481/5/42/5 part 2, A1838, NAA.

92   Iain Brotchie, DVA interview.

93   Civilian Irregular Defense Groups were part-time soldiers trained and sometimes led by American Special Forces training teams.

94   Tom Sale, monthly Bien Hoa report, April 1969, file 2481/5/42/5 part 2, A1838, NAA.

95   Letter, Carmel Hurst, c. December 1967.

96   Interview with Elizabeth and John Scott.

97   Interview with Carmel Hurst.

98   Peter Grant, DVA interview.

99   Interview with Elizabeth and John Scott.

100   Ibid.

101   Ibid.

102   Ibid.

103   Ibid.

104   Ibid.

105   Ibid.

106   Interview with Suzanne MacFarlane.

107   Interview with Paul Large.

108   Tom Sale, monthly Bien Hoa report, March 1968, file 2481/5/42/5 part 2, A1838, NAA.

109   Tom Sale, monthly Bien Hoa report, April 1968, file 2481/5/42/5 part 2, A1838, NAA.

110   Tom Sale, monthly Bien Hoa report, September 1968, file 2481/5/42/5 part 2, A1838, NAA.

111   Interview with Elizabeth and John Scott.

112   Kevin King, letter to DEA, 13 April 1969, A1838, NAA.

113   Tom Sale, post-tour report, April 1969, file 2481/5/42/5 part 2, A1838, NAA.

114   Pat Warren, interview for *The Sharp End*.

Chapter 4

1   This agency, set up by US President Lyndon Johnson, created an interagency headquarters that streamlined US efforts in support of the South Vietnamese government against Viet Cong insurgents.

2   Interview with Robyn Anderson.

3   Ibid.

4   Ibid.

5   Ibid.

6   Ibid.

7   Ibid.

8   Letter, Brian Smith to Graeme Grove, 5 March 1969, A1838, NAA.

9   Interview with Robyn Anderson.

10   Ibid.

11   Security Minute by Brian Smith, 18 February 1969, A1838, NAA.

12   Interview with Gavan O'Connor.

13   DEA, press release, 'Medical Aid to Vietnam', 3 July 1969, A1838, NAA.

14   Brian Smith, team report, Bien Hoa, February 1969, file 2481/5/42/5 part 2, A1838, NAA.

15   Letter, Professor Hugh Dudley to W. Philip, Alfred Hospital, 23 June 1969, file 2481/5/42/5 part 1, A1838, NAA.

16   Interview with Jenny Hunter.

17   Interview with Paul Large.

18   DEA Statement issued in Melbourne on 28 April 1969 at conclusion of conference on medical aid to Vietnam, 5 May 1969, A1838, NAA.

19   Interview with Joan Rose.

20   Interview with Paul Large.

21   Interview with Don Sidey.

22   Ibid.

23   Johanna Van Valen, DVA interview.

24   Bernard Dunn, DVA interview.

25   Graeme Grove, team report, Bien Hoa, October 1969, file 2481/5/42/5 part 2, A1838, NAA.

26   Taplin, 'My Story 1969–70'.

27   Interview with Carmel Hurst.

28   Interview with Elizabeth and John Scott.

29   Pat Warren, interview for *The Sharp End*.

30   Interview with Helen Banff (1989).

31   Ibid.

32   Graeme Grove, Bien Hoa team reports October–December 1969 inclusive, file 2481/5/42/5 part 2, A1838, NAA.

33   Graeme Grove, team report, Bien Hoa, December 1969, file 2481/5/42/5 part 2, A1838, NAA.

34   Interview with Betty Lockwood.

35   Ibid.

36   Letter, Gavan O'Connor to authors, 30 August 2006.

37   Interview with Betty Lockwood.

38   Interview with Elaine Ray.

39   Interview with Margaret Bolton.

40   Bill Betts, team report, Bien Hoa, May–August 1970, SA State Team, file 2481/5/42/5, A1838, NAA.

41   A.R. Waterhouse, team report, Bien Hoa, August–October 1970, Royal Melbourne Team, file 2481/5/42/6, A1838, NAA.

42   Ibid.

43   A.R. Waterhouse, Bulletin, Bien Hoa, file 2481/5/42/12 part 1, A1838, NAA.

44   D.G. Macleish, Bulletin, Bien Hoa, December 1970, file 2481/5/42/12 part 1, NAA.

45   A.R. Waterhouse and D.G. Macleish, Bulletin, Bien Hoa, October–November 1970, and D.G. Macleish, Bulletin, Bien Hoa, December 1970, file 2481/5/42/12 part 1, A1838, NAA.

46   Helen Banff, Report of Senior Nurse, Bien Hoa, January–July 1971, 18 July 1971, file 2481/5/42/6, A1838, NAA.

47   G.M. Bourke, team report, Bien Hoa, February–May 1971, 11 October 1971, file 2481/5/42/6, A1838, NAA.

48   Interview with Jill Storch.

49   Ibid.

50   Berenice Dawson, DVA interview.

51   Ibid.

52   Reginald Lord, team report, Bien Hoa, December 1971, file 2481/5/42/12 part 1, A1838, NAA.

53   J.S. Boxall, Department of Health Report, Bien Hoa, 5 August 1971, file 2481/5/42/6, A1838, NAA.

54   Ibid.

55   Interview with Jill Storch.

56   Ibid.

57   Paul Large, DVA interview.

58   W.D. Refshauge, Director General of Health, Canberra, ACT, 21 December 1971, file 2481/5/40/30, A1838, NAA.

59   Frances Byak, DVA interview.

60   Ibid.

61   John Matheson, team report, Bien Hoa, April 1972, file 2481/5/42/12 part 1, A1838, NAA.

62   John Matheson, team report, Bien Hoa, May 1972, file 2481/5/42/12 part 1, A1838, NAA.

63   Interview with Paul Large.

64   Ibid.

65   Interview with Don Sidey.

66   Ibid.

67   Interview with Ian McInnes.

68   Interview with Paul Large.

69   Interview with David Brownbill.

70   Interview with Aileen Monck.

71   Paul Large, final report, Bien Hoa, December 1972, file 2481/5/42/6, A1838, NAA.

Chapter 5

1   M.G. Williams, 'Report on Possibilities of Locating a Third Australian Surgical Team in Vung Tau', 19 August 1966, file 2481/5/29/7, A1838, NAA.

2   Ibid.

3   Interview with Doug Tracy.

4   Daily Telegraph, 17 November 1966.

5   Message, 'Another Australian Medical Team Arrives in Vietnam', 29 November 1966, file 2481/5/43 part 1, A1838, NAA.

6   Interview with Noel Lucas.

7   Interview with Doug Tracy.

8   Siobhan McHugh, *Minefields and Miniskirts: Australian women and the Vietnam War*, Doubleday, 1993, p. 8.

9   Interview with Tom Hugh.

10 McHugh, *Minefields and Miniskirts*, p. 8.

11 Interview with Tom Hugh.

12 Letter, Gavan O'Connor to colleagues, 6 February 1969.

13 Interview with Doug Tracy.

14 Interview with Tom Hugh.

15 Ibid.

16 Ibid.

17 Letter, Mike and Minh Hall to Noel Lucas, 27 November 2002.

18 Interview with Tom Hugh.

19 D.G. Tracy, 'Report on First Three Months' Experience of Third Australian Surgical Team Stationed at Le Loi Hospital, Vung Tau', 1 March 1967, file 2481/5/43 part 1, A1838, NAA.

20 Interview with Tom Hugh.

21 Derek Meyers, 'Vietnam Scrapbook', *British Medical Journal*, Vol. 3, No. 5613, 3 August 1968, p. 305.

22 Interview with Marita Mulcahy.

23 Interview with Doug Tracy.

24 Sheldon, 'R.P.A.H. Sends a Surgical Team to Vietnam'.

25 Ibid.

26 Meyers, 'Vietnam Scrapbook', p. 306.

27 Interview with Jan Bell.

28 Interview with Barbara Buscombe.

29 Meyers, 'Vietnam Scrapbook', p. 306.

30 Interview with James Ellis.

31 Barr, *Surgery*, p. 102.

32   Letter, Gavan O'Connor to his wife, 20 January 1969, private collection.

33   McHugh, *Minefields and Miniskirts*, p. 13.

34   Letter, Jan Bell to her family, 10 December 1967, private collection.

35   Email, Dick Cowdery to Mike Carlton, 1 May 2006, copy held by the authors.

36   Interview with Jan Bell.

37   Meyers, 'Vietnam Scrapbook', p. 306.

38   Interview with Doug Tracy.

39   Donald Sheldon, 'Report on the Australian Surgical Team (Vung Tau), May–August 1967', PR00926, AWM.

40   Letter, Gavan O'Connor to his wife, 20 January 1969, private collection.

41   Dr Norman Wyndham, 'Report on the work of the Third Australian Surgical Team Vung Tau, for the three months ending November 10th 1967', PR00926, AWM.

42   Interview with Gavan O'Connor.

43   Letter, Jan Bell to her family, 22 April 1968, private collection.

44   Interview with Marita Mulcahy.

45   Ministerial brief, K.C.O. Shann, First Assistant Secretary Saigon to the Minister for External Affairs, 'SEATO Aid, Vietnam: Auxiliary Surgical Team Ba Ria', 5 February 1968, file 2481/5/43/1 part 1, A1838, NAA.

46   'Report on security at Ba Ria by Australian military attaché Colonel A.F. Swinbourne', 24 June 1968, file 2481/5/43/1 part 1, A1838, NAA.

47   Interview with Sue Quinn.

48   Ibid.

49   Cordner, 'A Vista of Vietnam'.

50   Cordner, 'Australian General Practitioners in Vietnam', pp. 140–2.

51   Ibid., p. 144.

52   Interview with Sue Quinn.

53   Ibid.

54   Ibid.

55   Ibid.

56   Cordner, 'A Vista of Vietnam'.

57   Ibid.

58   Ibid.

59   Interview with Barbara Buscombe.

60   Cordner, 'A Vista of Vietnam'.

61   Ibid.

62   Cablegram, R.L. Harry to the DEA, 28 February 1969, file 2481/5/44, A1838, NAA.

63   Cablegram, R.L. Harry to the DEA, 12 March 1969, file 2481/5/44, A1838, NAA.

64   Cordner, 'A Vista of Vietnam'.

65   Ibid.

66   Letter, Jan Bell to her family, 1 February 1968, private collection.

67   Letter, Jan Bell to her family, 4 February 1968, private collection.

68   Ibid.

69   The *Heidelberger*, c. January 1969.

70   Letter, Jan Bell to her family, 6 February 1968, private collection.

71   Letter, Gavan O'Connor to his wife, 17 February 1969, private collection.

72   Sunderland, *Australian Civilian Medical Aid*, p. 6.

73   Ibid, p. 12.

74   Cablegram, Australian embassy Saigon to the DEA, 20 May 1969, file 2481/5/43 part 4, A1838, NAA.

75   Interview with William Townsend.

76   Ibid.

77   In the first part of 1969 the 1st Australian Field Hospital (1AFH) in Vung Tau was suffering from a lack of army anaesthetists and surgeons. Anaesthetist Rosemary Coffey, a member of the Repatriation Department surgical team at Le Loi Hospital, helped out by performing anaesthesia at the hospital for a week early in the year. In August of the same year Professor Hugh Dudley, Chairman of the Department of Surgery at Monash University and a member

of an Alfred Hospital team in Bien Hoa, spent eight days at 1AFH performing surgery in order to relieve some of the pressure on army surgeons. These events are recorded in O'Keefe, *Medicine at War*, pp. 164–5.

78   Interview with Gavan O'Connor.

Chapter 6

1   Interview with Peter Mangos.

2   Ian Ferguson, team report, Bien Hoa, 18 April 1966, file 2481/5/42/5 part 1, A1838, NAA.

3   Interview with Canny Coventry.

4   Interview with Ian McInnes.

5   Interview with Barbara Sutherland.

6   Interview with Jan Bell.

7   Interview with Janet Brewster.

8   Pat Warren, interview for *The Sharp End*.

9   Ibid.

10   Interview with Jan Bell.

11   Ibid.

12   Ibid.

13   Interview with Betty Lockwood.

14   Interview with Bob Gray.

15   Interview with Paul Large.

16   Maureen Spicer, personal memoir.

17   Interview with Don Sidey.

18   Interview with Betty Lockwood.

19   Wendy Jobberns, DVA interview.

20   Interview with Betty Lockwood.

21   Interview with Gavan O'Connor.

22   Interview with Robyn Anderson.

23   Interview with Ian McInnes.

24   Interview with Paul Large.

25 Maureen Spicer, personal memoir.

26 Interview with John Kendall Francis.

27 Interview with Jenny Hunter.

28 Interview with Marita Mulcahy.

29 Interview with William Townsend.

30 Interview with James Ellis.

31 Interview with Jenny Hunter.

32 Interview with David Brownbill.

33 Interview with Dot Angell.

34 Interview with Suzanne MacFarlane.

35 Interview with Elizabeth and John Scott.

36 Interview with Jill Storch.

37 Interview with Joan Rose.

38 Berenice Dawson, DVA interview.

39 Interview with Elizabeth and John Scott.

40 Interview with Bob Gray.

41 Interview with Barbara Buscombe.

42 Interview with John Kendall Francis.

43 Interview with Barbara Sutherland.

44 Interview with Janet Brewster.

45 Interview with Suzanne MacFarlane.

46 Interview with Robyn Anderson.

47 Interview with Barbara Sutherland.

48 Paul Large, 'Comments on Medical Aid Programmes in Vietnam,' c. December 1972, file 2481/5/42/6, A1838, NAA.

49 Tom Sale, team report, Bien Hoa, November 1967, file 2481/5/42/5 part 1, A1838, NAA.

50 Interview with Helen Banff.

51 Interview with Robyn Anderson.

52 Interview with Von Clinch.

53 Interview with Don Sidey.

54 Interview with Janet Brewster.

55 Interview with Barbara Sutherland.

56 Interview with Joan Rose.

57 Interview with Elaine Ray.

58 Interview with Von Clinch.

59 Interview with Aileen Monck.

60 Interview with Peter Last.

61 Interview with Jill Storch.

62 Sir Edward Dunlop, team report, Bien Hoa, August 1969, file 2481/5/42/12 part 1, A1838, NAA.

63 Interview with Doug Tracy.

64 Interview with Peter Last.

65 Interview with James Ellis.

66 Interview with Helen Banff.

67 Large, 'Comments on Medical Aid Programmes'.

68 Ibid.

Chapter 7

1   Large, 'Comments on Medical Aid Programmes'.

2   Ibid.

3   Interview with Josephine Howard.

4   Interview with Peter Mangos.

5   Ibid.

6   Interview with Paul Large.

7   Interview with Betty Lockwood.

8   Interview with Bob Gray.

9   Interview with Ian McInnes.

10 Interview with Suzanne MacFarlane.

11 Interview with Janet Brewster.

12 Interview with Marita Mulcahy.

13 Frances Byak, DVA interview.

14 Interview with Jill Storch.

15   Interview with Don Sidey.

16   Interview with Von Clinch.

17   Interview with Suzanne MacFarlane.

18   Letter, Dot Angell, 4 February 1967.

19   Frances Byak, DVA interview.

20   Interview with Josephine Howard.

21   Interview with Carmel Hurst.

22   Interview with Elaine Ray.

23   Interview with Paul Large.

24   Interview with Barbara Sutherland.

25   Ibid.

26   Interview with Jenny Hunter.

27   Interview with Dot Angell.

28   Interview with Gavan O'Connor.

29   Iain Brotchie, DVA interview.

30   Interview with Suzanne MacFarlane.

31   Interview with Joan Rose.

32   Frances Byak, DVA interview.

33   Interview with Bob Gray.

34   Interview with Betty Lockwood.

35   Ibid.

36   Interview with Don Sidey.

37   Interview with Ian McInnes.

38   Interview with Von Clinch.

39   Interview with Ian McInnes.

40   Interview with Suzanne MacFarlane.

41   Interview with Jill Storch.

42   Ibid.

43   Interview with Elizabeth and John Scott.

44   Ibid.

45   Ibid.

46   Ibid.

47   Interview with Marita Mulcahy.

48   Interview with Jan Bell.

49   Ibid.

50   Ibid.

51   Interview with Jenny Hunter.

52   Interview with Carmel Hurst.

53   Interview with Bob Gray.

54   Ibid.

55   Interview with Don Sidey.

56   Interview with Helen Banff.

Chapter 8

1   Interview with Peter Last.

2   Interview with Joan Rose.

3   Interview with Marita Mulcahy.

4   Interview with Carmel Hurst.

5   Interview with Von Clinch.

6   Interview with Betty Lockwood.

7   Interview with Noelle Laidlaw.

8   Interview with Jill Storch.

9   James Villiers, DVA interview.

10   Bernard Dunn, DVA interview.

11   Interview with Jenny Leak.

12   Interview with Gavan O'Connor.

13   Interview with Canny Coventry.

14   Interview with Dot Angell.

15   Interview with Robert Birrell.

16   Interview with Janet Brewster.

17   Interview with Barbara Sutherland.

18   Interview with Jenny Hunter.

19   Interview with Jill Storch.

20   Interview with Suzanne MacFarlane.

21   Interview with Jenny Leak.

22   Interview with Von Clinch, and Pat Warren, interview for *The Sharp End*.

23   Interview with Elizabeth and John Scott.

24   Kay Dabovich, DVA interview.

25   Interview with Von Clinch.

26   Interview with Barbara Sutherland.

27   Interview with Jo Howard.

28   Interview with Peter Last.

29   Carmel Hurst, interview for *The Sharp End*.

30   Interview with Joan Rose.

31   Interview with Jill Storch.

32   Interview with Carmel Hurst.

33   Interview with Joan Rose.

34   Interview with Robyn Anderson.

35   Interview with Ian McInnes.

Epilogue

1   The Gold Card enables the holder to access, within Australia, the full range of repatriation health care benefits, including choice of doctor, optical and dental care, chiropractic services and pharmaceuticals at the concessional rate.

2   Interview with David Brownbill.

3   In June 1966 the Australian National Line cargo vessel MV *Jeparit* sailed on its first voyage to Vietnam. The vessel had been chartered by the Department of Shipping and Transport to carry supplies for the Australian forces engaged in the war. However, after five voyages some seamen refused to man the vessel. To overcome this difficulty, crew members who were prepared to continue to serve on the *Jeparit* were supplemented by a Royal Australian Navy detachment. In February 1967 members of the Seamen's Union also refused to crew the cargo ship *Boonaroo* on its voyages to Vietnam. On 1 March 1967 the

vessel was commissioned by the Royal Australian Navy as HMAS *Boonaroo*.

4   Commonwealth of Australia, Senate Foreign Affairs, Defence and Trade Legislation Committee, Veterans' Affairs Legislation Amendment Bill (No. 1) 2000 and Veterans' Affairs Legislation Amendment (Budget Measures) Bill 2000, August 2000, p. 7.

5   Mohr Report, p. 7.

6   Submission by the Australian Nursing Federation to the Senate Foreign Affairs, Defence and Trade Legislation Committee, July 2000.

7   Senate Foreign Affairs, Defence and Trade Legislation Committee Report, August 2000, p. 8.

8   Mohr Report, p. 7.

9   *Commonwealth Parliamentary Debates*, Senate Hansard, 10 November 2000, p. 19727.

10   Bartlett, *Commonwealth Parliamentary Debates*, Senate Hansard, 6 December 2000, p. 20913.

11   *Commonwealth Parliamentary Debates*, House of Representatives Hansard, 31 August 2000, p. 19830.

12   Schacht and Hogg, Dissenting Report, Senate Foreign Affairs, Defence and Trade Legislation Committee Amendment Bill (No. 1), August 2000.

13   Dot Angell, in phone conversation with Gary McKay, 3 February 2009.

14   Data supplied by Dot Angell in phone conversation with Gary McKay, 19 January 2009.

15   Jane Cafarella, article, 'Nurses fight for cover', *Age*, 31 May 2003, p. 38.

16   Submission by the Australian Nursing Federation to the Senate Foreign Affairs, Defence and Trade Legislation Committee, July 2000.

17   *Commonwealth Parliamentary Debates*, Senate Hansard, 6 December 2000, p. 20913.

18   Interview with Ian McInnes.

19   Interview with Bob Gray.

20   Interview with Ian McInnes.

21   Interview with Don Sidey.

22   Interview with Ian McInnes.

23   Interview with David Brownbill.

24   Interview with Paul Large.

25   Ibid.

26   Interview with Bob Gray.

27   Interview with David Brownbill.

28   Interview with Jill Storch.

29   Interview with David Brownbill.

30   Johanna Van Valen, DVA interview.

31   Interview with Jenny Hunter.

32   Wendy Jobberns, DVA interview.

33   Interview with Don Sidey.

34   Ibid.

35   Interview with Ian McInnes.

36   Interview with David Brownbill.

37   Ibid.

38   Ibid.

39   Extract, Australian Ambassador's speech, 29 December 1972, file 2481/5/42/6, A1838, NAA.

Bibliography

Unpublished government records

National Archives of Australia records

Series A1838 Department of External Affairs correspondence files, 1948–1975

Items:

2481/5/29 Annex

2481/5/40 parts 1, 2, 5 and 9

2481/5/40/10

2481/5/40/24

2481/5/40/29

2481/5/40/30

2481/5/41 parts 1 and 2

2481/5/41/1 part 2

2481/5/42/5 parts 1 and 2

2481/5/42/6

2481/5/42/12 part 1

2481/5/43 parts 1–4

2481/5/44

2481/5/45/14

Australian War Memorial records

Accessioned interviews

Most of these interviews were recorded for this book, and have been registered in the AWM collections and carry AWM accession numbers. Interviews with

Carmel Hurst, Helen Banff and Pat Warren were not recorded for this book, however they are held by the AWM. All of these interviews are open to public access.

Anderson, Robyn, 24 May 2006, S03989

Angell, Dorothy 'Dot', 27 September 2005, F08155

Banff, Helen, February 1989, S00498

Bell, Jan and Quinn, Sue, 9 July 2006, S03993

Birrell, Robert, 27 May 2006, S03987

Brewster, Janet, 22 February 2006, S03979

Buscombe, Barbara, 11 July 2006, S03994

Clinch, Norma Veronica 'Von', 24 May 2006, S03990

Coventry, Canny, 24 May 2006, S03991

Ellis, James, 12 January 2007, S04269

Francis, John Kendall, 25 May 2006, S03984

Howard, Josephine; Bolton, Margaret; and Monck, Aileen, 7 November 2006, S03999

Hunter, Jennifer, 25 May 2006, S03985

Hurst, Carmel, 24 May 2006, S03988

Hurst, Carmel, May 1992, filmed interview for documentary *The Sharp End*, F10620

Last, Peter, 6 November 2006, S03997

Leak, Jeanette 'Jenny', 7 November 2006, S04245

Lockwood, Betty, 8 November 2006, S04246

MacFarlane, Suzanne, 7 December 2005, S03976

Mulcahy, Marita, 25 May 2006, S03986

O'Connor, Gavan, 22 August 2006, S03996

Ray, Elaine, 6 November 2006, S03998

Rose, Joan, 26 May 2006, S03983

Scott, Elizabeth and John, 8 December 2005, S03975

Storch, Jill, 12 March 2006, S03980

Sutherland, Barbara, 26 October 2005, S03974

Townsend, William, 15 June 2006, S03992

Tracy, Graham Douglas 'Doug', 15 September 2006, S03995

Warren, Pat, June 1992, filmed interview for documentary *The Sharp End*, F10644

Other interviews

These interviews were recorded for this book but have not been transcribed. The recordings are retained by Gary McKay, with the exception of Tom Hugh's, which is retained by Elizabeth Stewart.

Banff, Helen, 10 August 2006

Brownbill, David, 7 December 2005

Evans, Carmel, 25 May 2006

Gray, Bob, 24 May 2006

Hugh, Tom, 23 September 2006

Laidlaw, Noelle, 25 May 2006

Large, Paul, 26 August 2006

Lucas, Noel, 14 August 2006

Mangos, Peter, 24 May 2006

McInnes, Ian 'Cas', 25 May 2006

Mills, Jan, 16 September 2006

Sidey, Don, 6 November 2006

Private records

Clive Bond, PR03477, AWM

Sir Edward 'Weary' Dunlop, PR00926, AWM

Dr Bernard Dunn, PR89/121, AWM

Dr Donald Macleish, PR89/49, AWM

Dr Graham Wilson, PR89/100 and PR89/1175, AWM

Department of Veterans' Affairs interviews

These interviews were conducted for The Australians at War Film Archive. They are available on the website http://www.australiansatwarfilmarchive.gov.au/aawfa.

Brotchie, Iain, Archive no. 1543

Byak, Frances, Archive no. 1519

Dabovich, Kay, Archive no. 1573

Dawson, Berenice, Archive no. 0891

Dunn, Bernard, Archive no. 0832

Grant, Peter, Archive no. 1031

Howard, Josephine, Archive no. 1266

Jobberns, Wendy, Archive no. 0809

Large, Paul, Archive no. 0727

Van Valen, Johanna, Archive no. 0733

Villiers, James, Archive no. 1316

Personal correspondence

Letter by Daphne Amos, January 1966, private collection

Letters of Dorothy Angell, private collection

Letters of Jan Bell, private collection

Letter by Veronica Clinch, 21 December 1966, private collection

Letter Professor Hugh Dudley to W. Philip, Alfred Hospital, dated 23 June 1969, held by authors

Letter from Mike and Minh Hall to Dr Noel Lucas, 27 November 2002

Letter by Kathleen Hirst, 6 February 1966, private collection

Letter by Carmel Hurst, c. December 1967, private collection

Letter by Kevin King to DEA, dated 13 April 1969, held by authors

Letters of Dr Peter Last, private collection

John Morriss—questionnaire completed by mail, held by authors

Letters of Gavan O'Connor (personal), private collection

Letter to authors by Gavan O'Connor, 30 August 2006

Letters of Joan Rose, private collection

Letters of Elizabeth Scott, private collection

Letter Brian Smith to Graeme Grove, dated 5 March 1969, held by
authors

Private memoirs and collections

Cordner, Dr Donald, 'Vietnam Interlude—1969', Ch. 16 in 'The Most Fortu-
nate of Men', unpublished memoir, 1969, private collection

——'A Vista of Vietnam: A short history of Vietnamese affairs and a personal
account of three months as a member of the first Australian surgical team
at Baria (Phuoc Le), capital of Phuoc Tuy province, South Vietnam,
January–April 1969', unpublished memoir, 1969. Copy held by authors

Private papers of Carmel Evans, including administrative arrangements for
Australian surgical teams in Vietnam

Private papers of Jennifer Hunter, including newspaper cuttings and administrative arrangements

Diary of Jenny O'Neill, private collection

Taplin, Helen, 'My Story 1969–70, Bien Hoa, South Vietnam', unpublished
memoir, 2006, private collection

Personal memoir of Maureen Spicer, 11 August 2007

Newspapers

The Age

The Courier-Mail (Brisbane)

The Daily Telegraph (Sydney)

The Heidelberger (Melbourne)

Saigon Daily News

The Saigon Post

The Sun (Sydney)

The Vietnam Guardian

Theses

Angell, Dorothy, 'Breaking the Silence: the experience of the civilian nurses in Vietnam', PhD thesis, School of History/Women's Studies, La Trobe University, November 2001

Government reports

Angell, D., and Spicer, M., 'Australian Civilian Surgical Teams Vietnam 1964–1973', Submission to Commonwealth Review of Service in South East Asia 1955–1975, September 1999

Anon., 'Report on Possibilities of Locating a Third Australian Surgical Team in Vung Tau', 19 August 1966, 2481/5/29/7, A1838, NAA

Australian Nursing Federation, 'Submission to the Senate Foreign Affairs, Defence and Trade Legislation Committee', July 2000

Australian Nursing Federation and CN-ASTV, 'Australian Civilian Surgical Teams in Vietnam 1964–1972, Submission to Review of Service Entitlements', 2002

Birrell, Robert, 'Paediatrics at Long Xuyen and the Paediatric Unit done by Prince Henry's Hospital Team: South Vietnam—February–May 1967'. Copy held by authors

Boxall, J.S., Report of Meeting, Melbourne, 14 October 1971, 2481/5/40/29, A1838, NAA

Commonwealth Parliamentary Debates, Senate Hansard, 6 December 2000, and House of Representatives Hansard, 31 August 2000

Department of External Affairs, Annual Report, 1966–1967, 1967–1968, Commonwealth Government Printer, Canberra

Department of Veterans' Affairs, 'Report of the Review of Veterans' Entitlements (Clarke Report)', January 2003

Dudley, Professor Hugh, 'Australian Surgical Team, Bien Hoa: Alfred Hospital Team', report prepared for Director of Health, Canberra, 14 April 1967, 2481/5/42/5 part 1, A1838, NAA

Game, John A., 'Report on the Request to Provide Surgical Teams for

Viet-Nam', prepared for Department of External Affairs, 21 August 1962

Grove, Graeme, 'Report to His Excellency the Australian Ambassador, Mr Harry, regarding Australian teams at Long Xuyen Hospital', 9 November 1969

Last, Peter, 'Report on Service with Australian Surgical Team, Bien Hoa, July–October 1967', to Department of External Affairs, 7 December 1967. Copy held by authors

Lindell, John, 'Report to His Excellency the Australian Ambassador, Saigon', 8 November 1969

Mohr, Major General R.F., 'Review of Service Entitlement Anomalies in Respect of South-East Asian Service 1955–75', February 2000

Ryan, Peter, 'Visit to Bien Hoa Hospital', 23 November 1965, 2481/5/40 part 5, A1838, NAA

Ryan, Peter and Hurley, D., 'Report Upon the Australian Surgical Team in An Giang Province: Past, present and future', June 1966. Author's copy

Stubber, L.A., 'Final Report of the First Royal Perth Hospital Surgical Team at Long Xuyen', February–August 1969. Author's copy

Sunderland, Sir Sydney, 'Australian Civilian Medical Aid to Viet-Nam', Canberra, Department of External Affairs, 1969

Thompson Report, 'Vietnam: Medical aid', 10 November 1965, 2481/5/40 part 5, A1838, NAA

Books

Barr, Marshall, *Surgery, Sand and Saigon Tea: An Australian Army doctor in Viet Nam*, Allen & Unwin, Sydney, 2001

Brass, Alister, *Bleeding Earth: A doctor looks at Vietnam*, Heinemann, Melbourne, 1968

Campbell, Jennifer (ed.), *Letters From Our Heart: The lives of Australians through correspondence*, Hardie Grant, Melbourne, 2003

Ebury, Sue, *Weary: The life of Sir Edward Dunlop*, Viking, Melbourne, 1994

McHugh, Siobhan, *Minefields and Miniskirts: Australian women and the Vietnam War*, Doubleday, Sydney, 1993

Mesko, Jim, *VNAF: South Vietnamese Air Force, 1945–1975*, Squadron/Signal Publications Inc., Texas, 1987

Nam Phuong, *Red on Gold: The true story of one woman's courage and will to survive war-torn Vietnam*, Albatross Books, Sydney, 1991

O'Keefe, Brendan, *Medicine at War: Medical aspects of Australia's involvement in Southeast Asian conflicts 1950–1972*, Allen & Unwin, Sydney, 1994

Terry, Susan, *House of Love: Life in a Vietnamese hospital*, Lansdowne Press, Melbourne, 1966

Articles, journal chapters and university papers

Alfred Hospital (Melbourne), 'Faces and Places', in *Alfred Hospital Journal*, 1967

Articles in Department of External Affairs, *Current Notes on International Affairs*, issues August 1965, September 1965, July 1966, October 1966, July 1967, September 1967, October 1967 and July 1968

Cordner, Donald, 'Australian General Practitioners in Vietnam: An account of the work of the first Australian surgical team in Vietnam staffed entirely by general practitioners', in *Annals of General Practice*, Vol. 14, Part 3, September 1969

Grove, Graeme, 'Background to the Australian surgical teams in South Vietnam', in *Medical Journal of Australia*, Vol. 2, No. 8, 19 August 1967

Land, Kerri, '"We didn't like to talk about it": Australian military and civilian nursing in Vietnam during the 1962–1972 conflict', major assignment, Women in History course, Macquarie University, c. 1989

Large, Paul, 'Bizarre and Unusual Aspects of Surgery in South Vietnam', presentation notes to Alfred Hospital, c. 1967

Last, Peter, 'Some brief initial impressions of service in Australian surgical team, July–October 1967; 30 September 1967'. Copy held by the authors

Macleish, Donald, 'The Australian surgical team in South Vietnam: The first twelve months', in papers of Bernard Dunn, PR89/121, AWM

Meyers, Derek, 'Vietnam Scrapbook', in *British Medical Journal*, Vol. 3, No. 5613, 3 August 1968

Ryan, Peter, 'Surgical statistics of the Australian surgical team from St. Vincent's Hospital, Melbourne, in South Vietnam', *Medical Journal of Australia*, Vol. 2, No. 8, 19 August 1967

Sheldon, Donald M., 'RPAH sends a surgical team to Vietnam', in *R.P.A: Official Journal of the Royal Prince Alfred Hospital, Sydney*, Vol. 66, No. 252, September 1967

Slaughter, Captain John, 'The Alfred in Vietnam: The Australian Surgical Team', in Gilligan, Bernard (ed.), *Alfred Hospital Faces and Places Volume III*, Alfred Hospital, 2004

Terry, Susan, 'Nursing in Vietnam', in *Medical Journal of Australia*, Vol. 2, No. 8, 19 August 1967

Villiers, J.D., 'A Second Look', in *Medical Journal of Australia*, Vol. 2, No. 8, 19 August 1967

Note: The majority of research material collected for this book is lodged with the AWM Research Centre.

Index